The
100 *Best*
Mutual
Funds
to Own
in
America

2nd Edition

Gene Walden

Dearborn
Financial Publishing, Inc.®

This publication is designed to provide accurate and authoritative information in regard to the subject matter covered. It is sold with the understanding that the publisher is not engaged in rendering legal, accounting or other professional service. If legal advice or other expert assistance is required, the services of a competent professional person should be sought.

Managing Editor: Jack Kiburz
Cover Design: S. Laird Jenkins Corp.
Interior Design: Elizandro Carrington
Typesetting: Elizabeth Pitts

Library of Congress Cataloging-in-Publication Data

Walden, Gene.
    The 100 best mutual funds to own in America—2nd ed.
        p.   cm.
    Includes index.
    ISBN 0-7931-2357-7 (pbk.)
    1. Mutual funds—United States—Directories.
HG4930.W35   1997
332.63′27—dc20   96-46563
                                                     CIP

Contents

100 Best Funds, Listed Alphabetically

100 Best Funds by Investment Objective

Aggressive Growth Funds	Ranking
Acorn Fund	51
AIM Constellation Fund	42
Baron Asset Fund	5
Bull & Bear Special Equities Fund	77
Cowen Opportunity Fund "A"	89
Dean Witter Developing Growth Securities Fund	93
Delaware Trend Fund "A"	40
Evergreen Aggressive Growth Fund	46
Fidelity Emerging Growth Fund	54
Fidelity Low-Priced Stock Fund	27
Founders Frontier Fund	56
INVESCO Dynamics Fund	15
John Hancock Special Equities Fund "A"	9
Kaufmann Fund	2
Loomis Sayles Small Cap Fund	45
Managers Special Equity Fund	28
Meridian Fund	92
MFS Emerging Growth Fund "B"	11
Oberweis Emerging Growth Fund	23
PBHG Growth Fund	1
Piper Emerging Growth Fund	70
Princor Energing Growth Fund "A"	90
Putnam New Opportunities Fund "A"	7
Scudder Development Fund	87
Sierra Trust Emerging Growth Fund "A"	94
State Street Research Capital Fund	39
SunAmerica Small Company Growth Fund "A"	24
T. Rowe Price OTC Fund	57
Twentieth Century Giftrust Investors Fund	8
Twentieth Century Ultra Investors	52
Twentieth Century Vista Investors Fund	74
UAM Sirach Special Equity Portfolio	76
United New Concepts Fund "A"	48
Vanguard Explorer Fund	79

Preface

Since the first edition of *The 100 Best Mutual Funds to Own in America* was published in 1995, mutual funds have continued to follow a rocky but rousing path of spiraling popularity and performance. Many of the funds featured in the first edition of this book have climbed 50 to 80 percent since the book was published. The investment industry continued to turn out new funds (the total is now up to about 8,000), and investors continued to flock to mutual funds in droves. Americans have invested more than $3 trillion in mutual funds—including about $1 trillion in new investments in the past six years.

And with good reason. Mutual funds offer a number of very attractive advantages for investors. They provide instant diversification, professional management, retirement plan compatibility, automatic reinvestment, and checking account deduction, among other services. Put them all together, and it spells convenience, performance, and diversification—a tough combination for any investor to resist. The biggest problem may be deciding among all the attractive choices.

This new 1997 edition of *The 100 Best Mutual Funds to Own in America* should help make that decision a little easier for you. It features the nation's top funds over the past five years. About half of the funds from the first edition made a return visit to this list. Of the others, many continued to fare well, but were eliminated from the list either because they were closed to new investors, or they have new fund managers. And, a few simply didn't make the cut because other funds have performed even better.

Of the 100 funds in the last edition of this book, the top 50 ranked funds were, on average, up 35 percent the first year (1995), and the bottom 50 were up 31 percent. All 100 funds were, on average, up 32.8 percent for the year. That compares very favorably with the 20.3 percent average return of all mutual funds for the same period (according to Morningstar Research).

So if you want to select from the cream of the crop, you've come to the right source. Choose carefully, diversify by including several different types of funds in your portfolio, and be patient, and you, too, should be able to enjoy the same type of financial rewards that have made mutual funds the most popular form of investment ever invented. Good luck.

—Gene Walden

Introduction

For hurried Americans of the 1990s, mutual funds have become the fast food of investing.

Quick, convenient, and diversified, mutual funds give investors a chunk of the stock and bond markets without the hassle. No poring over stock tables, no thumbing through annual reports and corporate balance sheets, no restless nights fretting over the daily ups and downs of the markets. What could be simpler?

Well, maybe it's not quite as easy as it sounds. The selection process can be staggering. You must choose from more than eight thousand mutual funds—nearly four times the number of stocks on the New York Stock Exchange.

Despite their professional management, their diversification, and their finely-honed trading strategies, however, not all funds are created equal. In fact, the vast majority of mutual funds have trailed the overall stock market over the past ten years. However, there are exceptions that rise above the crowd.

The 100 Best Mutual Funds to Own in America is designed to ease your selection process by narrowing the field of choices to 100 truly exceptional funds. Each of the *100 Best* funds ranks in the top 2 percent of all mutual funds in terms of total return over the past five years.

In paging through this book, you'll find a detailed overview of each fund, with helpful insights on their investment objectives and strategies, their top ten holdings, sales charges and annual fees, fund manager's experience, special shareholder services, minimum investment requirements, performance records, asset mix, toll-free number, fax line, and a wealth of other vital information.

You'll also get a chance to tap the minds of America's top investment managers, and learn their secrets on what to buy, when to buy it, and when to sell it out.

A special honorable mention section of about 100 other outstanding stock and bond funds is also included. The honorable mention roster is divided into several sections, including growth funds, growth and income funds, bond funds, high-yield bond funds, tax-exempt bond funds, sector funds, international funds, and aggressive growth funds—all ranked based on five-year performance records.

WHY MUTUAL FUNDS?

What is a mutual fund? Technically, a mutual fund is a "company" that pools investment contributions from shareholders to buy stocks, bonds, or other investments. When you invest in a mutual fund, you are buying shares of the mutual fund "company," and you share in the success of that company.

But for all practical purposes, you can think of a mutual fund simply as a portfolio of investments such as stocks and bonds. You become a part owner of that portfolio when you buy shares in the fund. With a single investment, you suddenly hold a diversified portfolio of dozens of investments. Most funds have in the range of 25 to 300 stock or bond holdings. When you own shares in a fund, your share price directly reflects the net asset value of the stocks in the fund, and the investment value of your shares fluctuates as the fortune of the fund's holdings fluctuates.

In addition to diversification, convenience, and professional management, mutual funds offer several other benefits:

- *Liquidity.* With most funds, you can pull your money out simply by calling the company and telling them to sell your shares.
- *Low investment requirements.* It usually doesn't take a lot of money to invest in a mutual fund. Initial minimum investment requirements vary from about $250 to $2,500, although a few funds require as much as $100,000 to $500,000. Once you're a shareholder, most funds allow you to contribute even smaller subsequent amounts—usually in the range of $50 to $250—so it becomes very easy even for small investors to build a position in a fund.
- *Direct purchases.* Although brokers are often helpful in recommending good mutual funds to their clients, you don't have to use a broker to buy shares in a mutual fund. You can buy shares directly from the company simply by calling the company's toll-free sales line.
- *Low (or no) sales fees.* Many companies allow you to purchase fund shares with no sales fee. These are called *no-load funds* (which means they have no sales "load" or fee). Load funds vary in the fees they charge investors. Some *low-load* funds charge about 3 percent, although most load funds charge in the range of 4.5 to 8 percent. Some funds charge what is known as a *back-end load,* which is a sales charge you would pay when you sell out your shares in the fund. Typically, back-end load funds charge 5 percent if you sell the first year, 4 percent the second year, and so on, with the fee diminishing to zero after the fifth year. Funds also charge annual expense fees that usually vary from about 1 percent to 3 percent, depending on the fund.

- *Checking deduction plans.* With most funds, you can have money automatically withdrawn from your checking account and invested in the fund each month or each quarter.
- *Automatic withdrawal.* Retired investors sometimes opt for withdrawal plans that authorize the fund to pay out a set amount to the investor from his or her fund account each month or each quarter.
- *Retirement account access.* Most companies allow investors to use their funds in IRAs, SEPs, and other retirement accounts.
- *Telephone exchange.* Investors who wish to switch from one fund to another within the same family of funds are usually allowed to make that switch commission-free simply by calling the company and ordering the change.
- *Automatic reinvestment.* With most mutual funds, investors can have their dividends and capital gains distributions automatically reinvested in additional shares of the fund with no additional sales fee.

FUNDS FOR EVERY TASTE

A wide variety of mutual funds meets the taste and risk threshhold of nearly everyone who invests. The original mutual funds were designed to produce a combination of growth and income by investing in a diversified portfolio of dividend-paying blue-chip stocks. Many such "growth and income" funds are still offered today—along with a host of other types of funds, including:

- *Growth and income funds.* These funds are appropriate for investors who want a steady stream of income along with some appreciation. They are not appropriate for high-income investors who want to minimize their taxes because the additional income adds to the investor's tax burden. Because they invest in more well-established companies, growth and income funds are among the least risky types of mutual funds.
- *Growth funds.* These funds invest primarily in stocks of fast-growing companies in order to provide long-term appreciation (with minimal current income) for shareholders. While growth funds tend to be more volatile in the short term than income-oriented funds, they tend to provide better long-term returns. Because of their diversification, growth funds are among the least risky types of funds.
- *Aggressive growth funds.* These stock funds normally come in many forms. Some invest in depressed stocks that have turnaround potential. Others look for trendy stocks. Most of the top aggressive growth funds in recent years have had large positions in high tech stocks.

Other funds look for good startup companies that could blossom into major corporations. And still others invest in potential takeover stocks that could experience a sharp run-up in prices. With aggressive funds, the portfolio managers play a numbers game. Some of their picks pan out; others fall flat. Their hope is to make enough money on the winners to more than compensate for the losers. In truth, the label "aggressive growth" applies more to the types of stocks that these funds invest in than to their overall performance. Although a large share of the top-ranked funds in this book are aggressive growth funds, many aggressive growth funds have proven to be no more profitable than other stock funds—just more volatile. These funds tend to be riskier than growth funds, particularly over the short term.

- *International and global funds.* These funds give investors a stake in the international market. *Global funds* refers to funds that invest in both U.S. and foreign stocks, whereas *international funds* invest strictly in foreign stocks. Because they invest in foreign stocks, international funds can be somewhat riskier than U.S. growth stock funds. However, by investing in an international fund as part of a diversified portfolio, you add foreign diversification, which actually reduces the overall risk of your portfolio.

- *Sector funds.* These specialty funds invest strictly in stocks of one specific sector. There are funds for almost any market sector you could name—precious metals, utilities, high tech, medical technology, and financial, among others. If you think gas and oil stocks are ready to take off, you might invest in an energy fund. If you want a hedge against inflation, you might invest in a gold fund that buys the stocks of gold mining companies. While specialty funds have broad stock holdings within a specific sector, they lack the diversity and safety of traditional stock funds. If the sector is faring poorly, so will the fund. For instance, medical funds experienced phenomenal growth in 1991 when the medical sector was hot, but when medical stocks cooled off amid political discussions of medical cost containment, health care sector funds became the worst performing funds of 1992. Sector funds are the riskiest of all funds.

- *Money market funds.* Although money market funds are a form of mutual fund, they are considered a separate class. Brokerage firms use money market fund accounts for clients who want to continue drawing interest on the money in their account when it is not invested in securities or other investments. Banks also offer money market accounts for clients who want to get a slightly higher return than they would get through a standard savings account. These are the safest of all funds, but generally provide the lowest long-term return.

- *Bond funds.* Bond funds first became popular in the 1970s, when investors began opting for managed portfolios of corporate bonds rather than individual bonds. An offshoot of the traditional bond fund was the *high-yield bond funds*—portfolios of low-rated *junk bonds* that pay interest rates three or four points higher than those paid by many of the AAA-rated bonds. With individual junk bonds, safety is a major concern because of the risk of default, although the diversification of a portfolio of bonds reduces the risk substantially. In reality, all bond funds—even government bond funds—carry a great deal more risk than most investors expect. Bond values rise and fall as interest rates fluctuate. When interest rates rise, bond values drop. A 2 percent rise in market interest rates can push the value of a bond fund down by 10 percent or more. In 1994, when interest rates were dropping steadily, bond funds declined in value—many dropped as much as 5 to 10 percent. Conversely, when market rates are falling, bond funds enjoy excellent appreciation, although the best bond funds generally fall far short of the best stock funds over the long term. This book covers bond funds—both high quality and high yield—in the honorable mention section.

- *Tax-exempt bond funds.* These funds invest in municipal bonds, which provide a tax break for investors. The dividends they pay are exempt from federal taxes, and, in the case of funds that are comprised of tax-exempt bonds from the investor's state, they are also exempt from state taxes. The problem, however, is that the returns these funds provide are among the lowest in the industry—even after taking the tax break into account. Municipal bonds also carry a degree of risk. It is possible for bond issuers to default, creating major losses for bond holders, as was the case in Orange County, California in 1994.

- *Closed-end funds.* A closed-end fund is a professionally managed diversified portfolio that is closed to new investors. As with stock offerings, investment companies underwrite such funds to raise a limited amount of money. Once the cutoff point has been reached, no new investments are accepted, and the fund begins trading on the open market like a stock. Some of the best-known closed-end funds include the Mexico Fund, the Korea Fund, the Brazil Fund, and the Taiwan Fund, all of which trade on the New York Stock Exchange. By contrast, open-end funds can continue to issue new shares as shareholders contribute new investment dollars. Investors buy shares directly from the mutual fund company rather than through a stock exchange. (Closed-end funds are not covered in this book; only the traditional "open-end" funds are featured.)

RATING THE TOP 100 FUNDS

From 8,000 funds, my objective was to sift out the 100 best. I began by focusing on the top 2 percent of all funds based on total return over the past five years. Of those top-ranking funds, I eliminated from consideration all funds that were closed to new shareholders, all funds with excessive minimum investment requirements (anything over $25,000 was eliminated), and funds with new fund managers. (I made an exception for some Fidelity funds because the company has a policy of shifting fund managers from fund to fund every few years. It is a policy that has worked well for Fidelity because the funds are all managed more or less on a team basis anyway. But I did deduct at least one rating point from each fund that had a new manager.) Then I took one more look at the track histories of the funds, and eliminated funds that had been particularly volatile over the past few years.

Once I had assembled the list of 100, the next step was to rank the funds from 1 to 100. The ranking system revolved around the following three categories, each worth a maximum of five points (for a maximum total of 15 points):

- *Performance.* Each fund was graded based on its five-year total return record (through mid-1996). It is important to note that the system ranks the funds relative to other funds from the top 100—not relative to all mutual funds. If I had graded them relative to all funds, then all 100 of the funds in the book would have scored a perfect five because they all rank in the top 2 percent of all mutual funds over the five-year period. Instead, I graded on a curve, with roughly the top 25 funds receiving a perfect five, the next 25 receiving a four, and so on down to 2 points.

- *Consistency.* Rather than look at day-to-day volatility, I graded each fund's consistency on a year-to-year basis. I compared the performance of each fund to the Dow Jones Industrial Average each year over a six-year period from 1991 through 1995 (and part of 1996). A fund would score a perfect five if it outperformed the Dow (or ended the year virtually even with the Dow) each of the six years. Generally, if it trailed the Dow one of the six years, the fund would score a four; if it trailed the Dow two of the six years, it would score three points; if it trailed the Dow three of the six years, it would score a two for the category; and if it trailed four of the six years, it would score a one (although, if it were that volatile, I would have dropped it from the list—no fund scored less than a two in consistency).

There were a few exceptions. For instance, in some cases when a fund trailed the Dow three years, but only by a percentage point or two each time, I deducted two points instead of three. In the case of international funds, the Dow is not an appropriate comparative source, so I compared the performance of those funds both to the Dow and to the Morgan Stanley Capital Investment and Europe, Australasia, Far East (MSCI/EAFE) Index and determined a score based on both comparisons.

- *Fees/Services/Management.* This is the most subjective of the three categories—with certain guidelines. With this category, it was more a matter of deducting points than awarding them. To receive a perfect five, a fund would need to (1) be a true no-load fund (with no sales fee to buy or sell); (2) have a fund manager who had been with the fund at least four years; (3) offer the full range of standard services that most funds offer (checking account deduction, automatic withdrawal, retirement account availability, instant telephone redemption, and free switching between funds within the family by telephone); and (4) have reasonable minimum investment requirements (of no more than $5,000 initial investment minimum and $500 subsequent investment minimum).

A normal load fund—with a front-end or back-end sales fee of 4 percent or above—would automatically lose two points in this category, while a low-load fund (with a sales fee of 3 percent or less) would have just one point deducted. If the fund manager had been with the fund less than four years, another point would normally be deducted—with rare exception. (The only exceptions would be for a veteran fund manager who had been with the fund for a minimum of three years after establishing an impressive track record with another fund.) If a fund didn't offer most of the standard mutual fund services mentioned above, another point was deducted. If its minimum investment requirement is excessive (for instance, one fund in the book requires a $25,000 minimum investment), yet another point would be subtracted. Points might also be deducted for other reasons. Funds that were unable to send us an annual report—or didn't send it in a timely manner—lost a point. (For instance, I had to make five calls to one company before they finally sent me an annual report—and the report they sent was more than a year old; another company never sent an annual report, explaining that they were out of print—a full six months before the next report was due for release. Both of those funds were penalized one point.) Funds that had specific limitations (such as the Twentieth Century Giftrust Investors Fund, which can only be used as a trust for others) also lost a point.

BREAKING TIES

With 100 funds graded on a 15-point rating system, many funds scored the same. How did I break the ties? I looked at several factors:

- *Diversification.* A fund that is well-diversified across industry lines ranked above the sector funds, which invest exclusively in a specific industry. The reason: The risk factor is much higher with sector funds. While they may have done well over the most recent five-year period, they would stand to fall much faster than the broadly diversified funds if their sector should suddenly fall out of favor.
- *Management.* I looked at the experience of the fund manager. A fund with a manager who had been with the fund five to ten years would be rated above a fund with a relatively new manager.
- *Five-year total return.* If all other factors were about equal, I rated funds with the best five-year performance records ahead of those with lesser records. For funds with similar five-year records, I favored the funds with the better year-to-year consistency.

AND THE WINNERS ARE . . .

If mutual funds are the fast food of investing, then Fidelity must be the McDonald's. The Boston-based investment giant offers more than 200 different funds. Some 20 of the top 100 funds were Fidelity funds.

The hottest area was the high tech sector funds, which accounted for about a dozen of the top 100 funds. In fact, many of the other high-ranking diversified funds were also loaded with technology stocks.

Otherwise, the list was dominated by small company funds, aggressive growth funds and growth funds, with a few growth and income funds.

All of the funds in this book have doubled or tripled in value over the past five years. Keep in mind, however, that strong past performance does not guarantee similar future performance. It makes sense to invest in funds with solid, consistent track records and experienced management, but even the best funds have some down years. That is why investors should consider buying shares in more than one fund. Patience is also important. Nothing goes straight up, but over time, the best funds with the best managers tend to reward their patient shareholders with superior long-term returns.

MUTUAL FUNDS AND TAXES

There's no question that mutual funds are an investment conceived in convenience—you get diversity, professional management, and a host of special services, all for a simple investment. But the convenience ends when the taxes begin. Unless you invest strictly in tax-exempt municipal bond funds, or tuck your mutual funds safely away in a tax-sheltered retirement plan, you're likely to encounter some confusing twists when calculating your taxes.

Each year most stock and bond funds pay out interest, dividends, and capital gains distributions (from profits made on trades within the fund). As a shareholder, you are liable for taxes on those gains, even if you had those distributions automatically reinvested in additional shares. Your fund will send you a Form 1099-DIV (or similar form) annually that details your taxable gains for the year.

You are also liable for taxes on the appreciation of your fund shares when you sell out your holdings. But take special care in calculating your gains, particularly if you have your fund distributions automatically reinvested. The tendency among investors is to **overpay** because they forget they've already paid taxes on the reinvested share of their holdings.

For instance, if your total holdings went from $1,000 when you bought the fund to $2,000 when you sold, that doesn't mean you owe taxes on the full $1,000 gain. Part of that gain came from reinvested dividends and capital gains for which you would already have paid taxes.

To determine your true **taxable total:**

1. Add up all the dividends and distributions from the fund that you have had reinvested in additional shares.
2. Subtract the total value of your holdings when you bought the shares from the total value when you sold the shares to determine your total gain.
3. Subtract #1 (your reinvested distributions) from #2 (your total gain). That is your taxable income.

Example: You paid $1,000; you reinvested $100; you sold at $2,000.

Value at sale	$2,000
Initial investment	– $1,000
Reinvested distribution	– $ 100
Taxable income	$ 900

For investors who have accumulated shares over time, the IRS offers several options for calculating taxable gains on the sale of a portion of those shares:

- *First in, first out (FIFO).* You sell the first fund shares you purchased, and pay taxes on the gains. The best circumstance to use FIFO would be if your fund shares have declined recently. That means you may have paid the most for your earliest shares, and therefore they would represent the smallest taxable gain.
- *Average cost.* Your taxes would be based on the average price you paid for shares you accumulated over time. To calculate the average, divide your total investment in the fund (including reinvested gains) by the number of shares you own. That works best when share prices have surged over time because you probably paid the least for your earliest shares—and would show the biggest gain for those shares if you used FIFO. But by using cost averaging, you can push up the average purchase, and cut down the total taxable gain.
- *Specific identification.* This allows you to identify the specific shares you are selling. That enables you to select the shares that would give you the smallest taxable gain.

Tax-averse investors may prefer municipal bond funds. The dividends they pay are exempt from federal taxes, and, in the case of funds that are comprised of tax-exempt bonds from your state, they may also be exempt from state taxes. But you are still subject to taxes on any capital gains those funds earn by selling bonds at a profit.

Despite the tax breaks, however, it would probably be a mistake to put too much of your money in municipal bond funds. They tend to be among the worst-performing funds on the market over the long-term. Even with the tax savings, their total after-tax return is likely to trail that of most taxable stock and bond funds over the long term.

TAKING ACTION

This book helps reduce your universe of choices from the roughly 8,000 funds currently on the market to the much more manageable level of 100 (plus the honorable mention funds). But ultimately, it is you who must take action if you are to profit from the information in this book.

How should you select the fund or funds that are right for you? Here is a simple action plan:

1. Skim through the book to find a few funds that look promising to you.

2. Once you've selected a handful of good funds, call each fund's toll-free number (or send a fax) and request the fund's most recent annual or semiannual report and prospectus. The phone numbers you need are listed along with the profiles of each fund.
3. Read through the fund information. Many funds will also send some helpful marketing brochures that give you a better glimpse of their company and the fund for which you've requested information.
4. Weigh all the factors that are important to you—total five-year performance, sales loads, annual fees, minimum investment requirements, services, type of fund, and any other factors you consider important.
5. Decide which fund (or funds) you want to buy.
6. Call the fund's toll-free number and place your order.
7. To go one step further, you can track the progress of your fund each day in the mutual fund section of the *Wall Street Journal, Investor's Business Daily,* or *USA Today;* and many major metropolitan daily newspapers. There is also a newsletter you can subscribe to that specifically covers the 100 mutual funds in this book. It is called *The Best 100 Update,* it comes out twice a year, and it costs $12.95. (It also tracks the stocks in my other book, *The 100 Best Stocks to Own in America.*) You can order by calling 800-736-2970 or by writing P.O. Box 39373, Minneapolis, MN 55439.

THE COMPLETE PORTFOLIO

For a diversified approach, you will probably want to invest in several different funds, depending on your investment objectives. For instance, you should consider buying a broadly diversified stock growth fund, an aggressive growth fund, an international stock fund, perhaps an income fund such as a bond fund or high yield bond fund, and a sector fund such as a high tech fund. This book helps you choose from the best of each category.

Here are several factors to consider in making your selection—and several ways this book can help you assess those factors:

*   *Investment objectives.* Do you want income, capital appreciation, safety, or aggressive growth? While the top 100 funds are nearly all geared to total capital appreciation, the honorable mention section covers several dozen income funds.
*   *Performance.* You want a fund that has provided superior long-term performance. Good performance in a single year means very little. Very often, the best-performing funds one year become the worst-

performing funds the next. This book takes a long-term perspective, featuring funds based on superior five-year performance records.

- *Consistency.* Are you willing to put up with some volatility in hopes of getting better long-term returns? Or would you rather have a fund that tends to match the market year in and year out, but may not offer quite the long-term potential of some other more volatile funds? This book rates funds on year-to-year consistency.

- *Fees.* If you plan to hold a fund for years to come, the initial sales load won't make a lot of difference. But if you expect to move in and out of various funds from year to year, then the 4 to 8 percent fee that most load funds charge would make a significant difference in your total return. Investors who do a lot of buying and selling of mutual funds should seriously consider using only no-load or low-load funds. Also take a look at the fund's annual expense ratio. Those fees can vary from as little as 0.7 percent to as high as 3 percent—which can make a big difference over time. This book details all the fees associated with each of the featured funds—both the top 100 and the honorable mention picks.

- *Management.* A fund is truly a reflection of its manager. A fund with a great track record may not be such a great fund if the manager leaves. If you are selecting a fund based on its past performance, make sure the manager responsible for that performance is still running the fund.

- *Services.* As mentioned earlier, mutual funds offer a variety of services such as automatic checking account deduction, periodic fund withdrawal plans, and IRA accounts. Make sure the fund you are interested in offers the services you need.

AGGRESSIVE

PBHG Growth Fund

PBHG Funds, Inc.
680 East Swedesford Road
Wayne, PA 19087-1658

Fund manager: Gary Pilgrim

Fund objective: Aggressive growth

Toll-free: 800-433-0051

In-state: 610-254-1000

Fax: 610-989-6176

Performance	★ ★ ★ ★ ★
Consistency	★ ★ ★ ★ ★
Fees/Services	★ ★ ★ ★ ★
PBHGX	**15 Points**

"Twenty-five years in this business has taught me that a good company is a company that is doing good," says fund manager Gary Pilgrim. "The world pays for results."

The results of Pilgrim's investment philosophy have paid off spectacularly for shareholders of the PBHG Growth Fund, which has grown, on average, 34 percent per year over the past five years. And for the past decade, the fund has produced average annual growth of 21.5 percent. A $10,000 investment in the fund ten years ago would now be worth about $70,000.

Pilgrim founded the fund in 1985 and has been managing it ever since. He cofounded Pilgrim Baxter & Associates in 1982 after serving as a portfolio manager and analyst for 15 years with Philadelphia National Bank.

In analyzing emerging growth stocks for his fund, Pilgrim runs through the usual battery of screens and formulas, and he may even pay a visit to a promising young company to look it over. But for the most part, Pilgrim doesn't try to read too much between the lines. Fast growth—past and present—is the biggest factor that catches his eye.

His fund invests almost exclusively in small to mid-sized growth stocks. Pilgrim prefers stocks in the range of $250 million to $1 billion in market capitalization. He will hold on to the $1 billion-plus stocks if they're still on a fast growth track, but once they hit $2 billion, he unloads them.

"What we try to do is identify and hold on to the really high-growth stocks as long as it makes sense to do so. We'd like to hold them for four or five years, but that's pretty rare. Most growth companies go through stages of very rapid growth and then, for various reasons, they slow down. That growth phase may be nine months or it may be three years. When they start to slow down, that's when we weed them out of the portfolio."

The fund holds about 75 to 80 stocks at a time, all selected from a universe of about 450 emerging growth stocks that Pilgrim and his researchers track and grade on an ongoing basis. To make its way into Pilgrim's universe, a company must show earnings and sales growth of at least 20 percent per year.

He grades each stock on a wide range of factors. Among the most important areas are the following:

- *Sequential acceleration.* He prefers stocks with increasing sales growth rates.
- *Earnings surprises.* He likes companies that surprise the analysts by continuing to post higher-than-expected earnings.
- *Estimate revisions.* Similar to earnings surprises, Pilgrim likes companies that grow faster each year than analysts project.

After putting each of the 450 stocks through his complex scoring system, Pilgrim narrows the candidates to the top-rated 30 percent—about 150 stocks in all. After closer scrutiny, Pilgrim selects the most promising 120 of those stocks for the fund portfolio. The process never stops, however. "The art form of this process is your continuous awareness of how a company is doing. It's an ongoing process." When a stock's growth momentum begins to ebb, he dumps it in favor of a more promising stock from the top 150.

In terms of industrial sectors, the fund has 33 percent of its assets in technology stocks, 20 percent in consumer-related stocks, 17 percent in health care and 14 percent in services. The fund stays almost fully invested in the market most of the time.

PERFORMANCE

The fund has enjoyed phenomenal growth over the past five years. Including dividends and capital gains distributions, the PBHG Growth Fund has provided a total return for the past five years (through mid-1996) of 332 percent. A $10,000 investment in 1991 would have grown to $43,000 five years later. Average annual return: 34 percent.

CONSISTENCY

The fund has been very consistent, outperforming the Dow Jones Industrial Average for five consecutive years through 1995 (and again through the first half of 1996). Its biggest years were 1991 and 1995 when it jumped 51.6 and 50.4 percent, respectively.

FEES/SERVICES/MANAGEMENT

The fund is a pure no-load fund—no fees to buy, no fees to sell. Its annual expense ratio of 1.45 (with no 12b-1 fee) is about average among no-load funds.

The fund offers all the standard services such as retirement account availability, automatic withdrawal, and automatic checking account deduction. Its minimum initial investment of $2,500 is a little higher than average, but there is no minimum subsequent investment requirement.

Gary Pilgrim has managed the fund since its inception in 1985. The Growth Fund is one of 12 funds in the PBHG fund family.

Top Ten Holdings

1. Ascend Communications
2. FORE Systems
3. U.S. Robotics
4. PhyCor
5. C-Cube Microsystems
6. Money Store
7. Sunglass Hut International
8. Healthsource
9. Corrections of America
10. Cascade Communications

Asset Mix: Common stocks: 91%; Cash/equivalents: 9%
Total Net Assets: $3.3 billion

Fees

Front-end load	*None*
Redemption fee	*None*
12b-1 fee	*None*
Management fee	0.85%
Other expenses	0.60
Total annual expense	1.45%
Minimum initial investment	$2,500
Minimum subsequent investment	$1

Services

Telephone exchanges	*Yes*
Automatic withdrawal	*Yes*
Automatic checking deduction	*Yes*
Retirement plan/IRA	*Yes*
Instant redemption	*Yes*
Financial statements	*Semiannual*
Income distributions	*Annual*
Capital gains distributions	*Annual*
Portfolio manager—years	12
Number of funds in family	8

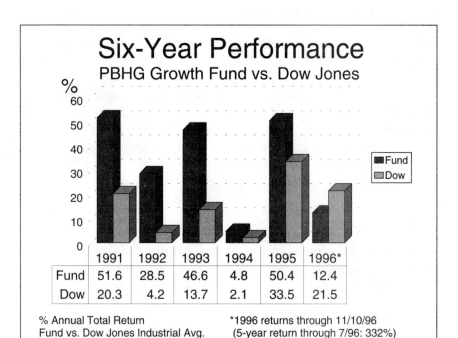

Six-Year Performance
PBHG Growth Fund vs. Dow Jones

	1991	1992	1993	1994	1995	1996*
Fund	51.6	28.5	46.6	4.8	50.4	12.4
Dow	20.3	4.2	13.7	2.1	33.5	21.5

% Annual Total Return
Fund vs. Dow Jones Industrial Avg.

*1996 returns through 11/10/96
(5-year return through 7/96: 332%)

2

Kaufmann Fund

Kaufmann Fund, Inc.
140 East 45th Street, 43rd Floor
New York, NY 10017

Fund managers: Lawrence Auriana, Hans Utsch
Fund objective: Aggressive growth

Toll-free: 800-261-0555
In-state: 212-922-0123
Fax: 212-344-6227

Performance	★ ★ ★ ★ ★
Consistency	★ ★ ★ ★ ★
Fees/Services	★ ★ ★ ★ ★
KAUFX	**15 Points**

Kaufmann Fund managers Lawrence Auriana and Hans Utsch continue to amaze and confound the skeptics, who question how long the dynamic duo can continue to defy the odds of gravity. Even with the fund's assets approaching $4 billion, Auriana and Utsch have managed to nimbly guide the bulging portfolio to dizzying new heights.

Kaufmann Fund investors have enjoyed an average annual return of nearly 26 percent over the past five years, and 19 percent over the past ten years. A $10,000 investment in the fund when Utsch and Auriana took it over in 1986 would have grown to about $55,000 ten years later.

Part of their secret, says Auriana, is that they steer away from the small-growth, small-niche companies. "We like companies that have proprietary products or unique services that appeal to a substantial market. We want companies that can grow at 20 percent per year or more for the next three to five years."

Auriana and Utsch look well beyond the numbers to sift out winning stocks for their portfolio. "Management is the most important criterion," says Auriana. "Every day we meet with the management of two to six companies. It can be risky meeting with management if you're not as experienced at it as we are. Management of these young companies are, almost without exception, terrific salespeople, and they're trying to sell you on their companies."

Auriana has enough experience in the business that he can usually cut through the hype to figure out which managers really have something to offer. "We already know a lot about these businesses—usually we know more than they expect us to know. In most cases, we've already met with their competitors and their suppliers, and we've followed their industries for years. We can usually tell if their estimates are overly optimistic."

Although strong management, fast growth, and solid cash flow attract Auriana to a stock, changes in those factors will prompt him to sell. "If there is some fundamental change in the business or the dynamics of the industry, or if the company is not living up to its plan—if it can't implement its business model—then we'll sell the stock."

A drop in earnings will often be the catalyst for the fund to sell its position, but exceptions do occur. "Sometimes we may already know the earnings are going to drop for that quarter, but we also know the long-term prospects are still good. Then we'll hold on to the stock, although we may also take a short position in the stock to hedge against a temporary drop in the price." The managers take a surprisingly conservative approach in their trading policy, with an annual portfolio turnover ratio of just 60 percent.

The fund managers like to ride their winners and sell their losers, but Auriana says they are not true momentum players. "Sometimes we'll buy a stock if a bad earnings quarter knocks the price down to what we consider to be a bargain level. A momentum player wouldn't do that." The fund stays fully invested in stocks at almost all times.

The fund has nearly 400 stock holdings, many of which are in technology-related industries. Its leading sector is medical equipment and services, which accounts for about 22 percent of total assets. Other leading sectors include computers and software, 10 percent; semiconductors and equipment, 12 percent; retail, 12 percent; and lodging, 6 percent.

PERFORMANCE

The fund has enjoyed exceptional growth over the past five years. Including dividends and capital gains distributions, the Kaufmann Fund has provided a total return for the past five years (through mid-1996) of 216 percent. A $10,000 investment in 1991 would have grown to about $32,000 five years later. Average annual return: 25.9 percent.

CONSISTENCY

The fund has been very consistent, outperforming the Dow Jones Industrial Average for five consecutive years through 1995 (and again through the first half of 1996). The fund's biggest year was 1991, when it jumped 79.2 percent (compared with a 20.3 percent rise in the Dow).

FEES/SERVICES/MANAGEMENT

The fund has no front-end sales load, but it does have a very small 0.2 percent redemption fee. The fund's total annual expense ratio of 2.29 percent (including a 0.65 percent 12b-1 fee and a 1.5 percent management fee) is very high compared with other funds.

The fund offers all the standard services such as retirement account availability, automatic withdrawal, and automatic checking account deduction. Its minimum initial investment of $1,500 and minimum subsequent investment of $100 are in line with other funds.

Comanagers Hans P. Utsch and Lawrence Auriana took over management of the fund in 1986. The Kaufmann Fund is the only fund the company offers.

Top Ten Holdings

1. HFS
2. Altera
3. Microchip Technology
4. Viking Office Products
5. Danka Business Systems
6. Blyth Industries
7. Nu-Kote Holdings
8. Wolverine World Wide
9. Lincare Holdings
10. Access Health Marketing

Asset Mix: Common stocks: 84%; Cash/equivalents: 12%; Other: 4%
Total Net Assets: $3.79 billion

Fees

Front-end load	*None*
Redemption fee (max)	0.20%
12b-1 fee	0.65
Management fee	1.50
Other expenses	0.14
Total annual expense	2.29%
Minimum initial investment	$1,500
Minimum subsequent investment	$100

Services

Telephone exchanges	*Yes*
Automatic withdrawal	*Yes*
Automatic checking deduction	*Yes*
Retirement plan/IRA	*Yes*
Instant redemption	*Yes*
Financial statements	*Semiannual*
Income distributions	*Annual*
Capital gains distributions	*Annual*
Portfolio managers—years	11
Number of funds in family	1

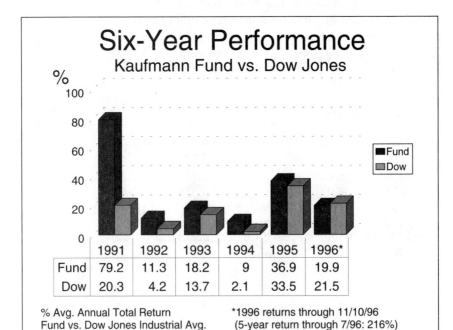

Six-Year Performance
Kaufmann Fund vs. Dow Jones

	1991	1992	1993	1994	1995	1996*
Fund	79.2	11.3	18.2	9	36.9	19.9
Dow	20.3	4.2	13.7	2.1	33.5	21.5

% Avg. Annual Total Return
Fund vs. Dow Jones Industrial Avg.

*1996 returns through 11/10/96
(5-year return through 7/96: 216%)

SECTOR

3
T. Rowe Price Science and Technology Fund

T. Rowe Price
100 East Pratt Street
Baltimore, MD 21202

Fund manager: Chip Morris
Fund objective: Sector fund

Toll-free: 800-638-5660
In-state: 410-547-2000
Fax: 410-347-1574

Performance	★ ★ ★ ★ ★
Consistency	★ ★ ★ ★ ★
Fees/Services	★ ★ ★ ★ ★
PRSCX	**15 Points**

The right place at the right time—the T. Rowe Price Science and Technology Fund opened in 1987, just as the high tech market was beginning to heat up. The fund has been blazing along like a runaway rocket ever since.

For seven consecutive years, the fund has outperformed the Dow Jones Industrial Average, fetching annual returns of more than 50 percent two of the past six years. A $10,000 investment in the Science and Technology Fund when it opened in 1987 would now be worth about $60,000—a 23 percent average annual return.

The secret, says fund manager Chip Morris, may be in the fund's charter. It is registered as a diversified fund with a maximum 25 percent threshold for any one sector. Whereas some technology funds specialize in computer stocks, others in health care, and still others in electronics or telecommunications, the T. Rowe Price Science and Technology Fund spreads its assets throughout a broad spectrum of high tech issues. That diversification has helped make the portfolio one of the nation's most consistent sector funds.

"With our diversification, we're not going to hit many home runs," says Morris, "but we've caught a good portion of all the key waves."

Generally speaking, the fund may have the lion's share of its assets spread through six or seven different technology sectors such as health care, wireless, computer software, semiconductors, communications, and data services, with roughly 15 percent of its assets in each of the key categories.

"That means we probably won't be among the top ten funds in any one quarter or even in any one year, because we are too diversified," says Morris. "But we're able to ease the volatility a little by spreading our bets. I think consistency will be an enduring quality of this fund."

Morris tries to keep at least 85 percent of the fund's assets invested in stocks at all times, but changes the mix continually. He loads up on the smaller, emerging stocks when they seem undervalued and poised for a rebound. When their valuations get a little too high, he moves some of the assets into the more stable names and raises cash modestly. But under normal circumstances, smaller stocks will dominate the fund. "We've tried to stay invested in the most dynamic small- and mid-cap stocks."

Morris is never shy about buying and selling stocks to stay on top of the trends. On average, the fund has an annual portfolio turnover ratio of about 130 percent.

"We understand that it's very important to keep moving. We try to stay on the leading edge of technology. It's easy to invest in the bigger technology companies like IBM or Hewlett-Packard, but we would rather invest in the one-product wonders like Cisco Systems—if we do our homework and make sure that their one product really is hot."

Although the fund's assets recently exceeded two billion dollars, Morris still prefers to keep the portfolio at a manageable level of about 50 stocks.

You may never see the fund at the top of the short-term mutual fund charts, but Morris doesn't expect it to land close to the bottom, either. "Our strategy is to try to stay close in a bad market, and significantly outperform in a good market." Fortunately for Morris, the high tech market has been very good for a very long time.

PERFORMANCE

The fund has enjoyed exceptional growth over the past five years. Including dividends and capital gains distributions, the Science and Technology Fund has provided a total return for the past five years (through mid-

1996) of 259 percent. A $10,000 investment in 1991 would have grown to about $36,000 five years later. Average annual return: 29.1 percent.

CONSISTENCY

The fund has been very consistent, outperforming the Dow Jones Industrial Average every year over the seven-year period from 1989 through 1995 (but it trailed the Dow through the first half of 1996). Its biggest gains came in 1991, when it jumped 60.2 percent, and 1995, when it rose 55.5 percent.

FEES/SERVICES/MANAGEMENT

Like all T. Rowe Price funds, the Science and Technology Fund is a pure no-load fund—no fee to buy, no fee to sell. Its annual expense ratio of 1.01 percent (with no 12b-1 expenses) compares very favorably with other no-load funds.

The fund offers all the standard services such as retirement account availability, automatic withdrawal and automatic checking account deduction. Its minimum initial investment of $2,500 and minimum subsequent investment of $100 are a little high compared with other funds.

Chip Morris has been associated with the fund since 1987 and has been the lead fund manager since 1991. The T. Rowe Price fund family includes 50 funds and allows shareholders to switch from fund to fund by telephone.

Top Ten Holdings

1. Vodafone
2. BMC Software
3. Maxim Integrated Products
4. Xilinx
5. First Data
6. Microsoft
7. Bay Networks
8. Adobe Systems
9. Cisco Systems
10. Electronic Arts

Asset Mix: Common stocks: 92%; Cash/equivalents: 8%
Total Net Assets: $2.3 billion

Fees

Front-end load	*None*
Redemption fee	*None*
12b-1 fee	*None*
Management fee	0.69%
Other expenses	0.32
Total annual expense	1.01%
Minimum initial investment	$2,500
Minimum subsequent investment	$100

Services

Telephone exchanges	*Yes*
Automatic withdrawal	*Yes*
Automatic checking deduction	*Yes*
Retirement plan/IRA	*Yes*
Instant redemption	*Yes*
Financial statements	*Semiannual*
Income distributions	*Annual*
Capital gains distributions	*Annual*
Portfolio manager—years	6
Number of funds in family	50

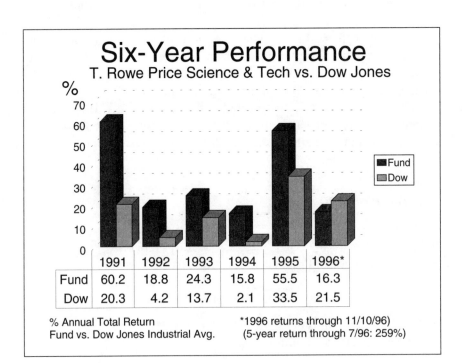

Six-Year Performance
T. Rowe Price Science & Tech vs. Dow Jones

	1991	1992	1993	1994	1995	1996*
Fund	60.2	18.8	24.3	15.8	55.5	16.3
Dow	20.3	4.2	13.7	2.1	33.5	21.5

% Annual Total Return
Fund vs. Dow Jones Industrial Avg.

*1996 returns through 11/10/96)
(5-year return through 7/96: 259%)

SECTOR

4
INVESCO
Strategic Portfolios:
Technology Fund

INVESCO Funds Group
7800 East Union Avenue, Suite 800
P.O. Box 173706
Denver, CO 80217-3706

Fund manager: Daniel B. Leonard
Fund objective: Sector fund

Toll-free: 800-525-8085
In-state: 303-930-6300
Fax: 303-930-6584

Performance	★ ★ ★ ★ ★
Consistency	★ ★ ★ ★ ★
Fees/Services	★ ★ ★ ★ ★
FTCHX	**15 Points**

Daniel Leonard has been riding the crest of a high-tech tidal wave. It's a trend, says the veteran portfolio manager of INVESCO's fast-climbing Technology Fund, that could last for years to come. "Technology will take us well into the next century. We'll all be more wireless and more interactive."

Over the past ten years, the fund has grown at a rate of about 20 percent per year. A $10,000 investment in the fund ten years ago would now be worth about $60,000.

The fund focuses on small, emerging companies from a wide range of technology sectors, although its heaviest weighting is in the computer area. Computer software accounts for 14 percent of total assets, computer systems accounts for 12 percent, and computer services account for 10 percent. Other leading sectors include electronics (15 percent), medical products and drugs (7 percent), telecommunications (7 percent), and finance (7 percent).

"If we can spot an area that looks particularly good, we may move some more money into it, or we may become underweighted in areas we think don't look good." Leonard is not shy about moving his money around. His portfolio turnover ratio approaches 200 percent per year. To stay on top of the trends, Leonard likes to attend technology conferences and exhibitions, interview corporate managers, and study sales trends. "I try to get a feel for what types of products are moving ahead of the other areas."

Leonard's investment strategy is to focus on companies with strong earnings and sales growth. "We like companies with accelerating sales. When they begin to slow down, that probably means the stock price will slow down too."

Normally, Leonard keeps nearly 90 to 100 percent of the fund's assets invested in stocks, although it recently dropped to just under 80 percent. "We might go to 20 percent cash (investments) on rare occasions, but only if we thought we were coming into a real bear market."

PERFORMANCE

The fund has enjoyed exceptional growth over the past five years. Including dividends and capital gains distributions, the INVESCO Technology Fund has provided a total return for the past five years (through mid-1996) of 226 percent. A $10,000 investment in 1991 would have grown to about $33,000 five years later. Average annual return: 26.6 percent.

CONSISTENCY

The fund has been very consistent, outperforming the Dow Jones Industrial Average five consecutive years through 1995 (but it trailed the Dow through the first half of 1996). Its biggest gain came in 1991, when it jumped 76.9 percent (compared with a 20.3 percent rise in the Dow).

FEES/SERVICES/MANAGEMENT

Like all INVESCO funds, the Technology Fund is a true no-load fund—no fee to buy, no fee to sell. The fund's total annual expense ratio of 1.12 percent (with no 12b-1 fee) compares favorably with other no-load funds.

The fund offers all the standard services such as retirement account availability, automatic withdrawal, and automatic checking account deduction. Its minimum initial investment of $1,000 and minimum subsequent investment of $50 compare favorably with other funds.

Daniel Leonard joined INVESCO in 1975. He managed the company's Growth Fund before moving to the Technology Fund in 1985. He also manages the INVESCO Gold Fund. The INVESCO fund family includes 33 funds and allows shareholders to switch from fund to fund by telephone.

Top Ten Holdings

1. MEMC Electronic Materials
2. First Data
3. General Motors "E"
4. Newbridge Neworks
5. Kent Electronics
6. Cellular Services
7. U.S. Robotics
8. Ceridian
9. Harris
10. BMC

Asset Mix: Common stocks: 78%; Cash/equivalents: 22%
Total Net Assets: $704 million

Fees

Front-end load	*None*
Redemption fee	*None*
12b-1 fee	*None*
Management fee	0.73%
Other expenses	0.39
Total annual expense	1.12%
Minimum initial investment	$1,000
Minimum subsequent investment	$50

Services

Telephone exchanges	*Yes*
Automatic withdrawal	*Yes*
Automatic checking deduction	*Yes*
Retirement plan/IRA	*Yes*
Instant redemption	*Yes*
Financial statements	*Semiannual*
Income distributions	*Annual*
Capital gains distributions	*Annual*
Portfolio manager—years	12
Number of funds in family	33

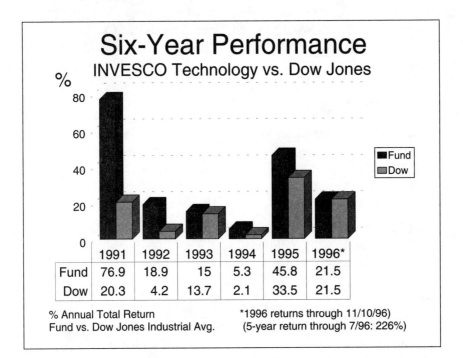

Six-Year Performance
INVESCO Technology vs. Dow Jones

	1991	1992	1993	1994	1995	1996*
Fund	76.9	18.9	15	5.3	45.8	21.5
Dow	20.3	4.2	13.7	2.1	33.5	21.5

% Annual Total Return
Fund vs. Dow Jones Industrial Avg.

*1996 returns through 11/10/96)
(5-year return through 7/96: 226%)

5
Baron Asset Fund

The Baron Funds
767 Fifth Avenue, 24th Floor
New York, NY 10153

Fund manager: Ronald Baron
Fund objective: Aggressive growth

Toll-free: 800-992-2766
In-state: 212-759-7700
Fax: 212-759-7529

Performance	★ ★ ★ ★
Consistency	★ ★ ★ ★ ★
Fees/Services	★ ★ ★ ★ ★
BARAX	**14 Points**

Ronald Baron, the founder and portfolio manager of the Baron Asset Fund, has built a strong track record the past ten years by taking a long-term approach investing in fast-rising small and mid-size growth stocks.

"We invest only in securities we believe can increase in value at least 50 percent within two years," he explains. "We hope to hold our investments much longer than that to minimize both taxes and transaction costs."

His long-term approach is reflected in the fund's low annual portfolio turnover ratio of just 35 percent.

Since its inception in 1987, the fund has grown about 18 percent per year. A $10,000 investment in the Baron Asset Fund when it opened would have grown to about $44,000 nine years later.

The fund, which has about 60 stock holdings, is well-diversified across industry groups. Its largest segment is business services, which account for about 15 percent of assets. Other leading segments include retail and restaurants (14 percent), health services (13 percent), communications (12 percent), and financial stocks (9 percent). The fund stays 80 to 90 percent invested in stocks most of the time.

PERFORMANCE

The fund has enjoyed exceptional growth over the past five years. Including dividends and capital gains distributions, the Baron Asset Fund has provided a total return for the past five years (through mid-1996) of 187 percent. A $10,000 investment in 1991 would have grown to about $29,000 five years later. Average annual return: 23.5 percent.

CONSISTENCY

The fund has been very consistent, outperforming the Dow Jones Industrial Average five consecutive years through 1995 (and it was well ahead of the Dow through the first half of 1996).

FEES/SERVICES/MANAGEMENT

The Baron Asset Fund is a true no-load fund—no fees to buy or sell fund shares. Its annual expense ratio of 1.44 percent (including a .25 percent 12b-1 fee and a 1 percent management fee) is about average among all funds.

The fund offers all the standard services such as retirement account availability, automatic withdrawal, and automatic checking account deduction. Its minimum initial investment of $2,000 and subsequent investment minimum of $10 compares favorably to other funds.

Ronald Baron has managed the fund since its inception in 1987. The Baron family of funds includes only one other fund, the Baron Growth and Income Fund.

Top Ten Holdings

1. Robert Half Int'l
2. Manor Care
3. Charles Schwab
4. Smart & Final
5. American Mobile Satellite
6. Cellular Comm Puerto Rico
7. Olsten
8. Saga Communications
9. Genesis Health Ventures
10. DeVRY

Asset Mix: Common stocks: 85%; Cash/equivalents: 15%
Total Net Assets: $638 million

Fees

Front-end load	*None*
Redemption fee	*None*
12b-1 fee	0.25%
Management fee	1.00
Other expenses	0.19
Total annual expense	1.44%
Minimum initial investment	$2,000
Minimum subsequent investment	$10

Services

Telephone exchanges	*Yes*
Automatic withdrawal	*Yes*
Automatic checking deduction	*Yes*
Retirement plan/IRA	*Yes*
Instant redemption	*Yes*
Financial statements	*Semiannual*
Income distributions	*Annual*
Capital gains distributions	*Annual*
Portfolio manager—years	10
Number of funds in family	2

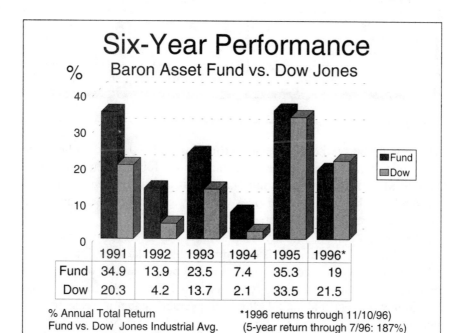

Six-Year Performance
Baron Asset Fund vs. Dow Jones

	1991	1992	1993	1994	1995	1996*
Fund	34.9	13.9	23.5	7.4	35.3	19
Dow	20.3	4.2	13.7	2.1	33.5	21.5

% Annual Total Return
Fund vs. Dow Jones Industrial Avg.

*1996 returns through 11/10/96)
(5-year return through 7/96: 187%)

6
Fidelity Select Home Finance Portfolio

SECTOR

Fidelity Investments
82 Devonshire Street
Boston, MA 02109

Fund manager: David Ellison
Fund objective: Sector fund

Toll-free: 800-544-8888
In-state: 801-534-1910
Fax: 617-476-9753

Performance	★ ★ ★ ★ ★
Consistency	★ ★ ★ ★ ★
Fees/Services	★ ★ ★ ★
FSVLX	**14 Points**

The new-home market has been sizzling in the 1990s, and so have the companies bankrolling the latest housing boom. Mortgage lenders such as Fannie Mae, BankAmerica, and Nationsbank have enjoyed increased demand for their lending services courtesy of a robust economy and attractive mortgage interest rates.

The result for the Fidelity Select Home Finance Portfolio has been nothing short of spectacular. The fund has eclipsed the Dow Jones Industrial Average five consecutive years, and has posted returns of more than 50 percent three of the past five years. A $10,000 investment five years ago would now be worth about $43,000—an average annual increase of 33.7 percent.

Not all of the fund's success, however, should be attributed to the housing boom. Fund manager David Ellison, who has been with the fund since its inception in 1985, has done an astute job of finding hot pockets within the lending industry. His strategy is to look for bargains.

"I have the biggest positions in the cheapest stocks," says Ellison. To determine which stocks are cheapest, he compares hundreds of bank and thrift stocks for PE ratios, price-to-book value, and a variety of other screens. "Then you put some value on management," adds Ellison. "I try to talk to the managers of as many of these companies as possible."

The biggest challenge Ellison faces is surviving the down times. "When the sector is underperforming, my strategy is to have fewer stock positions and move more assets into the cheaper names with the best managers. And then brace for the time the market turns around." Ellison wants to be fully invested when the market hits bottom. "People are afraid of rising interest rates. When rates go up, they start selling. That's when you want to be in the market. You have to stay optimistic in this business. You have to always feel that things are going to turn around. You buy when fear is high—when people are anticipating the worst in respect to interest rates, and stocks are near their 52-week lows. One whiff of good news, and those stocks are all going to double."

He adds: "There are going to be some down times. I know that. But the game here is, when the group is hot, you want to be red hot. Certainly if the sector is down, you're down. But you want to be there at the bottom. That's what puts you in a position to outperform everyone else when this group is in favor. That's how I play it. I want to hit a home run."

When a stock begins to enjoy a little too much success, that's a signal to Ellison to bail out. "I sell stocks that have had a lot of 'buy' action." He particularly looks for the following:

- *High valuations.* If the stock is too pricey based on its PE ratio and other criteria, it's a sell.
- *Takeover speculation.* "When I hear a stock is up (in price) on takeover rumors, I sell. But I don't sell it all. That way, if the stock continues to run up (in price), I'll still have some left in the portfolio."

Ellison takes that same slow approach with nearly every stock he sells. "I don't sell the whole block at once. I get in a position slowly, and I get out slowly. It gives you a chance to rethink your position. And if the stock moves up, you're still in the game."

The home mortgage sector tends to do best when interest rates are low or falling and worst when they begin to edge back up. Volatility is something Ellison has had to get used to. "I don't spend time worrying about the market. I've seen the mood swings before. And I don't worry about a one-year record. I want a good five-year record."

Ellison has about 100 stock holdings in the portfolio. Banks and thrifts account for about 66 percent of the portfolio. Credit agencies, financial services, insurance, real estate, and related sectors make up the other 34 percent.

PERFORMANCE

The fund has enjoyed exceptional growth over the past five years. Including dividends and capital gains distributions, the Fidelity Select Home Finance Portfolio has provided a total return for the past five years (through mid-1996) of 327 percent. A $10,000 investment in 1991 would have grown to $43,000 five years later. Average annual return: 33.7 percent.

CONSISTENCY

The fund has been very consistent, outperforming the Dow Jones Industrial Average five consecutive years through 1995 (but it trailed the Dow through the first half of 1996). The fund has had gains of more than 50 percent three of the past five years. However, in 1990—a bad year for the mortgage business—the fund suffered a 15 percent decline.

FEES/SERVICES/MANAGEMENT

The fund has a front-end load of 3 percent, and a maximum redemption fee of 0.75 percent if it's sold out within 30 days. Otherwise, a fee of $7.50 is charged upon redemption. The fund's total annual expense ratio of 1.42 percent (with no 12b-1 fee) is about average among load funds.

The fund offers all the standard services such as retirement account availability, automatic withdrawal, and automatic checking account deduction. Its minimum initial investment of $2,500 and minimum subsequent investment of $250 are a little high compared with other funds.

David Ellison has managed the fund since its inception in 1985. The Fidelity fund family includes 210 funds.

Top Ten Holdings

1. Standard Federal Bancorp
2. Charter One Financial
3. Bank of New York
4. Astoria Financial
5. Federal National Mortgage Association
6. NationsBank
7. BankAmerica
8. First Chicago NBD
9. North Side Savings Bank
10. Greenpoint Financial

Asset Mix: Common stocks: 90%; Cash/equivalents: 10%
Total Net Assets: $617 million

Fees

Front-end load	3.00%
Redemption fee	$7.50
12b-1 fee	*None*
Management fee	0.61
Other expenses	0.81
Total annual expense	1.42%
Minimum initial investment	$2,500
Minimum subsequent investment	$250

Services

Telephone exchanges	*Yes*
Automatic withdrawal	*Yes*
Automatic checking deduction	*Yes*
Retirement plan/IRA	*Yes*
Instant redemption	*Yes*
Financial statements	*Semiannual*
Income distributions	*Semiannual*
Capital gains distributions	*Semiannual*
Portfolio manager—years	12
Number of funds in family	210

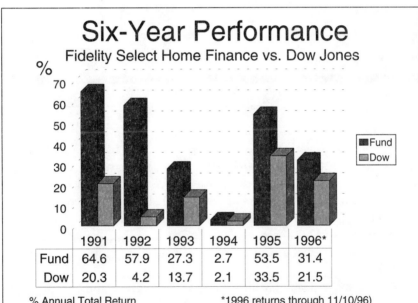

Six-Year Performance
Fidelity Select Home Finance vs. Dow Jones

	1991	1992	1993	1994	1995	1996*
Fund	64.6	57.9	27.3	2.7	53.5	31.4
Dow	20.3	4.2	13.7	2.1	33.5	21.5

% Annual Total Return
Fund vs. Dow Jones Industrial Avg.

*1996 returns through 11/10/96)
(5-year return through 7/96: 327%)

7

Putnam New Opportunities Fund "A"

AGGRESSIVE

Putnam Mutual Funds
One Post Office Square
Boston, MA 02109

Fund manager: Daniel L. Miller
Fund objective: Aggressive growth

Toll-free: 800-225-1581
In-state: 617-292-1000
Fax: 617-760-5869

Performance	★ ★ ★ ★ ★
Consistency	★ ★ ★ ★ ★
Fees/Services	★ ★ ★
PNOPX	**13 Points**

The Putnam New Opportunities Fund has become one of the hottest mutual funds in America. Opened in 1990, the fund has already attracted investment assets of nearly $5 billion. Its rapid growth corresponds directly to its high-octane performance. Since its inception in 1990, the fund has racked up average annual returns of about 33 percent.

A $10,000 investment in the fund when it opened in 1990 would have grown to about $53,000 six years later. The fund invests in fast-growing small and midsized companies, many of which are in high tech-related areas.

Fund manager Daniel Miller, who has been with the fund from the beginning, focuses on stocks in industries that he believes have the greatest potential for growth. Those industries include personal communications (long distance telephone, cellular telephone, paging, and personal communications networks), media and entertainment (cable television, filmmakers, theme parks, casinos, and radio and TV stations), medical technology and health care services, environmental and waste disposal services, applied and advanced technology (software, networking, semiconductors, and information services), personal financial services, and value-oriented consuming (retailers, restaurants, lodging, and travel services).

The fund stays almost fully invested in stocks most of the time. Miller takes a moderate trading approach, with an annual portfolio turnover ratio of 57 percent.

The fund has about 180 stock holdings in all. The leading industrial segments include software, 13 percent; business services, 7 percent; computer services, 7 percent; health care services and HMOs, 9 percent; networking equipment, 7 percent; and semiconductors, 5 percent.

PERFORMANCE

The fund has enjoyed phenomenal growth over the past five years. Including dividends and capital gains distributions, the Putnam New Opportunities Fund has provided a total return for the past five years (through mid-1996) of 300 percent. A $10,000 investment in 1991 would have grown to about $40,000 five years later. Average annual return: 32 percent.

CONSISTENCY

The fund has been very consistent, outperforming the Dow Jones Industrial Average five consecutive years through 1995 (and again through the first half of 1996). Its best years were 1991 and 1995 when it climbed 67.6 percent and 46.2 percent, respectively.

FEES/SERVICES/MANAGEMENT

The fund has a front-end load of 5.75 percent. Its total annual expense ratio of 1.13 percent (including a 0.25 percent 12b-1 fee and a 0.61 percent management fee) compares favorably with other funds.

The fund offers all the standard services such as retirement account availability, automatic withdrawal, and automatic checking account deduction. Its minimum initial investment of $500 and minimum subsequent investment of $50 compare very favorably with other funds.

Daniel Miller has managed the fund since 1990. The Putnam fund family includes 77 funds and allows shareholders to switch from fund to fund by telephone.

Top Ten Holdings

1. HFS
2. America Online
3. Cisco Systems
4. Paging Network
5. U.S. Robotics

6. Infinity Broadcasting
7. Corporate Express
8. Vencor
9. Oxford Health Plans
10. StrataCom

Asset Mix: Common stocks: 92%; Cash/equivalents: 8%
Total Net Assets: $3.2 billion

Fees

Front-end load	5.75%
Redemption fee	*None*
12b-1 fee	0.25
Management fee	0.61
Other expenses	0.27
Total annual expense	1.13%
Minimum initial investment	$500
Minimum subsequent investment	$50

Services

Telephone exchanges	*Yes*
Automatic withdrawal	*Yes*
Automatic checking deduction	*Yes*
Retirement plan/IRA	*Yes*
Instant redemption	*Yes*
Financial statements	*Semiannual*
Income distributions	*Quarterly*
Capital gains distributions	*Annual*
Portfolio manager—years	7
Number of funds in family	77

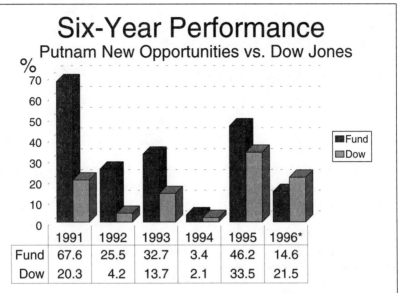

Six-Year Performance
Putnam New Opportunities vs. Dow Jones

	1991	1992	1993	1994	1995	1996*
Fund	67.6	25.5	32.7	3.4	46.2	14.6
Dow	20.3	4.2	13.7	2.1	33.5	21.5

% Annual Total Return
Fund vs. Dow Jones Industrial Avg.

*1996 returns through 11/10/96
(5-year return through 7/96: 300%)

8

Twentieth Century Giftrust Investors Fund

AGGRESSIVE

Twentieth Century Group
4500 Main Street
P.O. Box 419200
Kansas City, MO 64141-6200

Fund managers: James E. Stowers III, Glen Fogle, and Robert C. Puff Jr.
Fund objective: Aggressive growth

Toll-free: 800-345-2021
In-state: 816-531-5575
Fax: 816-340-4753

Performance	★ ★ ★ ★ ★
Consistency	★ ★ ★ ★ ★
Fees/Services	★ ★ ★
TWGTX	**13 Points**

This has been a truly phenomenal fund for many, many years, with an average return the past decade of 21 percent per year. Too bad you can't buy shares of the fund for yourself.

The Giftrust Fund is designed as a trust to be used to set aside money for children or foundations. The fund has a minimum ten-year holding period intended to encourage a long-term growth philosophy. Because of its ten-year requirement, it may not be appropriate as a college savings vehicle for children who will be attending college in less than ten years. The Giftrust is irrevocable.

The fund is very aggressive and fairly volatile, but its long-term performance has been exceptional. The fund was opened in 1983. A $10,000 investment in the fund ten years ago would now be worth about $67,000.

The fund invests primarily in small to midsized companies on a fast growth track. Generally speaking, the fund stays fully invested in stocks. The fund maintains a fairly aggressive trading policy, with an annual portfolio turnover ratio of 105 percent.

In all, the fund has about 70 stock holdings, heavily weighted in the high tech area. Leading sectors include computer software and services,

19 percent of total assets; business services and supplies, 16 percent; computer peripherals, 12 percent; medical equipment, 10 percent; and biotechnology, 7 percent. About 8 percent of the fund's assets are in foreign stocks.

PERFORMANCE

The fund has enjoyed exceptional growth over the past five years. The fund has provided a total return over the past five years (through mid-1996) of 302 percent. A $10,000 investment in the fund in 1991 would have grown to about $40,000 five years later. Average annual return: 32.1 percent.

CONSISTENCY

The fund has been extremely consistent, outperforming the Dow Jones Industrial Average five consecutive years through 1995 (and was ahead of the Dow through the first half of 1996). The fund's biggest gain was in 1991 when it soared 84.9 percent.

FEES/SERVICES/MANAGEMENT

Like all Twentieth Century funds, the Giftrust Investors Fund is a true no-load fund—no fee to buy, no fee to sell. And it has a very low total annual expense ratio of 1.0 percent (with no 12b-1 fee).

Because of its unusual nature, the fund offers very few of the standard services most other funds offer. As mentioned above, you can't invest in the fund in your own name. It is strictly to be used as a trust for others.

The fund's $250 minimum initial investment and $25 minimum contribution for existing accounts compare very favorably with other funds.

James Stowers III and Robert Puff Jr. have been involved in the management of the fund since its inception in 1983. Glen Fogle joined the management team in 1990. The Twentieth Century fund family includes 18 funds.

Top Ten Holdings

1. Shiva
2. U.S. Office Products
3. APAC Teleservices
4. Security Dynamics Technology
5. PMT Services
6. Computer Horizons
7. CBT Group
8. Centocor
9. ABR Information Services
10. Neuromedical Systems

Asset Mix: Common stocks: 98%; Cash/equivalents: 2%
Total Net Assets: $798 million

Fees

Front-end load	*None*
Redemption fee	*None*
12b-1 fee	*None*
Management fee	1.00%
Other expenses	*None*
Total annual expense	1.00%
Minimum initial investment	$500
Minimum subsequent investment	$50

Services

Telephone exchanges	*Yes*
Automatic withdrawal	*No*
Automatic checking deduction	*Yes*
Retirement plan/IRA	*No*
Instant redemption	*No*
Financial statements	*Semiannual*
Income distributions	*Annual*
Capital gains distributions	*Annual*
Portfolio managers—years	14
Number of funds in family	18

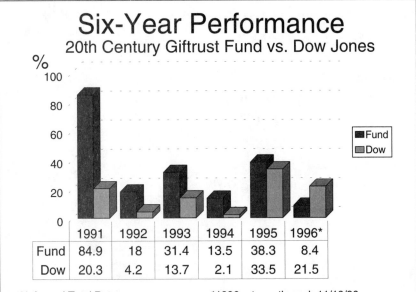

Six-Year Performance
20th Century Giftrust Fund vs. Dow Jones

	1991	1992	1993	1994	1995	1996*
Fund	84.9	18	31.4	13.5	38.3	8.4
Dow	20.3	4.2	13.7	2.1	33.5	21.5

% Annual Total Return
Fund vs. Dow Jones Industrial Avg.

*1996 returns through 11/10/96
(5-year return through 7/96: 302%)

9
John Hancock Special Equities Fund "A"

AGGRESSIVE

John Hancock Funds
101 Huntington Avenue, 5th Floor
Boston, MA 02199-7603

Fund manager: Michael P. DiCarlo
Fund objective: Aggressive growth

Toll-free: 800-225-5291
In-state: 617-375-1500
Fax: 617-375-1819

Performance	★ ★ ★ ★ ★
Consistency	★ ★ ★ ★ ★
Fees/Services	★ ★ ★
JHNSX	**13 Points**

What's so special about the Special Equities Fund? For starters, it's had a very special 30 percent average annual return the past five years. Fund manager Michael DiCarlo looks for "special situations"—companies that may be involved in an unique growth situation, or occupy a dominant position in an emerging industry, or have a significant and growing market share in a large fragmented industry.

"We're bottom-up investors," said DiCarlo. "We build the portfolio stock by stock, searching across the broad investment spectrum for small-cap companies that fit our investment criteria." He says candidates must have the potential for earnings and revenue growth of at least 25 percent per year.

The portfolio is packed with small, young companies you've probably never heard of, such as Dura Pharmaceuticals, Mossimo, Adaptec, and Cognos. Most stocks in the portfolio have annual sales of $100 million or more, although the fund also invests in some companies that are even smaller.

DiCarlo takes a fairly conservative trading approach, with an annual portfolio turnover ratio of 70 percent.

Over the past ten years, the fund has grown at an average annual rate of about 16 percent. A $10,000 investment in the fund ten years ago would now be worth about $45,000.

One of the objectives of the fund is to invest in a broad range of industries, although recently the portfolio has been dominated by high tech stocks. The leading segments include computer related products and services, 41 percent of assets; health and medical, 15 percent; telecommunications, 6 percent; and retail, 6 percent.

PERFORMANCE

The fund has enjoyed exceptional growth over the past five years. Including dividends and capital gains distributions, the Special Equities Fund has provided a total return for the past five years (through mid-1996) of 273 percent. A $10,000 investment in 1991 would have grown to about $37,000 five years later. Average annual return: 30.1 percent.

CONSISTENCY

The fund has been very consistent, beating or matching the Dow Jones Industrial Average for five consecutive years through 1995 (and the fund was even with the Dow through the first half of 1996). The fund's biggest year was 1991 when it jumped 84.5 percent.

FEES/SERVICES/MANAGEMENT

Special Equity "A" shares have a front-end load of 5 percent, and a total annual expense ratio of 1.48 percent (including a 0.3 percent 12b-1 fee and a 0.82 percent management fee). "B" shares have a 5 percent redemption fee and a much higher 2.2 percent total annual expense ratio.

The fund offers all the standard services such as retirement account availability, automatic withdrawal, and automatic checking account deduction. Its minimum initial investment of $1,000 and minimum subsequent investment of $50 compare favorably with other funds.

Michael P. DiCarlo has managed the fund since 1988. The John Hancock fund family includes 40 funds and allows shareholders to switch from fund to fund by telephone.

Top Ten Holdings

1. Electronics for Imaging	6. Media Computer Systems
2. Cascade Communications	7. Atria Software
3. America Online	8. PETsMART
4. Adaptec	9. Chesapeake Energy
5. Cognos	10. CUC International

Asset Mix: Common stocks: 96%; Cash/equivalents: 4%
Total Net Assets: $876 million

Fees

Front-end load	5.00%
Redemption fee	*None*
12b-1 fee	0.30
Management fee	0.82
Other expenses	0.36
Total annual expense	1.48%
Minimum initial investment	$1,000
Minimum subsequent investment	$50

Services

Telephone exchanges	*Yes*
Automatic withdrawal	*Yes*
Automatic checking deduction	*Yes*
Retirement plan/IRA	*Yes*
Instant redemption	*Yes*
Financial statements	*Semiannual*
Income distributions	*Annual*
Capital gains distributions	*Annual*
Portfolio manager—years	9
Number of funds in family	40

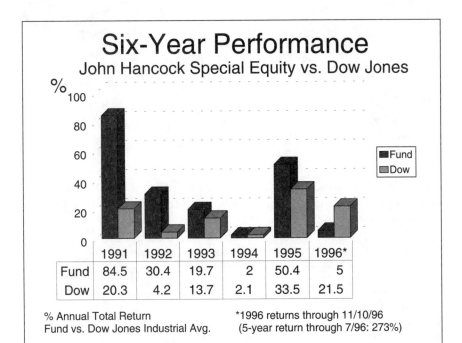

Six-Year Performance
John Hancock Special Equity vs. Dow Jones

	1991	1992	1993	1994	1995	1996*
Fund	84.5	30.4	19.7	2	50.4	5
Dow	20.3	4.2	13.7	2.1	33.5	21.5

% Annual Total Return
Fund vs. Dow Jones Industrial Avg.

*1996 returns through 11/10/96
(5-year return through 7/96: 273%)

10
Parkstone Small Capitalization Fund "A"

LONG TERM

Parkstone Funds
1900 East Dublin-Granville Road
Columbus, OH 43229

Fund manager: Roger Stamper
Fund objective: Long-term growth

Toll-free: 800-451-8377
In-state: 614-470-8000

Performance	★ ★ ★ ★ ★
Consistency	★ ★ ★ ★ ★
Fees/Services	★ ★ ★
PKSAX	**13 Points**

Compiling average annual returns of nearly 30 percent over the past five years is an achievement few money managers have ever—or will ever—match. But to hear Parkstone Small Capitalization Fund manager Roger Stamper talk about it, putting up the big numbers year in and year out is little more than a walk in the park.

"People try to make a lot out of managing money, but it's really very simple," says Stamper. "In the long term, it's earnings growth that drives a stock. When the market is topsy-turvy, when everyone else is pessimistic, we still focus on the same factor—earnings. If the earnings keep going up, then eventually the stock has to follow. The earnings will always bail you out."

The Parkstone Small Capitalization Fund invests primarily in small to midsized companies. "In terms of size, our focus is on companies with market capitalizations of $100 to $500 million," says Stamper. "Once the company hits $500 million, I won't add it to the portfolio, but if we already hold it, I might add to our position if I still like the stock. When it hits $1 billion, I won't add anymore. And when it hits $2.5 billion, it's gone. I sell it all out. Obviously, the best companies are those I never have to sell until they get too big."

Stamper takes a long-term, buy-and-hold approach, with an annual portfolio turnover ratio of just 50 percent.

The Parkstone Small Cap Fund is different from other funds in that the fund manager does very little of the initial market research. Stamper relies on regional brokerage companies around the country to feed him stock ideas. "Our focus has always been on Main Street, not Wall Street. We go to where the best information is. We deal with a group of regional brokers who know their markets very well and are able to identify the smaller, emerging stocks well before they catch the attention of Wall Street."

Stamper is most interested in small stocks with sustainable growth. The trick is figuring out which companies have sustainable growth. "You really can't quantify it. You want strong management, increasing market share, strong revenue growth, good products—all the intangibles that give you confidence the company is likely to continue its strong growth."

Stamper tends to invest most often in companies he understands. "If I can paint a picture in my mind of what the company does and why its sales and earnings will continue to grow, that's a big plus for me."

The fund will sell out stocks when the growth begins to wane or when management begins to change key strategies. Stamper is also quick to sell a stock that takes a sudden turn for the worse. "Even if we have to take a 30 percent loss, we'll get out. It's the cockroach theory. I've seen too many times when you wait around a quarter or two to see if the company will improve, and it just gets worse."

The fund has about 70 stock holdings primarily in the technology area. Computer software accounts for about 18 percent of assets, health care and medical make up 24 percent, and retail stocks account for 11.5 percent.

PERFORMANCE

The fund has enjoyed exceptional growth over the past five years. Including dividends and capital gains distributions, the Parkstone Small Capitalization Fund has provided a total return for the past five years (through mid-1996) of 258 percent. A $10,000 investment in 1989 would have grown to $36,000 five years later. Average annual return: 29.1 percent.

CONSISTENCY

The fund has been very consistent, outperforming the Dow Jones Industrial Average every year over the five-year period through 1995 (and again through the first half of 1996). Its biggest gain came in 1991, when it moved up 43.9 percent (compared with a 20.3 percent rise in the Dow).

FEES/SERVICES/MANAGEMENT

The Parkstone Small Capitalization Fund offers three classes of funds. The "A" shares carry a 4.5 percent front-end load; "B" shares carry a maximum 4 percent redemption fee (that declines 1 percent per year to zero after the four years), but with a higher annual expense ratio; and "C" shares carry no load, but are available only to institutional customers.

The fund's total annual expense ratio of 1.55 percent (including a 0.25 percent 12b-1 fee and a 1 percent management fee) is about average among mutual funds. The fund offers all the standard services such as retirement account availability, automatic withdrawal, and automatic checking account deduction. Its minimum initial investment of $1,000 (with no minimum subsequent investment requirement) compares favorably with other funds.

Roger Stamper has managed the fund since 1988. The Parkstone fund family includes 11 funds and allows shareholders to switch from fund to fund by telephone.

Top Ten Holdings

1. Omnicare
2. Credit Acceptance
3. Concord EFS
4. Micro Warehouse
5. McAfee Associates
6. Phycor
7. LCI International
8. Macromedia
9. Medpartners
10. Regal Cinemas

Asset Mix: Common stocks: 95%; Cash/equivalents: 5%
Total Net Assets: $125.1 million

Fees

Front-end load	4.50%
Redemption fee	*None*
12b-1 fee	0.25
Management fee	1.00
Other expenses	0.30
Total annual expense	1.55%
Minimum initial investment	$1,000
Minimum subsequent investment	*None*

Services

Telephone exchanges	*Yes*
Automatic withdrawal	*Yes*
Automatic checking deduction	*Yes*
Retirement plan/IRA	*Yes*
Instant redemption	*Yes*
Financial statements	*Semiannual*
Income distributions	*Monthly*
Capital gains distributions	*Annual*
Portfolio manager—years	9
Number of funds in family	11

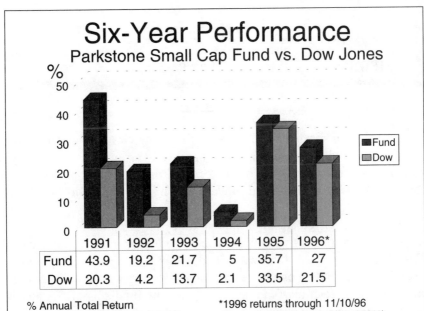

Six-Year Performance
Parkstone Small Cap Fund vs. Dow Jones

	1991	1992	1993	1994	1995	1996*
Fund	43.9	19.2	21.7	5	35.7	27
Dow	20.3	4.2	13.7	2.1	33.5	21.5

% Annual Total Return
Fund vs. Dow Jones Industrial Avg.

*1996 returns through 11/10/96
(5-year return through 7/96: 258%)

11

MFS Emerging Growth Fund "B"

AGGRESSIVE

MFS Fund Distributors, Inc.
500 Boylston Street
Boston, MA 02116-3741

Fund manager: John W. Ballen
Fund objective: Aggressive growth

Toll-free: 800-637-2929
In-state: 617-954-5000
Fax: 617-954-6617

Performance	★ ★ ★ ★ ★
Consistency	★ ★ ★ ★ ★
Fees/Services	★ ★ ★
MEGBX	**13 Points**

How would you spend $4 billion? MFS Emerging Growth Fund manager John Ballen—who has seen the assets in his fund grow more than twenty-fold the past five years—has been like a kid in a candy shop. A little of this, a few shares of that—and suddenly, he has more than 400 stocks in the portfolio.

Ballen has stayed ahead of the market by stocking his portfolio with a diverse range of fast-rising companies with little-known names such as Harmonic Lightwaves, Transwitch, and Xilinx. The fund's success, however, has given Ballen one more challenge—staying ahead of the quickly rising flood of cash the fund has attracted. The fund's assets (A and B shares combined) have grown from $145 million in 1991 to more than $4 billion in 1996.

Despite the rapid growth, Ballen has tried to stay true to the mission of the fund, which is to "invest primarily (at least 80 percent of assets under normal circumstances) in stocks of small and medium-sized companies that are early in their life cycle but which have the potential to become major enterprises." Once Ballen uncovers a solid prospect, he likes to hold for the long term. The fund's annual portfolio turnover ratio is a very modest 36 percent.

The fund is broadly diversified across industry groups. The leading segments include computer software and systems (28 percent of assets), health and medical related stocks (20 percent), restaurants and lodging (14.5 percent), retail stores (10 percent), business services (6 percent), and telecommunications (5 percent).

PERFORMANCE

The fund has enjoyed exceptional growth over the past five years. Including dividends and capital gains distributions, the MFS Emerging Growth Fund has provided a total return for the past five years (through mid-1996) of 229 percent. A $10,000 investment in 1991 would have grown to about $33,000 five years later. Average annual return: 26.9 percent.

CONSISTENCY

The fund has been very consistent, outperforming the Dow Jones Industrial Average every year over the five-year period from 1991 through 1995 (and again through the first half of 1996). Its biggest gain came in 1991, when it jumped 87.6 percent (compared with a 20.3 percent rise in the Dow).

FEES/SERVICES/MANAGEMENT

The fund's B shares have a redemption fee of 4 percent and a very high annual expense ratio of 2.08 percent (including a 1 percent 12b-1 fee). The fund also has A shares that carry a front-end load of 5.75 percent, and a much lower 12b-1 fee of 0.25 percent and total expense ratio of 1.28 percent.

The fund offers all the standard services such as retirement account availability, automatic withdrawal, and automatic checking account deduction. Its minimum initial investment of $1,000 and minimum subsequent investment of $50 are comparable with other funds.

John Ballen has managed the fund since 1986. The MFS family of funds includes 33 funds with the option of switching freely between funds.

Top Ten Holdings

1. HFS	6. BMC Software
2. Oracle	7. Office Depot
3. United HealthCare	8. Computer Associates Int'l
4. Cadence Design Systems	9. System Software Associates
5. Autodesk	10. WorldCom

Asset Mix: Common stocks: 98%; Cash/equivalents: 2%
Total Net Assets: $ 2.5 billion

Fees

Front-end load	*None*
Redemption fee	4.00%
12b-1 fee	1.00
Management fee	0.75
Other expenses	0.33
Total annual expense	2.08%
Minimum initial investment	$1,000
Minimum subsequent investment	$50

Services

Telephone exchanges	*Yes*
Automatic withdrawal	*Yes*
Automatic checking deduction	*Yes*
Retirement plan/IRA	*Yes*
Instant redemption	*Yes*
Financial statements	*Annually*
Income distributions	*Annually*
Capital gains distributions	*Annually*
Portfolio managers—years	11
Number of funds in family	33

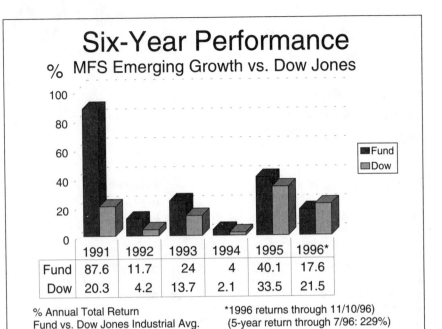

Six-Year Performance
% MFS Emerging Growth vs. Dow Jones

	1991	1992	1993	1994	1995	1996*
Fund	87.6	11.7	24	4	40.1	17.6
Dow	20.3	4.2	13.7	2.1	33.5	21.5

% Annual Total Return
Fund vs. Dow Jones Industrial Avg.

*1996 returns through 11/10/96)
(5-year return through 7/96: 229%)

12

Warburg Pincus Emerging Growth Fund

AGGRESSIVE

Warburg Pincus Funds
466 Lexington Avenue
New York, NY 10017-3147

Fund managers: Beth Dater,
   Steven Lurito
Fund objective: Aggressive growth

Toll-free: 800-927-2874
In-state: 212-878-0600
Fax: 212-370-9833

Performance	★ ★ ★ ★
Consistency	★ ★ ★ ★
Fees/Services	★ ★ ★ ★ ★
CUEGX	**13 Points**

The Warburg Pincus Emerging Growth Fund invests in small and mid-sized companies that have progressed beyond the start-up phase and have established a profitable niche in their industry.

The fund, which opened in 1988, has posted an average annual return of about 19 percent since its inception. A $10,000 investment in the fund in 1988 would have grown to about $43,000 eight years later.

Fund managers Beth Dater and Steven Lurito look for stocks that have "positive earnings momentum and have the potential to achieve significant capital gains within a relatively short period of time" through new products or services, technological improvements, or changes in management.

The fund, which stays almost fully invested in stocks most of the time, is heavily weighted in the technology area. Its leading industrial segments include computers (16 percent of assets), electronics (10 percent), business services (11 percent), health care and pharmaceuticals (10 percent), and finance (8 percent). In all, the fund has about 75 stock holdings.

The fund managers take a fairly conservative approach in their trading strategy, with an annual portfolio turnover ratio of 85 percent.

PERFORMANCE

The Warburg Pincus Emerging Growth Fund has experienced outstanding growth over the past five years. Including dividends and capital gains distributions, the fund has provided a total return for the past five years (through mid-1996) of 176 percent. A $10,000 investment five years ago would have grown to about $27,600. Average annual return: 22.5 percent.

CONSISTENCY

The fund has been relatively consistent, outperforming the Dow Jones Industrial Average four of the five years through 1995 (and it was nearly even with the Dow through the first half of 1996). The fund's biggest gain came in 1991, when it rose 56.1 percent (compared with a 20.3 percent rise in the Dow).

FEES/SERVICES/MANAGEMENT

The Warburg Pincus Emerging Growth Fund is a true no-load fund—no fee to buy, no fee to sell. The fund's total annual expense ratio of 1.26 percent (with no 12b-1 fee) compares favorably with other no-load funds.

The fund offers all the standard services such as retirement account availability, automatic withdrawal, and automatic checking account deduction. Its minimum initial investment of $2,500 is a little higher than average, but its minimum subsequent investment of $100 is in line with other funds.

Beth Dater has managed the fund since its inception in 1988, and has been a portfolio manager with Warburg Pincus since 1978. Comanager Steven Lurito joined the fund in 1990. The Warburg Pincus fund family includes 11 funds and allows shareholders to switch from fund to fund by telephone.

Top Ten Holdings

1. Solectron	6. Paging Network
2. Input/Output	7. Gilead Sciences
3. Viking Office Products	8. Borders Group
4. Glenayre Technologies	9. Cognex
5. Synopsys	10. Continuum

Asset Mix: Common stocks: 93%; Cash/equivalents: 7%
Total Net Assets: $945 million

Fees

Front-end load	*None*
Redemption fee	*None*
12b-1 fee	*None*
Management fee	0.90%
Other expenses	0.36
Total annual expense	1.26%
Minimum initial investment	$2,500
Minimum subsequent investment	$100

Services

Telephone exchanges	*Yes*
Automatic withdrawal	*Yes*
Automatic checking deduction	*Yes*
Retirement plan/IRA	*Yes*
Instant redemption	*Yes*
Financial statements	*Annual*
Income distributions	*Annual*
Capital gains distributions	*Annual*
Portfolio manager—years	9
Number of funds in family	11

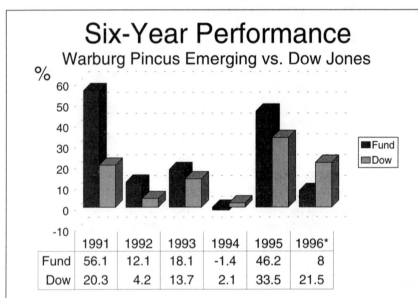

Six-Year Performance
Warburg Pincus Emerging vs. Dow Jones

	1991	1992	1993	1994	1995	1996*
Fund	56.1	12.1	18.1	-1.4	46.2	8
Dow	20.3	4.2	13.7	2.1	33.5	21.5

% Avg. Annual Total Return   *1996 returns through 11/10/96
Fund vs. Dow Jones Industrial Avg.   (5-year return through 7/96: 176%)

LONG TERM

13

Stein Roe Capital Opportunities Fund

Stein Roe Mutual Funds
P.O. Box 804058
Chicago, IL 60680-4058

Fund managers: Gloria Santella, Eric Maddix
Fund objective: Long-term growth

Toll-free: 800-338-2550
In-state: 312-368-7800
Fax: 312-368-5632

Performance	★ ★ ★ ★ ★
Consistency	★ ★ ★
Fees/Services	★ ★ ★ ★ ★
SRFCX	**13 Points**

When fund managers Gloria Santella and Eric Maddix scour the market for promising small stocks to tuck into their Stein Roe Capital Opportunities portfolio, their primary quest is for fast-rising stars in booming industries. Most of the fund's portfolio is concentrated in fast-growth sectors such as health care, technology, and business services.

But rapid growth isn't the only quality Santella and Maddix look for in a stock. They also like companies with veteran management, a strong balance sheet, and the ability to exploit market opportunities with successful products or services.

The fund has enjoyed outstanding growth the past five years, averaging 26.9 percent per year. But fasten your seat belt: the Capital Opportunities Fund has had some wild swings. Down 29 percent in 1990, it roared back with a 62.8 percent gain in 1991; dead even in 1994, it jumped 50.7 percent in 1995. Over the past ten years, the fund has grown at an average annual rate of 14 percent. A $10,000 investment in the fund ten years ago would now be worth about $37,000.

The fund stays almost fully invested in common stocks most of the time. It has about 50 stock holdings in all. The fund managers take a fairly conservative trading approach, with an annual portfolio turnover ratio of 60 percent.

The leading industrial sector in the portfolio is technology, which accounts for 20 percent of total assets. Other leading sectors are health care, 17 percent; business services, 15 percent; leisure and entertainment, 12 percent; specialty retailing, 7 percent; and industrial products, 6 percent.

PERFORMANCE

The Stein Roe Capital Opportunities Fund has enjoyed exceptional growth over the past five years. Including dividends and capital gains distributions, the fund has provided a total return for the past five years (through mid-1996) of 229 percent. A $10,000 investment in 1991 would have grown to about $33,000 five years later. Average annual return: 26.9 percent.

CONSISTENCY

The fund has been fairly consistent, outperforming the Dow Jones Industrial Average three of the five years through 1995 (and again through the first half of 1996). The fund's biggest gains came in 1991 and 1995 when it climbed 62.8 percent and 50.7 percent, respectively.

FEES/SERVICES/MANAGEMENT

Like all Stein Roe funds, the Capital Opportunity Fund is a true no-load— no fee to buy, no fee to sell. The fund's total annual expense ratio of 1.25 percent (with no 12b-1 fee) compares favorably with other funds.

The fund offers all the standard services such as retirement account availability, automatic withdrawal, and automatic checking account deduction. Its minimum initial investment of $2,500 is a little higher than average, but its minimum subsequent investment of $100 compares favorably with other funds.

Gloria Santella has managed the fund since 1991. Eric Maddix joined the fund as comanager in 1996. The Stein Roe fund family includes 18 funds and allows shareholders to switch from fund to fund by telephone.

Top Ten Holdings

1. Gartner Group
2. HFS
3. Clear Channel
   Communications
4. PhyCor
5. Paychex

6. Papa John's Int'l
7. Tellabs
8. HBO
9. StrataCom
10. Sunglass Hut Int'l

Asset Mix: Common stocks: 89%; Cash/equivalents: 11%
Total Net Assets: $682 million

Fees

Front-end load	*None*
Redemption fee	*None*
12b-1 fee	*None*
Management fee	0.90%
Other expenses	0.35
Total annual expense	1.25%
Minimum initial investment	$2,500
Minimum subsequent investment	$100

Services

Telephone exchanges	*Yes*
Automatic withdrawal	*Yes*
Automatic checking deduction	*Yes*
Retirement plan/IRA	*Yes*
Instant redemption	*Yes*
Financial statements	*Semiannual*
Income distributions	*Annual*
Capital gains distributions	*Annual*
Portfolio manager—years	6
Number of funds in family	18

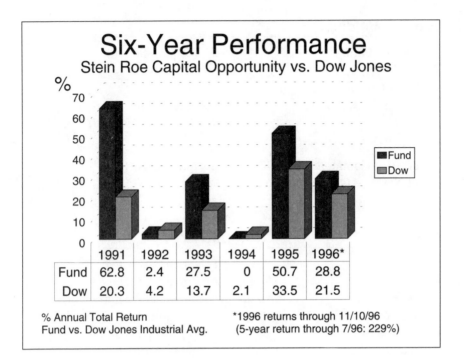

Six-Year Performance
Stein Roe Capital Opportunity vs. Dow Jones

	1991	1992	1993	1994	1995	1996*
Fund	62.8	2.4	27.5	0	50.7	28.8
Dow	20.3	4.2	13.7	2.1	33.5	21.5

% Annual Total Return   *1996 returns through 11/10/96
Fund vs. Dow Jones Industrial Avg.   (5-year return through 7/96: 229%)

LONG TERM

14
Founders Growth Fund

Founders Funds
2930 E. Third Avenue
Denver, CO 80206

Fund manager: Edward Keely
Fund objective: Long-term growth

Toll-free: 800-525-2440
In-state: 303-394-4404
Fax: 303-331-9862

Performance	★ ★ ★ ★
Consistency	★ ★ ★ ★
Fees/Services	★ ★ ★ ★ ★
FRGRX	**13 Points**

Solid, well-established companies with a track record of consistent growth make up the bulk of the portfolio of the Founders Growth Fund. The no-load fund invests in a diverse selection of mid- and large-capitalization stocks such as Cisco Systems, Home Depot, and AT&T.

"As we research individual companies, we pay special attention to business fundamentals, innovative management, increased productivity, and high recurring income," explains fund manager Edward Keely.

The fund has enjoyed stellar performance for many years. Since 1980, the fund has posted average annual gains of 15 percent. A $10,000 investment in the fund in 1980 would have grown to about $80,000 by 1996. A $10,000 investment in the fund ten years ago would now be worth about $40,000.

In all, the fund has about 100 stock holdings across a broad spectrum of industries. Keely maintains a fairly aggressive trading policy, with an annual portfolio turnover ratio of 130 percent.

Like many of the top funds, the Founders Growth Fund has had large positions in technology-related sectors. Computer software accounts for 11 percent of total assets, computer networking and equipment makes up

14 percent of assets, and semiconductors and equipment account for another 4 percent. Other leading segments include telecommunications, 7 percent; retail, 5 percent; health-related, 10 percent; leisure, 4 percent; and aerospace, 4 percent. About 8 percent of the fund's assets are invested in foreign stocks.

PERFORMANCE

The Founders Growth Fund has experienced outstanding growth over the past five years. Including dividends and capital gains distributions, the fund has provided a total return for the past five years (through mid-1996) of 165 percent. A $10,000 investment in 1991 would have grown to about $26,500 five years later. Average annual return: 21.6 percent.

CONSISTENCY

The fund has been very consistent, outperforming (or matching) the Dow Jones Industrial Average four of the five years through 1995 (and it was about even with the Dow through the first half of 1996). The fund's biggest gains came in 1991 and 1995, when it moved up 47.4 percent and 45.6 percent, respectively.

FEES/SERVICES/MANAGEMENT

The Founders Growth Fund is a true no-load fund—no fee to buy, no fee to sell. The fund's total annual expense ratio of 1.28 percent (including a 0.25 percent 12b-1 fee and a 0.74 percent management fee) compares favorably with other no-load funds.

The fund offers all the standard services such as retirement account availability, automatic withdrawal, and automatic checking account deduction. Its minimum initial investment of $1,000 and minimum subsequent investment of $100 are comparable to other funds.

Edward Keely has managed the fund since 1993. The Founders fund family includes 12 funds and allows shareholders to switch from fund to fund by telephone.

Top Ten Holdings

1. Ascend Communications	6. WorldCom
2. FORE Systems	7. U.S. Robotics
3. Hospitality Franchise	8. Columbia Healthcare
4. AT&T	9. Parametric Technology
5. Computer Associates Int'l	10. Newbridge Networks

Asset Mix: Common stocks: 83%; Cash/equivalents: 17%
Total Net Assets: $842 million

Fees

Front-end load	*None*
Redemption fee	*None*
12b-1 fee	0.25%
Management fee	0.74
Other expenses	0.29
Total annual expense	1.28%
Minimum initial investment	$1,000
Minimum subsequent investment	$100

Services

Telephone exchanges	*Yes*
Automatic withdrawal	*Yes*
Automatic checking deduction	*Yes*
Retirement plan/IRA	*Yes*
Instant redemption	*Yes*
Financial statements	*Semiannual*
Income distributions	*Annual*
Capital gains distributions	*Annual*
Portfolio manager—years	4
Number of funds in family	12

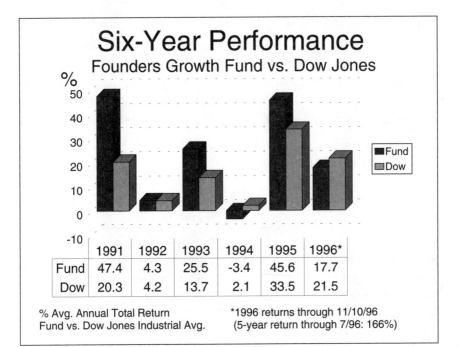

Six-Year Performance
Founders Growth Fund vs. Dow Jones

	1991	1992	1993	1994	1995	1996*
Fund	47.4	4.3	25.5	-3.4	45.6	17.7
Dow	20.3	4.2	13.7	2.1	33.5	21.5

% Avg. Annual Total Return
Fund vs. Dow Jones Industrial Avg.

*1996 returns through 11/10/96
(5-year return through 7/96: 166%)

AGGRESSIVE

15

INVESCO Dynamics Fund

INVESCO Funds Group
P.O. Box 173706
Denver, CO 80217-3706

Fund manager: Timothy J. Miller
Fund objective: Aggressive growth

Toll-free: 800-525-8085
In-state: 303-930-6300
Fax: 303-930-6584

Performance	★ ★ ★ ★
Consistency	★ ★ ★ ★
Fees/Services	★ ★ ★ ★ ★
FIDYX	**13 Points**

The INVESCO Dynamics Fund is a broadly diversified aggressive growth fund that was first introduced in 1967. Fund manager Timothy Miller invests in both small upcoming high tech companies and established blue chip stocks such as McDonald's, Phillips Petroleum, and Dayton Hudson.

In addition to U.S. stocks, the fund also dabbles in foreign issues, which make up about 15 percent of the portfolio.

Over the past ten years, the fund has provided an average return of about 15 percent per year. A $10,000 investment in the fund ten years ago would now be worth about $40,000.

The fund's basic strategy is to buy and sell stocks based on such market factors as price movements of the stock, indicated investor interest, current information about the company, and general market and monetary conditions. As much as 25 percent of the portfolio may be in foreign stock holdings. Fund manager Timothy J. Miller maintains an aggressive trading strategy, with an annual portfolio turnover ratio of about 176 percent.

The fund has about 70 stock holdings, most heavily weighted in computer-related stocks. Computer stocks account for 13 percent of assets;

health care-related stocks make up 12 percent, oil and gas stocks account for 9 percent, and retail makes up 10 percent.

PERFORMANCE   ★ ★ ★ ★

The fund has enjoyed exceptional growth over the past five years. Including dividends and capital gains distributions, the Dynamics Fund has provided a total return for the past five years (through mid-1996) of 165 percent. A $10,000 investment in 1991 would have grown to about $26,500 five years later. Average annual return: 21.5 percent.

CONSISTENCY   ★ ★ ★ ★

The fund has been relatively consistent, outperforming the Dow Jones Industrial Average four of the five years through 1995 (but it trailed the Dow through the first half of 1996). The fund's biggest gain came in 1991, when it rose 67 percent (compared with a 20.3 percent rise in the Dow).

FEES/SERVICES/MANAGEMENT   ★ ★ ★ ★ ★

Like all INVESCO funds, the Dynamics Fund is a true no-load fund—no fee to buy, no fee to sell. The fund's total annual expense ratio of 1.21 percent (including a 0.25 percent 12b-1 fee and a 0.6 percent management fee) compares favorably with other no-load funds.

The fund offers all the standard services such as retirement account availability, automatic withdrawal, and automatic checking account deduction. Its minimum initial investment of $1,000 and minimum subsequent investment of $50 compare favorably with other funds.

Timothy Miller has managed the fund since 1993. The INVESCO fund family includes 33 funds and allows shareholders to switch from fund to fund by telephone.

Top Ten Holdings

1. Glaxo Holdings
2. Aftra
3. Dayton Hudson
4. Agrium Inc.
5. Heineken

6. McDonald's
7. Corporate Express
8. Dillard Department Stores
9. Petroleum GEO Services
10. Harrah's Entertainment

Asset Mix: Common stocks: 95%; Cash/equivalents: 5%
Total Net Assets: $790 million

Fees

Front-end load	*None*
Redemption fee	*None*
12b-1 fee	0.25%
Management fee	0.60
Other expenses	0.36
Total annual expense	1.21%
Minimum initial investment	$1,000
Minimum subsequent investment	$50

Services

Telephone exchanges	*Yes*
Automatic withdrawal	*Yes*
Automatic checking deduction	*Yes*
Retirement plan/IRA	*Yes*
Instant redemption	*Yes*
Financial statements	*Semiannual*
Income distributions	*Annually*
Capital gains distributions	*Annual*
Portfolio manager—years:	4
Number of funds in family	33

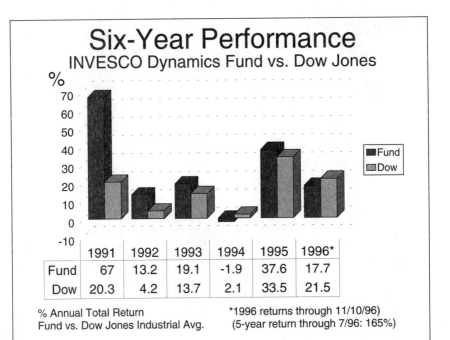

	1991	1992	1993	1994	1995	1996*
Fund	67	13.2	19.1	-1.9	37.6	17.7
Dow	20.3	4.2	13.7	2.1	33.5	21.5

% Annual Total Return   *1996 returns through 11/10/96)
Fund vs. Dow Jones Industrial Avg.   (5-year return through 7/96: 165%)

GLOBAL

16
Janus Worldwide Fund

Janus Funds
100 Fillmore Street, Suite 300
Denver, CO 80206-4923

Fund manager: Helen Young Hayes
Fund objective: Global equity

Toll-free: 800-525-8983
In-state: 303-333-3863
Fax: 303-394-7659

Performance	★ ★ ★ ★
Consistency	★ ★ ★ ★
Fees/Services	★ ★ ★ ★ ★
JAWWX	**13 Points**

You won't find a more diversified fund on the planet than Janus Worldwide. The fund has stock holdings in more than than 70 industries throughout 29 countries.

Janus Worldwide invests primarily in mid- to large-capitalization stocks that have shown steady earnings and revenue growth. U.S. stocks account for only about a quarter of the fund's assets. The largest concentration of holdings—about 50 percent of the fund's assets—is in Europe. Asian stocks account for 20 percent. The fund also holds some foreign currency contracts.

The fund, which opened in 1991, has produced an average annual return of about 21 percent over the past five years.

Fund manager Helen Young Hayes takes an aggressive trading approach, with an annual portfolio turnover ratio of 142 percent. The fund stays almost fully invested in stocks most of the time.

The Worldwide Fund has about 200 stock holdings across a broad range of industries. Its leading industrial segments include pharmaceuticals, 11 percent; diversified holding companies, 7 percent; commercial services, 6 percent; automotive, 4 percent; and chemicals, 3 percent.

PERFORMANCE

The Janus Worldwide Fund has experienced outstanding growth over the past five years. Including dividends and capital gains distributions, the fund has provided a total return for the past five years (through mid-1996) of 160 percent. A $10,000 investment in 1991 would have grown to about $26,000 five years later. Average annual return: 21.1 percent.

CONSISTENCY

The fund has been relatively consistent, outperforming the Dow Jones Industrial Average three of the four years from 1992 through 1995 (and it was well ahead of the Dow through the first half of 1996). The fund out-performed the MSCI/EAFE world index two of the four years through 1995 and again through the first half of 1996.

FEES/SERVICES/MANAGEMENT

Like all Janus funds, the Janus Worldwide Fund is a true no-load fund—no fee to buy, no fee to sell. The fund's total annual expense ratio of 1.24 percent (with no 12b-1 fee) compares favorably with other no-load funds.

The fund offers all the standard services such as retirement account availability, automatic withdrawal, and automatic checking account deduction. Its minimum initial investment of $2,500 and minimum subsequent investment of $100 is a little higher than average.

Helen Young Hayes has managed the fund since 1991. The Janus fund family includes 14 funds and allows shareholders to switch from fund to fund by telephone.

Top Ten Holdings

1. Kinnevik	6. Securitas
2. IBM	7. Adidas
3. NTT Data Communications	8. HFS
4. Roche Holdings	9. SAP AG
5. Hoechst AG	10. Nutricia

Asset Mix: Common stocks: 89%; Preferred stock: 5%; U.S. government agency obligations: 6%
Total Net Assets: $3.3 billion

Fees

Front-end load	*None*
Redemption fee	*None*
12b-1 fee	*None*
Management fee	0.68%
Other expenses	0.56
Total annual expense	1.24%
Minimum initial investment	$2,500
Minimum subsequent investment	$100

Services

Telephone exchanges	*Yes*
Automatic withdrawal	*Yes*
Automatic checking deduction	*Yes*
Retirement plan/IRA	*Yes*
Instant redemption	*Yes*
Financial statements	*Semiannual*
Income distributions	*Annual*
Capital gains distributions	*Annual*
Portfolio manager—years	6
Number of funds in family	14

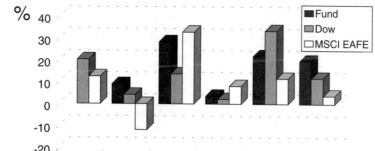

Six-Year Performance
Janus Worldwide Fund vs. Dow & World index

	1991	1992	1993	1994	1995	1996*
Fund	NA	9	28.4	3.6	21.9	19.6
Dow	20.3	4.2	13.7	2.1	33.5	11.8
MSCI EAFE	12.5	-11.9	32.9	8.1	11.6	3.7

% Annual Total Return   *1996 returns through 7/1/96
Fund vs. Dow Jones Industrial Avg.   (5-year return through 7/96: 161%)
MSCI EAFE refers to Morgan Stanley world index

17

Alliance Technology Fund "A"

SECTOR

Alliance Capital Group
P.O. Box 1520
Secaucus, NJ 07096-1520

Fund managers: Peter Anastos,
  Gerald Malone
Fund objective: Sector fund

Toll-free: 800-221-5672
  or 800-227-4618
In-state: 201-319-4000
Fax: 201-319-4075

Performance	★ ★ ★ ★ ★
Consistency	★ ★ ★ ★ ★
Fees/Services	★ ★ ★
ALTFX	**13 Points**

The Alliance Technology Fund is one of a group of high tech superfunds that have not only provided exceptional long-term returns throughout the 1990s, but have also outperformed the market on a consistent year-to-year basis as well.

Founded in 1982, Alliance Technology is among the oldest funds in the growing ranks of the technology fund sector. Over the past ten years, the fund has compiled an average annual return of about 17 percent. A $10,000 investment in the fund ten years ago would now be worth about $50,000.

The fund's aim is to invest in the fastest-growing leading-edge technology stocks when they are reasonably priced. The fund can be volatile in the short term, but the growth prospects in the technology area should lead to above-average growth over the long term.

The fund tends to stay heavily invested in stocks (80 to 95 percent of the portfolio) most of the time. In all, the fund has about 60 stock holdings. The fund managers take a fairly patient approach, with an annual portfolio turnover ratio of 55 percent.

The fund does not invest in medical technology stocks, restricting its investments to computer and communications stocks. Computer software and services account for 24 percent of assets, semiconductor stocks account for 11 percent, computer systems account for 10 percent, and communications issues make up 25 percent.

PERFORMANCE

The fund has enjoyed exceptional growth over the past five years. Including dividends and capital gains distributions, the Alliance Technology Fund has provided a total return for the past five years (through mid-1996) of 265 percent. A $10,000 investment in 1991 would have grown to about $36,500 five years later. Average annual return: 29.6 percent.

CONSISTENCY

The fund has been very consistent, outperforming the Dow Jones Industrial Average six consecutive years through 1995 (but it trailed the Dow through the first half of 1996). Its biggest gains came in 1991 and 1995 when it moved up 54.2 percent and 45.8 percent, respectively.

FEES/SERVICES/MANAGEMENT

The fund has a 4.25 percent front-end sales load. It has a total annual expense ratio of 1.75 percent (including a 0.3 percent 12b-1 fee and a 1 percent management fee).

The fund offers all the standard services such as retirement account availability, automatic withdrawal, and automatic checking account deduction. Its minimum initial investment of $250 and minimum subsequent investment of $50 compare very favorably with other funds.

Peter Anastos has managed the fund since 1989. Comanager Gerald Malone joined the fund in 1992. The Alliance Capital fund family includes 44 funds and allows shareholders to switch from fund to fund by telephone.

Top Ten Holdings

1. Cisco Systems
2. Oracle Systems
3. Hewlett-Packard
4. First Data
5. Altera

6. General Motors
7. Glenayre Technologies
8. 3Com
9. FORE Systems
10. Seagate Technology

Asset Mix: Common stocks: 83%; Cash/equivalents: 17%
Total Net Assets: $436 million

Fees

Front-end load	4.25%
Redemption fee	*None*
12b-1 fee	0.30
Management fee	1.00
Other expenses	0.45
Total annual expense	1.75%
Minimum initial investment	$250
Minimum subsequent investment	$50

Services

Telephone exchanges	*Yes*
Automatic withdrawal	*Yes*
Automatic checking deduction	*Yes*
Retirement plan/IRA	*Yes*
Instant redemption	*Yes*
Financial statements	*Semiannual*
Income distributions	*Annual*
Capital gains distributions	*Annual*
Portfolio managers—years	8
Number of funds in family	44

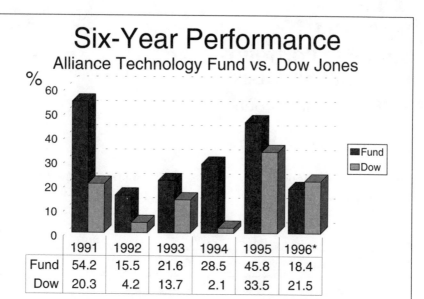

Six-Year Performance
Alliance Technology Fund vs. Dow Jones

	1991	1992	1993	1994	1995	1996*
Fund	54.2	15.5	21.6	28.5	45.8	18.4
Dow	20.3	4.2	13.7	2.1	33.5	21.5

% Annual Total Return
Fund vs. Dow Jones Industrial Avg.

*1996 returns through 11/10/96)
(5-year return through 7/96: 265%)

18

INVESCO
Strategic Portfolios:
Financial Services

SECTOR

INVESCO Funds Group
P.O. Box 173706
Denver, CO 80217-3706

Fund manager: Doug Pratt
Fund objective: Sector fund

Toll-free: 800-525-8085
In-state: 303-930-6300
Fax: 303-930-6584

Performance	★ ★ ★ ★
Consistency	★ ★ ★ ★
Fees/Services	★ ★ ★ ★ ★
FSFSX	**13 Points**

The strong economy in recent years has kept the financial services industry on a roll. The INVESCO Financial Services Portfolio has taken advantage of that growth, posting average returns over the past five years of 22.5 percent per year.

Since its inception in 1986, the fund has grown about 16 percent per year. A $10,000 investment in the fund when it was introduced would now be worth about $45,000.

As its name implies, the fund specializes in stocks of banks, savings and loans, and other financial-related companies. Among its leading holdings are Chase Manhattan, Citicorp, and Wells Fargo. The fund also invests in HMOs such as Columbia Healthcare, and in consumer and industrial finance companies, leasing companies, securities brokerage companies, insurance agencies, and real estate stocks and trusts.

Fund manager Doug Pratt, who has been running the fund since 1992, maintains a very active trading policy, with an annual portfolio turnover ratio of about 170 percent.

Normally, Pratt stays 90 to 95 percent invested in the stock market. The fund has a total of about 40 stock holdings. The leading segment is banking, which accounts for 41 percent of total assets. Insurance stocks rank second (31 percent of assets) followed by HMO stocks (8 percent).

PERFORMANCE

The fund has enjoyed exceptional growth over the past five years. Including dividends and capital gains distributions, the Financial Services Portfolio has provided a total return for the past five years (through mid-1996) of 175 percent. A $10,000 investment in 1991 would have grown to about $27,500 five years later. Average annual return: 22.5 percent.

CONSISTENCY

The fund has been consistent recently, outperforming the Dow Jones Industrial Average four of the five years through 1995 (but it trailed the Dow through the first half of 1996). Its biggest gain came in 1991, when it jumped 74 percent (compared with a 20.3 percent rise in the Dow).

FEES/SERVICES/MANAGEMENT

Like all INVESCO funds, the Financial Services Portfolio is a true no-load fund—no fee to buy, no fee to sell. The fund's total annual expense ratio of 1.26 percent (with no 12b-1 fee) compares favorably with other funds.

The fund offers all the standard services such as retirement account availability, automatic withdrawal, and automatic checking account deduction. Its minimum initial investment of $1,000 and minimum subsequent investment of $50 compare favorably with other funds.

Douglas Pratt has managed the fund since 1992. He also comanages the INVESCO Growth Fund. The INVESCO fund family includes 33 funds and allows shareholders to switch from fund to fund by telephone.

Top Ten Holdings

1. First Chicago Bank	6. Wells Fargo
2. BankAmerica	7. Citicorp
3. Conseco	8. Columbia Healthcare
4. Chase Manhattan	9. Republic N.Y. Bank
5. Compass Bank Shares	10. Bank of New York

Asset Mix: Common stocks: 98%; Cash/equivalents: 2%
Total Net Assets: $432 million

Fees

Front-end load	*None*
Redemption fee	*None*
12b-1 fee	*None*
Management fee	0.75%
Other expenses	0.51
Total annual expense	1.26%
Minimum initial investment	$1,000
Minimum subsequent investment	$50

Services

Telephone exchanges	*Yes*
Automatic withdrawal	*Yes*
Automatic checking deduction	*Yes*
Retirement plan/IRA	*Yes*
Instant redemption	*Yes*
Financial statements	*Semiannual*
Income distributions	*Annual*
Capital gains distributions	*Annual*
Portfolio manager—years	5
Number of funds in family	33

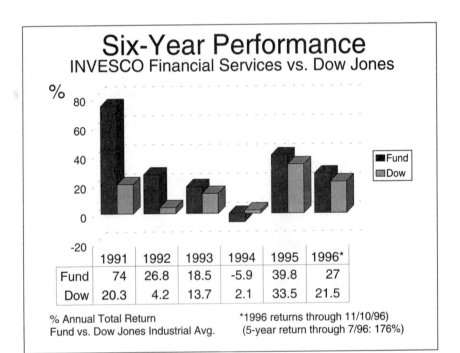

Six-Year Performance
INVESCO Financial Services vs. Dow Jones

	1991	1992	1993	1994	1995	1996*
Fund	74	26.8	18.5	-5.9	39.8	27
Dow	20.3	4.2	13.7	2.1	33.5	21.5

% Annual Total Return
Fund vs. Dow Jones Industrial Avg.

*1996 returns through 11/10/96)
(5-year return through 7/96: 176%)

SECTOR

Fidelity Select Developing Communications Portfolio

Fidelity Investments
82 Devonshire Street
Boston, MA 02109

Fund manager: Paul Antico
Fund objective: Sector fund

Toll-free: 800-544-8888
In-state: 801-534-1910
Fax: 617-476-9753

Performance	★ ★ ★ ★ ★
Consistency	★ ★ ★ ★
Fees/Services	★ ★ ★ ★
FSDCX	**13 Points**

The telecommunications industry has been flourishing worldwide the past few years, helping propel the Fidelity Developing Communications Portfolio to exceptional growth. Over the past five years, the fund has grown at an average annual rate of about 25 percent.

Fund manager Paul Antico invests at least 80 percent of the fund's assets in stocks of companies that are involved in the development, manufacture, or sale of communications products and services, with special focus on firms with new technologies or new applications of existing technologies.

"I've worked on two strategies with the fund," explains Antico. "Half of my focus has been on what I call the 'broadband revolution.' That describes the equipment upgrade that's happening in telecommunications networks as people and companies look for more bandwidth to send data, to get on to the Internet, or even for video conferencing. The other area I've concentrated on is cellular service providers."

Cellular and communications services stocks account for 23 percent of the fund's total assets. Other leading sectors include TV and radio equipment, 15 percent; data communications equipment, 8 percent; and telephone service, 7.5 percent.

Antico is very aggressive in his trading policy, with an annual portfolio turnover ratio of 266 percent.

PERFORMANCE

The fund has enjoyed exceptional growth over the past five years. Including dividends and capital gains distributions, the Developing Communications Portfolio has provided a total return for the past five years (through mid-1996) of 204 percent. A $10,000 investment in 1991 would have grown to about $30,000 five years later. Average annual return: 24.9 percent.

CONSISTENCY

The fund has been very consistent recently, outperforming the Dow Jones Industrial Average four of the five years through 1995 (and it was about even with the Dow through the first half of 1996). Its best year was in 1991 when it jumped 61.3 percent.

FEES/SERVICES/MANAGEMENT

The fund has a low front-end load of 3 percent and a maximum redemption fee of 0.75 percent if it's sold out within 29 days. Otherwise, shareholders pay a $7.50 redemption fee. Its annual expense ratio of 1.61 percent (with no 12b-1 fees) is about average among all funds.

The fund offers all the standard services such as retirement account availability, automatic withdrawal, and automatic checking account deduction. Its minimum initial investment of $2,500 and minimum subsequent investment of $250 are a little high compared with other funds.

Paul Antico has managed the fund since 1993. He has been with Fidelity since 1991. The Fidelity fund family includes about 210 funds.

Top Ten Holdings

1. Glenayre Technologies
2. AirTouch Communications
3. United States Cellular
4. Cisco Systems
5. Vanguard Cellular Systems

6. Dynatech
7. U.S. Robotics
8. Palmer Wireless
9. Arch Communications Group
10. California Microwave

Asset Mix: Common stocks: 85%; Cash/equivalents: 15%
Total Net Assets: $372 million

Fees

Front-end load	3.00%
Redemption fee	$7.50
12b-1 fee	*None*
Management fee	0.61
Other expenses	1.00
Total annual expense	1.61%
Minimum initial investment	$2,500
Minimum subsequent investment	$250

Services

Telephone exchanges	*Yes*
Automatic withdrawal	*Yes*
Automatic checking deduction	*Yes*
Retirement plan/IRA	*Yes*
Instant redemption	*Yes*
Financial statements	*Semiannual*
Income distributions	*Semiannual*
Capital gains distributions	*Semiannual*
Portfolio manager—years	4
Number of funds in family	210

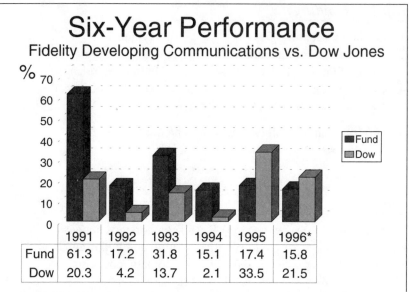

Six-Year Performance
Fidelity Developing Communications vs. Dow Jones

	1991	1992	1993	1994	1995	1996*
Fund	61.3	17.2	31.8	15.1	17.4	15.8
Dow	20.3	4.2	13.7	2.1	33.5	21.5

% Annual Total Return
Fund vs. Dow Jones Industrial Avg.

*1996 returns through 11/10/96
(5-year return through 7/96: 204%)

SECTOR

20
Fidelity Select
Electronics Portfolio

Fidelity Investments
82 Devonshire Street
Boston, MA 02109

Fund manager: Marc Kaufman
Fund objective: Sector fund

Toll-free: 800-544-8888
In-state: 801-534-1910
Fax: 617-476-9753

Performance	★ ★ ★ ★ ★
Consistency	★ ★ ★ ★ ★
Fees/Services	★ ★ ★
FSELX	**13 Points**

Fidelity calls it the "Electronics Portfolio," but traditional electrical and electronics stocks such as TV and radio equipment, electrical instruments, and connectors and capacitors account for only about 5 percent of the fund's total assets. Instead, the Fidelity Select Electronics Portfolio is heavily weighted in computer related stocks—along with a sprinkling of medical and telecommunications issues.

For shareholders who have enjoyed spectacular returns, however, the fund by any other name would smell as sweet. The fund has enjoyed enormous growth the past five years, with a 32.5 percent average annual growth rate for the period. That's a sharp contrast to the previous five years when the fund was actually down about 2 percent. In fact, a $10,000 investment in the fund ten years ago would now be worth about $39,500, while a $10,000 investment in the fund just five years ago would now be worth even more—about $41,000.

Fund manager Marc Kaufman takes a very active trading approach, with a 205 percent annual portfolio turnover ratio.

In all, the fund holds about 100 stocks. The leading segment is semi-conductors, which account for about 28 percent of assets. Other leading segments include computers and office equipment (8 percent); computer storage devices (7 percent), and data communications equipment (5 percent).

The fund invests in both large capitalization stocks such as IBM, Compaq, and Hewlett-Packard, and in smaller emerging companies such as Cisco Systems, Analog Devices, and Adaptec.

PERFORMANCE

The fund has enjoyed phenomenal growth over the past five years. Including dividends and capital gains distributions, the Electronics Portfolio has provided a total return for the past five years (through mid-1996) of 309 percent. A $10,000 investment in 1991 would have grown to about $41,000 five years later. Average annual return: 32.5 percent.

CONSISTENCY

The fund has been very consistent, outperforming the Dow Jones Industrial Average for six consecutive years through 1995 (but it trailed the Dow through the first six months of 1996). The fund's biggest year was 1995 when it jumped 69.4 percent.

FEES/SERVICES/MANAGEMENT

The fund has a front-end load of 3 percent and a maximum redemption fee of 0.75 percent if shares are redeemed within 30 days. Otherwise shareholders pay $7.50 to redeem shares. The fund's total annual expense ratio of 1.34 percent (with no 12b-1 fee) is about average among load funds.

The fund offers all the standard services such as retirement account availability, automatic withdrawal, and automatic checking account deduction. Its minimum initial investment of $2,500 and minimum subsequent investment of $250 are a little high compared with other funds.

Marc Kaufman has managed the fund only since 1995. He has been with Fidelity since 1992. The Fidelity fund family includes 210 funds.

Top Ten Holdings

1. Analog Devices	6. Adaptec
2. IBM	7. Hewlett-Packard
3. U.S. Robotics	8. Cisco Systems
4. Compaq Computer	9. Seagate Technology
5. Maxim Integrated Products	10. Tencor Instruments

Asset Mix: Common stocks: 80%; Cash/equivalents: 20%
Total Net Assets: $1.2 billion

Fees

Front-end load	3.00%
Redemption fee	0.75
12b-1 fee	*None*
Management fee	0.61
Other expenses	0.73
Total annual expense	1.34%
Minimum initial investment	$2,500
Minimum subsequent investment	$250

Services

Telephone exchanges	*Yes*
Automatic withdrawal	*Yes*
Automatic checking deduction	*Yes*
Retirement plan/IRA	*Yes*
Instant redemption	*Yes*
Financial statements	*Semiannual*
Income distributions	*Semiannual*
Capital gains distributions	*Semiannual*
Portfolio manager—years	2
Number of funds in family	210

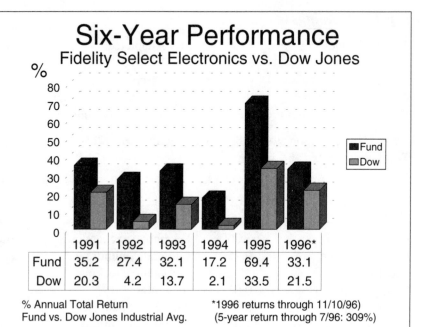

Six-Year Performance
Fidelity Select Electronics vs. Dow Jones

	1991	1992	1993	1994	1995	1996*
Fund	35.2	27.4	32.1	17.2	69.4	33.1
Dow	20.3	4.2	13.7	2.1	33.5	21.5

% Annual Total Return   *1996 returns through 11/10/96)
Fund vs. Dow Jones Industrial Avg.   (5-year return through 7/96: 309%)

SECTOR

Fidelity Select
Computers Portfolio

Fidelity Investments
82 Devonshire Street
Boston, MA 02109

Fund manager: Jason Weiner
Fund objective: Sector fund

Toll-free: 800-544-8888
In-state: 801-534-1910
Fax: 617-476-9753

Performance	★ ★ ★ ★ ★
Consistency	★ ★ ★ ★ ★
Fees/Services	★ ★ ★
FDCPX	**13 Points**

The steady surge in computer stocks this decade has helped the Fidelity Select Computers Portfolio post five straight years of 20 percent-plus annual returns. The fund's success should continue as long as the computer revolution thrives—and that could be for a long time to come.

Fund manager Jason Weiner stepped in as fund manager in 1996, after two years as portfolio manager of the Fidelity Select Air Transportion Portfolio. He replaced Harry Lange, who now manages the Fidelity Capital Appreciation Fund. But much of the success of the Computer Portfolio is attributable to Lange. Lange credited the fund's strong performance to diligent research. "We want to know about earnings surprises even before the company discloses its earnings. We talk to buyers, to retailers, and to user groups, we attend trade shows, we read the trade magazines and we try to talk to the management of the companies on a regular basis."

Over the past ten years, the fund has posted average annual returns of about 15 percent. A $10,000 investment in the fund ten years ago would now be worth about $41,000.

The fund invests in stocks of all sizes, from the very small, one-product companies to major manufacturers such as IBM and Digital Equipment. It takes a different approach with the big companies than with the small emerging growth stocks.

For the larger firms, the fund manager looks at gross profit margins, PE ratios, price-to-cash flow ratios, and price-to-sales ratios. The fund bought IBM and Digital Equipment after their price had plummeted and their gross profit margins had stabilized.

For the smaller companies, earnings growth is the major factor, although PE ratios also come into play. The fund also takes advantage of the volatility in the computer sector to scoop up stocks when their prices plunge. "A company can miss out on a product cycle and see its earnings drop, but it may be able to get back on top in the next product cycle," explained Lange. "Dell Computer went through a situation like that. The stock dropped from the low $40s to about $13 a share. But it got back in the game in the next product cycle, and the stock bounced back up into the $40s."

The fund will dump a stock if the price gets too high relative to its earnings or if the company's growth is slowing down. But if earnings continue to climb, the fund may hold the stock for years. The fund has a very aggressive trading policy, with an annual portfolio turnover ratio of about 190 percent.

The fund holds about 100 stocks. Mini- and micro-computer stocks account for 21 percent of the portfolio, followed by computer storage device stocks (11 percent), computers and office equipment (8 percent), and prepackaged computer software (7 percent).

PERFORMANCE

The fund has experienced remarkable growth over the past five years. Including dividends and capital gains distributions, the Fidelity Select Computers Portfolio has provided a total return for the past five years (through mid-1996) of 237 percent. A $10,000 investment in 1991 would have grown to about $34,000 five years later. Average annual return: 27.5 percent.

CONSISTENCY

The fund has been very consistent, outperforming the Dow Jones Industrial Average five consecutive years through 1995 (but it trailed the Dow through the first half of 1996). Even in 1994, when the Dow moved up only 2.1 percent, the fund jumped 20.5 percent.

FEES/SERVICES/MANAGEMENT

The fund has a front-end load of 3 percent and a maximum redemption fee of 0.75 percent if it's sold out within 30 days. Otherwise a $7.50 fee is charged at redemption. The fund has a total annual expense ratio of 1.47 percent (with no 12b-1 fee), which is about average among all load funds.

The fund offers all the standard services such as retirement account availability, automatic withdrawal, and automatic checking account deduction. Its minimum initial investment of $2,500 and minimum subsequent investment of $250 are slightly on the high side as compared with other funds.

Jason Weiner has been managing the fund since 1996, after spending two years as manager of the Fidelity Select Air Transportation Portfolio. He joined Fidelity in 1991. The Fidelity fund family includes 210 funds.

Top Ten Holdings

1. Seagate Technology
2. Compaq Computer
3. Digital Equipment
4. IBM
5. Dell Computer
6. Gateway 2000
7. Teradyne
8. Sumitomo Sitix
9. Hutchinson Technology
10. Cisco Systems

Asset Mix: Common stocks: 83%; Cash/equivalents: 17%
Total Net Assets: $528.7 million

Fees

Front-end load	3.00%
Redemption fee	$7.50
12b-1 fee	*None*
Management fee	0.61
Other expenses	0.86
Total annual expense	1.47%
Minimum initial investment	$2,500
Minimum subsequent investment	$250

Services

Telephone exchanges	*Yes*
Automatic withdrawal	*Yes*
Automatic checking deduction	*Yes*
Retirement plan/IRA	*Yes*
Instant redemption	*Yes*
Financial statements	*Semiannual*
Income distributions	*Semiannual*
Capital gains distributions	*Semiannual*
Portfolio manager—years	1
Number of funds in family	210

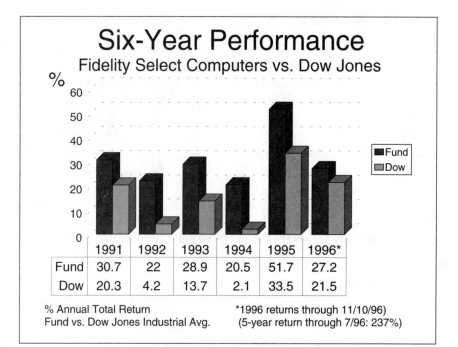

Six-Year Performance
Fidelity Select Computers vs. Dow Jones

	1991	1992	1993	1994	1995	1996*
Fund	30.7	22	28.9	20.5	51.7	27.2
Dow	20.3	4.2	13.7	2.1	33.5	21.5

% Annual Total Return   *1996 returns through 11/10/96)
Fund vs. Dow Jones Industrial Avg.   (5-year return through 7/96: 237%)

Smith Barney Special Equities Fund

LONG TERM

Smith Barney Mutual Funds
388 Greenwich Street, 37th Floor
New York, NY 10013

Fund manager: George Novello
Fund objective: Long-term growth

Toll-free: 800-451-2010
In-state: 212-723-9218
Fax: 212-698-3987

Performance	★ ★ ★ ★ ★
Consistency	★ ★ ★ ★
Fees/Services	★ ★ ★
HSEAX	**12 Points**

Smith Barney Special Equities Fund manager George Novello is committed for the long term to small emerging stocks with rapid earnings growth. It is a strategy that has worked great for the fund the past five years—but not so great the previous five years (before Novello took over as fund manager).

Over the past five years the fund has jumped 206 percent (25.1 percent per year)—which is 34 percentage points higher than the fund's growth for the past 10-year period (172 percent). In other words, the fund was in the red for the five-year period through 1990, but has climbed rapidly since then, riding the crest of the small stock bull market.

"We remain committed to an investment approach that owns high-quality, high-growth companies over a full market cycle," explains Novello. "We are not market timers nor short-term traders, but investors, and, as such, we own stocks on a long-term basis."

The Special Equities Fund has about 60 stock holdings in the portfolio. Novello maintains a fairly aggressive trading policy, with an annual portfolio turnover ratio of 123 percent.

The fund is heavily weighted in high tech stocks, although its largest segment is retail, which accounts for 17 percent of assets. Other leading segments include communications, 15 percent; software, 12 percent; health care and pharmaceuticals, 9 percent; restaurants, 9 percent; semiconductors and electronics, 8 percent; and technology, 7 percent.

PERFORMANCE

The fund has enjoyed exceptional growth over the past five years. Including dividends and capital gains distributions, the Smith Barney Special Equities Fund has provided a total return for the past five years (through mid-1996) of 206 percent. A $10,000 investment in 1991 would have grown to about $31,000 five years later. Average annual return: 25.1 percent.

CONSISTENCY

The fund has been very consistent, outperforming the Dow Jones Industrial Average four of the five years through 1995 (but it trailed the Dow through the first half of 1996). The fund did have an off year in 1994 when it dropped 6.3 percent, but it also had a huge year in 1995 when it jumped 62.3 percent.

FEES/SERVICES/MANAGEMENT

The fund's A shares have a front-end sales load of 5 percent, and a total annual expense ratio of 1.49 percent (including a 0.25 percent 12b-1 fee and a 0.75 percent management fee). Its "B" shares have a 5 percent redemption charge and very high 2.21 percent annual expense ratio.

The fund offers all the standard services such as retirement account availability, automatic withdrawal, and automatic checking account deduction. Its minimum initial investment of $1,000 and minimum subsequent investment of $50 are comparable to other funds.

George Novello has managed the fund since 1990. The Smith Barney fund family includes 47 funds and allows shareholders to switch from fund to fund by telephone.

Top Ten Holdings

1. Ascend Communications
2. Macromedia
3. Baby Superstore
4. Starbucks
5. Callaway Golf

6. Boston Chicken
7. PETsMART
8. Adtran
9. Sunglass Hut Int'l
10. C-Cube Microsystems

Asset Mix: Common stocks: 90%; Cash/equivalents: 10%
Total Net Assets: $192.0 million

Fees

Front-end load	5.0%
Redemption fee	*None*
12b-1 fee	0.25
Management fee	0.75
Other expenses	0.49
Total annual expense	1.49%
Minimum initial investment	$1,000
Minimum subsequent investment	$50

Services

Telephone exchanges	*Yes*
Automatic withdrawal	*Yes*
Automatic checking deduction	*Yes*
Retirement plan/IRA	*Yes*
Instant redemption	*Yes*
Financial statements	*Semiannual*
Income distributions	*Annual*
Capital gains distributions	*Annual*
Portfolio manager—years	7
Number of funds in family	47

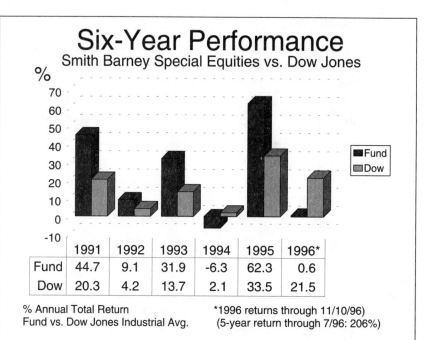

Six-Year Performance
Smith Barney Special Equities vs. Dow Jones

	1991	1992	1993	1994	1995	1996*
Fund	44.7	9.1	31.9	-6.3	62.3	0.6
Dow	20.3	4.2	13.7	2.1	33.5	21.5

% Annual Total Return   *1996 returns through 11/10/96)
Fund vs. Dow Jones Industrial Avg.   (5-year return through 7/96: 206%)

AGGRESSIVE

23

Oberweis Emerging Growth Fund

Oberweis Asset Management, Inc.
951 Ice Cream Drive, Suite 200
North Aurora, IL 60542

Fund manager: James D. Oberweis
Fund objective: Aggressive growth

Toll-free: 800-323-6166
In-state: 630-801-6000
Fax: 630-896-5282

Performance	★ ★ ★ ★
Consistency	★ ★ ★
Fees/Services	★ ★ ★ ★ ★
OBEGX	**12 Points**

The Oberweis Emerging Growth Fund is an aggressive stock fund that has achieved outstanding returns by riding the high tech wave. More than half of the fund's assets are in high tech stocks in the computer, medical, electronics, or telecommunications sectors.

Most of the stocks in the portfolio are considered small cap stocks with market capitalizations between $100 million and $1 billion. Fund manager James Oberweis considers eight factors in selecting stocks. He wants stocks with rapid earnings growth, rapid revenue growth and a PE ratio no higher than half of the company's projected earnings growth based on estimates for the next five years.

He also looks at price-to-sales ratios and recent growth trends, and he studies the balance sheets to assess the strength of each company. He searches for companies with products or services that have the potential for substantial future growth. Finally, he watches the stock price. "We have a philosophy of believing the tape. This means that no matter how good a company looks on paper, if its stock is declining in a steady or rising market, we feel there must be something wrong. Conversely, if its stock is doing well in a steady or falling market, we consider that to be a very positive feature." The fund's annual portfolio turnover ratio is a fairly active 79 percent.

The fund holds about 150 stocks, strongly weighted in the high technology sector. The leading segment is computer products and services, which account for about 35 percent of the fund's assets, while electrical equipment and electronic components and semiconductors account for another 13 percent. Medical related stocks make up about 4 percent and telecommunications account for about 7 percent.

PERFORMANCE

The fund has experienced excellent growth over the past five years. Including dividends and capital gains distributions, the Oberweis Emerging Growth Fund has provided a total return for the past five years (through mid-1996) of 184 percent. A $10,000 investment five years ago would have grown to about $28,000. Average annual return: 23.3 percent.

CONSISTENCY

The fund has been fairly consistent, outperforming the Dow Jones Industrial Average three of the five years from 1991 through 1995 (and again through the first half of 1996). In 1991, it was one of the nation's leading funds, rising 87 percent (compared with a 20.3 percent rise in the Dow).

FEES/SERVICES/MANAGEMENT

The fund is a true no-load fund—no fee to buy, no fee to sell. The fund's total annual expense ratio of 1.58 percent (including a 0.25 12b-1 fee and a 0.75 management fee) is about average among no-load funds.

The fund offers all the standard services such as retirement account availability, automatic withdrawal, and automatic checking account deduction. Its minimum initial investment of $1,000 and minimum subsequent investment of $100 are very close to the industry averages.

Fund founder James D. Oberweis has managed the fund since its inception in 1987. The Emerging Growth Fund is one of only two funds offered by Oberweis. The other is a new Micro-Cap Portfolio introduced in 1995.

Top Ten Holdings

1. Eltron International	6. ValuJet
2. Lone Star Steakhouse/Saloon	7. Applix
3. Madge Networks	8. Mylex
4. JLG Industries	9. Employee Solutions
5. Flextronics Int'l	10. CIBER

Asset Mix: Common stocks: 97%; Corporate bonds: 3%
Total Net Assets: $155 million

Fees

Front-end load	*None*
Redemption fee	*None*
12b-1 fee	0.25%
Management fee	0.75
Other expenses	0.58
Total annual expense	1.58%
Minimum initial investment	$1,000
Minimum subsequent investment	$100

Services

Telephone exchanges	*Yes*
Automatic withdrawal	*Yes*
Automatic checking deduction	*Yes*
Retirement plan/IRA	*Yes*
Instant redemption	*Yes*
Financial statements	*Semiannual*
Income distributions	*Annual*
Capital gains distributions	*Annual*
Portfolio manager—years	10
Number of funds in family	2

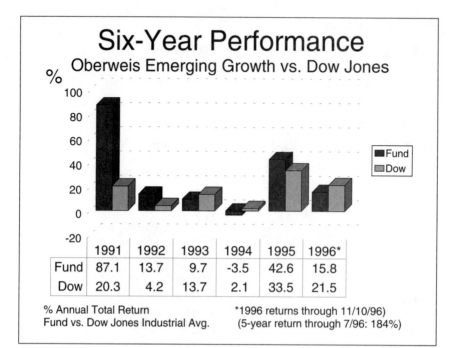

Six-Year Performance
Oberweis Emerging Growth vs. Dow Jones

	1991	1992	1993	1994	1995	1996*
Fund	87.1	13.7	9.7	-3.5	42.6	15.8
Dow	20.3	4.2	13.7	2.1	33.5	21.5

% Annual Total Return   *1996 returns through 11/10/96)
Fund vs. Dow Jones Industrial Avg.   (5-year return through 7/96: 184%)

AGGRESSIVE

SunAmerica Small Company Growth Fund "A"

SunAmerica Funds
733 Third Avenue
New York, NY 10017-3204

Fund manager: Audrey Snell
Fund objective: Aggressive growth

Toll-free: 800-858-8850
In-state: 212-551-5912
Fax: 212-551-5933

Performance	★ ★ ★ ★
Consistency	★ ★ ★ ★ ★
Fees/Services	★ ★ ★
SEGAX	**12 Points**

Fund manager Audrey Snell has managed to garner big returns by thinking small. Snell's SunAmerica Small Company Growth Fund focuses on small, emerging growth stocks that have the potential to hit it big.

The fund's investment strategy is to buy small lesser-known companies or new growth companies in fast-growing industries such as telecommunications, media, and biotechnology. Most of the stocks in the portfolio have a market capitalization of under $1 billion.

Over the past five years, fund shares have grown at an average annual rate of 23 percent. The fund is very actively traded, with an annual portfolio turnover ratio of 350 percent.

You would find no household names among the fund's approximately 130 stock holdings. Instead, the fund is filled with names such as Teltrend, Depotech, Metra Biosystems, and Simware—all small, young companies in the early stages of their corporate development.

The leading industrial segments within the fund's portfolio include electronics and electrical equipment, 10 percent of total assets; communications and telecommunications, 11 percent; computers and software, 18 percent; health and medical, 10 percent; and broadcast and media, 6 percent.

PERFORMANCE

The fund has experienced outstanding growth over the past five years. Including dividends and capital gains distributions, the SunAmerica Small Company Fund has posted a total return for the past five years (through mid-1996) of 182 percent. A $10,000 investment in 1991 would have grown to about $28,000 five years later. Average annual return: 23.1 percent.

CONSISTENCY

The fund has been very consistent, outperforming or matching the Dow Jones Industrial Average for five consecutive years through 1995 (and again through the first half of 1996). The fund exceeded 50 percent annual growth two of the past six years—1991 and 1995, when it climbed 54.9 and 50.2 percent, respectively.

FEES/SERVICES/MANAGEMENT

The fund has a 5.75 percent front-end sales load, and an annual expense ratio of 1.57 percent (including a 0.35 percent 12b-1 fee and a 0.75 percent management fee), which is about average among all funds.

The fund offers all the standard services such as retirement account availability, automatic withdrawal, and automatic checking account deduction. Its minimum initial investment of $500 and subsequent investment minimum of $100 compare favorably to other funds.

Audrey Snell has managed the fund since 1992. The SunAmerica fund family includes ten funds and allows shareholders to switch from fund to fund by telephone.

Top Ten Holdings

1. Neurex
2. HospitABR Information Services
3. Gadzooks
4. Guilford Pharmaceuticals
5. Structural Dynamics Research
6. Veterinary Centers America
7. Centocor
8. Octel Communications
9. Documentation
10. Cisco Systems

Asset Mix: Common stocks: 86%; Cash/equivalents: 12%
Total Net Assets: $110 million

Fees

Front-end load	5.75%
Redemption fee	*None*
12b-1 fee	0.35
Management fee	0.75
Other expenses	0.47
Total annual expense	1.57%
Minimum initial investment	$500
Minimum subsequent investment	$100

Services

Telephone exchanges	*Yes*
Automatic withdrawal	*Yes*
Automatic checking deduction	*Yes*
Retirement plan/IRA	*Yes*
Instant redemption	*Yes*
Financial statements	*Semiannual*
Income distributions	*Annual*
Capital gains distributions	*Annual*
Portfolio manager—years	5
Number of funds in family	10

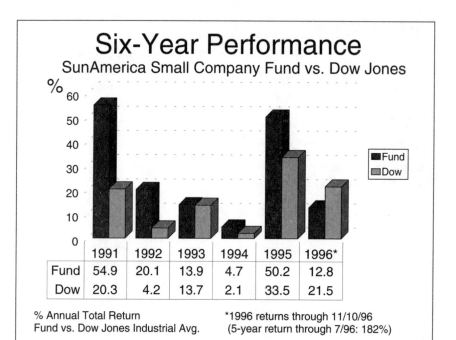

Six-Year Performance
SunAmerica Small Company Fund vs. Dow Jones

	1991	1992	1993	1994	1995	1996*
Fund	54.9	20.1	13.9	4.7	50.2	12.8
Dow	20.3	4.2	13.7	2.1	33.5	21.5

% Annual Total Return
Fund vs. Dow Jones Industrial Avg.

*1996 returns through 11/10/96
(5-year return through 7/96: 182%)

LONG TERM

Putnam OTC Emerging Growth Fund "A"

Putnam Mutual Funds
One Post Office Square
Boston, MA 02109

Fund manager: James Callinan
Fund objective: Long-term growth

Toll-free: 800-225-1581
In-state: 617-292-1000
Fax: 617-760-5869

Performance	★ ★ ★ ★ ★
Consistency	★ ★ ★ ★ ★
Fees/Services	★ ★
POEGX	**12 Points**

Small, over-the-counter growth stocks have led to outstanding gains for the Putnam OTC Emerging Growth Fund. Over the past ten years, the fund has grown at an average annual rate of 17 percent. A $10,000 investment in the fund ten years ago would now be worth about $48,000.

Portfolio manager James Callinan looks for companies with market capitalizations of under $1 billion that have growth potential "significantly greater than the market averages." The fund focuses on stocks that are "in a relatively early stage of development with a record of profitability and a strong financial position." Most of the fund's holdings benefit from new technology, a unique or proprietary product, or a profitable market niche. While most of the stocks in the portfolio are little-known companies, a few are household names, such as HBO and America Online.

In all, the fund has about 130 stock holdings. The fund is fairly aggressive in its trading policy, with an annual portfolio turnover ratio of 116 percent.

The fund is diversified across several industry groups. Its leading segments include computer software, 14 percent of assets; computer services, 8 percent; health care and medical, 21 percent; semiconductors, 8 percent; broadcasting, 7 percent, and networking equipment, 12 percent.

PERFORMANCE

The fund has enjoyed exceptional growth over the past five years. Including dividends and capital gains distributions, the Putnam OTC Emerging Growth Fund has provided a total return for the past five years (through mid-1996) of 237 percent. A $10,000 investment in 1991 would have grown to about $34,000 five years later. Average annual return: 27.5 percent.

CONSISTENCY

The fund has been very consistent, outperforming the Dow Jones Industrial Average for five consecutive years through 1995 (and again through the first half of 1996). The fund's biggest year was 1995 when it jumped 55.9 percent.

FEES/SERVICES/MANAGEMENT

The fund has a front-end load of 5.75 percent. Its total annual expense ratio of 1.14 percent (including a 0.25 percent 12b-1 fee and a 0.68 percent management fee) compares favorably with other funds.

The fund offers all the standard services such as retirement account availability, automatic withdrawal, and automatic checking account deduction. Its minimum initial investment of $500 and minimum subsequent investment of $50 compare very favorably with other funds.

James Callinan has managed the fund only since 1994. The Putnam fund family includes 77 funds and allows shareholders to switch from fund to fund by telephone.

Top Ten Holdings

1. U.S. Robotics
2. MBNA
3. HBO
4. America Online
5. Vencor
6. First Data
7. Bed Bath & Beyond
8. Infinity Broadcasting
9. Atmel
10. Analog Devices

Asset Mix: Common stocks: 91%; Cash/equivalents: 9%
Total Net Assets: $1.2 billion

Fees

Front-end load	5.75%
Redemption fee	*None*
12b-1 fee	0.25
Management fee	0.68
Other expenses	0.21
Total annual expense	1.14%
Minimum initial investment	$500
Minimum subsequent investment	$50

Services

Telephone exchanges	*Yes*
Automatic withdrawal	*Yes*
Automatic checking deduction	*Yes*
Retirement plan/IRA	*Yes*
Instant redemption	*Yes*
Financial statements	*Semiannual*
Income distributions	*Quarterly*
Capital gains distributions	*Quarterly*
Portfolio manager—years	3
Number of funds in family	77

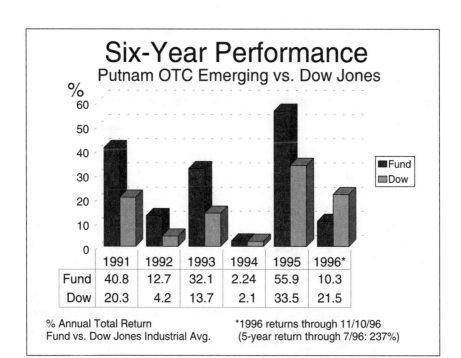

Six-Year Performance
Putnam OTC Emerging vs. Dow Jones

	1991	1992	1993	1994	1995	1996*
Fund	40.8	12.7	32.1	2.24	55.9	10.3
Dow	20.3	4.2	13.7	2.1	33.5	21.5

% Annual Total Return
Fund vs. Dow Jones Industrial Avg.

*1996 returns through 11/10/96
(5-year return through 7/96: 237%)

26
Brandywine Fund

Brandywine Funds, Inc.
3908 Kennett Pike
P.O. Box 4166
Greenville, DE 19807

LONG TERM

Fund manager: Foster S. Friess
Fund objective: Long-term growth

Toll-free: 800-656-3017
In-state: 302-656-6200
Fax: 302-656-7644

Performance	★ ★ ★ ★
Consistency	★ ★ ★ ★
Fees/Services	★ ★ ★ ★
BRWIX	**12 Points**

The Brandywine Fund is a well-balanced growth fund that has established a long history of solid performance by investing in a wide cross-section of stocks. The fund, however, may be a little rich for many investors with its minimum $25,000 initial investment.

But those who have managed to ante up the cash have enjoyed a great ride. Over the past ten years, the fund has posted an average annual return of about 17 percent. A $10,000 investment in the fund ten years ago would now be worth about $47,000.

Led by fund founder Foster S. Friess, the fund management team looks for stocks that have a proven record of profitability and strong earnings momentum. They also look for strong historical sales and net income growth rates, solid debt-to-equity, low PE ratios, and favorable stock price-to-book value ratios. The fund managers also place a strong emphasis on examining the internal developments of companies, such as acquisitions and new product and management changes. The fund manager maintains a very active trading strategy, with an annual portfolio turnover ratio of about 190 percent.

In all, the fund has more than 200 stock holdings. Its heaviest weighting is in computers and software, which account for 20 percent of its stock portfolio. Other leading segments include retail (14 percent), oil field services (10 percent), pharmaceutical and health care (14 percent), apparel (7 percent), and communications (6 percent).

PERFORMANCE

The fund has enjoyed outstanding growth over the past five years. Including dividends and capital gains distributions, the Brandywine Fund has provided a total return for the past five years (through mid-1996) of 166 percent. A $10,000 investment in the fund in 1991 would have grown to about $27,000 five years later. Average annual return: 21.6 percent.

CONSISTENCY

The fund has been very consistent, outperforming the Dow Jones Industrial Average four of the five years through 1995 (but it narrowly trailed the Dow through the first half of 1996). Its biggest year was 1991, when it moved up 49 percent.

FEES/SERVICES/MANAGEMENT

The fund is a true no-load fund—no fee to buy, no fee to sell. Its total annual expense ratio of 1.07 percent (with no 12b-1 fee) is on the low side for a no-load fund.

The fund's drawback is its $25,000 minimum investment for new investors. Subsequent contributions must be at least $1,000. The fund offers many of the standard mutual fund services. Friess Associates (headed by Foster S. Friess) has managed the fund since its inception in 1985. The Brandywine Fund is one of only two funds Brandywine Funds offers.

Top Ten Holdings

1. Gap
2. Sears, Roebuck
3. Nike
4. Halliburton
5. Computer Associates Int'l
6. Pharmacia & Upjohn
7. Eli Lilly
8. EMC
9. Cisco Systems
10. Seagate Technology

Asset Mix: Common stocks: 98%; Cash/equivalents: 2%
Total Net Assets: $4.94 billion

Fees

Front-end load	*None*
Redemption fee	*None*
12b-1 fee	*None*
Management fee	1.00%
Other expenses	0.07
Total annual expense	1.07%
Minimum initial investment	$25,000
Minimum subsequent investment	$1,000

Services

Services	
Telephone exchanges	*Yes*
Automatic withdrawal	*Yes*
Automatic checking deduction	*No*
Retirement plan/IRA	*No*
Instant redemption	*Yes*
Financial statements	*Semiannual*
Income distributions	*Annual*
Capital gains distributions	*Annual*
Portfolio manager—years	13
Number of funds in family	2

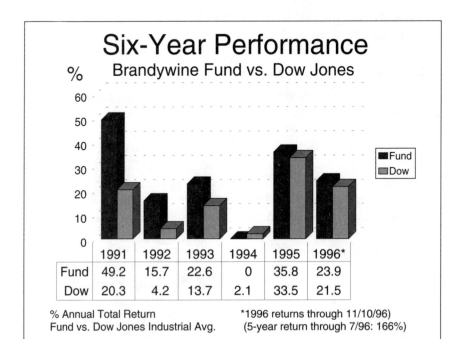

Six-Year Performance
Brandywine Fund vs. Dow Jones

	1991	1992	1993	1994	1995	1996*
Fund	49.2	15.7	22.6	0	35.8	23.9
Dow	20.3	4.2	13.7	2.1	33.5	21.5

% Annual Total Return
Fund vs. Dow Jones Industrial Avg.

*1996 returns through 11/10/96)
(5-year return through 7/96: 166%)

AGGRESSIVE

Fidelity Low-Priced Stock Fund

Fidelity Investments
82 Devonshire Street
Boston, MA 02109

Fund manager: Joel Tillinghast
Fund objective: Aggressive growth

Toll-free: 800-544-8888
In-state: 801-534-1910
Fax: 617-476-9743

Performance	★ ★ ★ ★
Consistency	★ ★ ★ ★
Fees/Services	★ ★ ★ ★
FLPSX	**12 Points**

True to its name, the Fidelity Low-Priced Stock Fund invests strictly in stocks that are selling for less than $25 a share. Most of its holdings are small, little-known companies or new companies that the large institutional investors have not yet discovered. The median market capitalization of the stocks in the fund is about $340 million.

The fund also invests in some out-of-favor stocks that appear poised for a turnaround. Whereas the smaller stocks tend to be more volatile than established blue chips, the potential long returns are greater as well, according to fund manager Joel Tillinghast. "Small-cap stocks tend to be more cyclical—rising and falling in tandem with the economy—than large-cap stocks. Being smaller, their sales can move up or down more quickly depending on the strength of the economy."

Introduced in 1989, the fund has moved up about 19 percent per year. A $10,000 investment when the fund opened would now be worth about $33,000. The fund has also grown quickly in terms of assets invested. Its assets have already grown to more than $4 billion.

The fund invests in a broad range of industries. In all, it has about 700 stock holdings. Its leading industrial segments include finance, which accounts for 17 percent of assets; technology, 8 percent; health, 7 percent; basic industries, 6 percent; and utilities, 5 percent.

Tillinghast takes a fairly aggressive trading approach, with a 65 percent annual portfolio turnover ratio.

PERFORMANCE

The fund has enjoyed exceptional growth over the past five years. Including dividends and capital gains distributions, the Low-Priced Stock Fund has provided a total return for the past five years (through mid-1996) of 164 percent. A $10,000 investment in 1991 would have grown to about $26,000 five years later. Average annual return: 21.4 percent.

CONSISTENCY

The fund has been very consistent recently, outperforming the Dow Jones Industrial Average four of the five years from 1991 through 1995 (and it was even with the Dow through the first half of 1996). Its best year was in 1991 when it jumped 46.3 percent.

FEES/SERVICES/MANAGEMENT

The fund has a low front-end load of 3 percent and a maximum redemption fee of 1.5 percent if it's sold out within 90 days. It has a low total annual expense ratio of 1.11 percent (with no 12b-1 fee).

The fund offers all the standard services such as retirement account availability, automatic withdrawal, and automatic checking account deduction. Its minimum initial investment of $2,500 and minimum subsequent investment of $250 are a little high compared with other funds.

Joel Tillinghast has managed the fund since it opened in 1989. He joined Fidelity in 1986. The Fidelity fund family includes 210 funds.

Top Ten Holdings

1. Universal Health Services B	6. United Insurance Companies
2. Lyondell Petrochemical	7. Canadian National Rail
3. Vencor	8. Century Tel Enterprises
4. Welsh Water	9. SouthTrust
5. Firstbank Puerto Rico	10. Commerce Group

Asset Mix: Common stocks: 72%; Preferred stock: 1%; U.S. Treasury obligations: 10%; Repurchase agreements: 17%
Total Net Assets: $4.2 billion

Fees

Front-end load	3.00%
Redemption fee	*None*
12b-1 fee	*None*
Management fee	0.82
Other expenses	0.29
Total annual expense	1.11%
Minimum initial investment	$2,500
Minimum subsequent investment	$250

Services

Telephone exchanges	*Yes*
Automatic withdrawal	*Yes*
Automatic checking deduction	*Yes*
Retirement plan/IRA	*Yes*
Instant redemption	*Yes*
Financial statements	*Semiannual*
Income distributions	*Annual*
Capital gains distributions	*Annual*
Portfolio manager—years	8
Number of funds in family	210

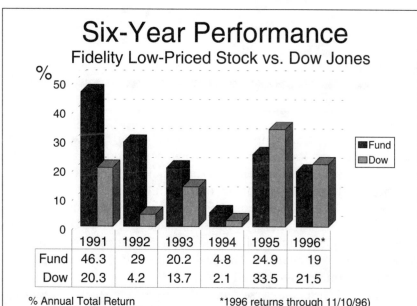

Six-Year Performance
Fidelity Low-Priced Stock vs. Dow Jones

	1991	1992	1993	1994	1995	1996*
Fund	46.3	29	20.2	4.8	24.9	19
Dow	20.3	4.2	13.7	2.1	33.5	21.5

% Annual Total Return
Fund vs. Dow Jones Industrial Avg.

*1996 returns through 11/10/96)
(5-year return through 7/96: 164%)

28

Managers Special Equity Fund

SECTOR

Managers Funds
40 Richards Avenue
Norwalk, CT 06854

Fund managers: Timothy Ebright, Gary Pilgrim, and Andrew Knuth
Fund objective: Aggressive growth

Toll-free: 800-835-3879
In-state: 203-857-5321
Fax: 203-857-5316

Performance	★ ★ ★
Consistency	★ ★ ★ ★
Fees/Services	★ ★ ★ ★ ★
MGSEX	**12 Points**

The Managers Special Equity Fund uses a *hired gun* approach to investment management. Rather than hire its own portfolio managers, Managers Funds scours the investment industry for the top independent money managers, and contracts with them to run its funds.

For instance, the Special Equity Fund has three portfolio managers including Gary Pilgrim, the very successful manager of the PBHG Growth Fund; Timothy Ebright of Liberty Investment; and Andrew Knuth of Westport Asset Management. The three work together to select the portfolio and determine buy-and-sell strategy.

The fund invests a diverse range of fast-growing small and midsize stocks. The managers are fairly conservative in their trading policy, with an annual portfolio turnover ratio of 65 percent. The fund stays almost fully invested in stocks most of the time.

Over the past ten years, the fund has grown at an average annual rate of about 15 percent. A $10,000 investment in the fund ten years ago would now be worth about $40,000.

The fund has about 175 stock holdings. Its leading industrial segment is technology, which accounts for 16 percent of assets. Other leading sectors include consumer nondurables, 10 percent; finance and insurance, 15 percent; general business, 15 percent; health care, 14 percent; and transportation, 8 percent.

PERFORMANCE

The Managers Special Equity Fund has experienced outstanding growth over the past five years. Including dividends and capital gains distributions, the fund has provided a total return for the past five years (through mid-1996) of 156 percent. A $10,000 investment in 1991 would have grown to about $26,000 five years later. Average annual return: 20.7 percent.

CONSISTENCY

The fund has been very consistent, outperforming the Dow Jones Industrial Average four of the five years through 1995 (and it was ahead of the Dow again through the first half of 1996). The fund's biggest gain came in 1991, when it rose 49.3 percent (compared with a 20.3 percent rise in the Dow).

FEES/SERVICES/MANAGEMENT

Like all Managers Funds, the Special Equity Fund is a true no-load fund—no fee to buy, no fee to sell. The fund's total annual expense ratio of 1.44 percent (with no 12b-1 fee) is well in line with other no-load funds.

The fund offers all the standard services such as retirement account availability, automatic withdrawal, and automatic checking account deduction. Its minimum initial investment of $2,000 and minimum subsequent investment of $1 compare favorably with other funds.

Timothy Ebright and Andrew Knuth have been managing the fund since 1985. Gary Pilgrim joined the team in 1994. The Managers Fund family includes eight funds and allows shareholders to switch from fund to fund by telephone.

Top Ten Holdings

1. National Education
2. Charter One Financial
3. AT&T Capital
4. Premier Bancorp
5. Harper Group

6. Consolidated Freightways
7. Airborne Freight
8. Electro Rent
9. Allied Capital Commercial
10. Owens & Minor

Asset Mix: Common stocks: 91%; Cash/equivalents: 9%
Total Net Assets: $166 million

Fees

Front-end load	*None*
Redemption fee	*None*
12b-1 fee	*None*
Management fee	0.90%
Other expenses	0.54
Total annual expense	1.44%
Minimum initial investment	$2,000
Minimum subsequent investment	$1

Services

Telephone exchanges	*Yes*
Automatic withdrawal	*Yes*
Automatic checking deduction	*Yes*
Retirement plan/IRA	*Yes*
Instant redemption	*Yes*
Financial statements	*Annual*
Income distributions	*Annual*
Capital gains distributions	*Annual*
Portfolio managers—years	12
Number of funds in family	8

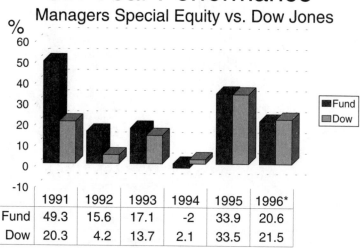

Six-Year Performance
Managers Special Equity vs. Dow Jones

	1991	1992	1993	1994	1995	1996*
Fund	49.3	15.6	17.1	-2	33.9	20.6
Dow	20.3	4.2	13.7	2.1	33.5	21.5

% Annual Total Return   *1996 returns through 11/10/96
Fund vs. Dow Jones Industrial Avg.   (5-year return through 7/96: 156%)

29

Harbor Capital Appreciation Fund

LONG TERM

Harbor Funds
One Seagate, 15th Floor
Toledo, OH 43666

Fund manager: Spiros Segalas
Fund objective: Long-term growth

Toll-free: 800-422-1050
In-state: 419-247-2477
Fax: 419-247-3093

Performance	★ ★ ★
Consistency	★ ★ ★ ★
Fees/Services	★ ★ ★ ★ ★
HACAX	**12 Points**

The Harbor Capital Appreciation Fund guns for the big game—companies such as Intel and Microsoft with histories of above-average growth and market capitalizations of over $1 billion.

Started in 1987, the fund has enjoyed excellent long-term growth. Since inception, it has posted an average annual return of about 18 percent.

Fund manager Spiros Segalas looks for companies with rapid sales and earnings growth that are likely to benefit from strong marketing competence, commitment to research and development, superior new product flow, and veteran management. He invests in both U.S. and foreign blue chip stocks.

Although Segalas keeps an eye on stock values when making investments, he rarely tries to time the market. The fund remains fully invested (95 to 100 percent of assets in stocks) almost all the time. Segalas is fairly conservative in his trading activity, with an annual portfolio turnover ratio of 52 percent.

The fund has only about 65 stock holdings. Its leading industrial groups include computer and business equipment, 13 percent of total assets; software, 10 percent; drugs and health care, 13 percent; electronics, 11 percent; and telecommunications, 8 percent.

PERFORMANCE

The fund has enjoyed outstanding growth over the past five years. Including dividends and capital gains distributions, the Harbor Capital Appreciation Fund has provided a total return for the past five years (through mid-1996) of 153 percent. A $10,000 investment in 1991 would have grown to about $25,000 five years later. Average annual return: 20.4 percent.

CONSISTENCY

The fund has been very consistent, outperforming the Dow Jones Industrial Average four of the five years from 1991 through 1995 (but narrowly trailed the Dow through the first half of 1996). The fund's biggest recent year was 1991, when it climbed 54.8 percent (compared with a 20.3 percent rise in the Dow).

FEES/SERVICES/MANAGEMENT

The fund is a true no-load fund—no fee to buy, no fee to sell. It has a very low total annual expense ratio of just 0.75 percent (with no 12b-1 fee).

The fund offers all the standard services such as retirement account availability, automatic withdrawal, and automatic checking account deduction. Its minimum initial investment of $2,000 and minimum subsequent investment of $500 are a little high compared with other funds.

Spiros Segalas has managed the fund since 1990. The Harbor fund family includes eight funds and allows shareholders to switch from fund to fund by telephone.

Top Ten Holdings

1. Cisco Systems
2. Ford Motor Credit
3. Hewlett-Packard
4. Boeing
5. Intel
6. Reuters Holdings
7. Microsoft
8. Walt Disney
9. Astra
10. Computer Associates Int'l

Asset Mix: Common stocks: 97%; Cash/equivalents: 3%
Total Net Assets: $1.3 billion

Fees

Front-end load	*None*
Redemption fee (max)	*None*
12b-1 fee	*None*
Management fee	0.60%
Other expenses	0.15
Total annual expense	0.75%
Minimum initial investment	$2,000
Minimum subsequent investment	$500

Services

Telephone exchanges	*Yes*
Automatic withdrawal	*Yes*
Automatic checking deduction	*Yes*
Retirement plan/IRA	*Yes*
Instant redemption	*Yes*
Financial statements	*Annual*
Income distributions	*Annual*
Capital gains distributions	*Annual*
Portfolio manager—years	7
Number of funds in family	8

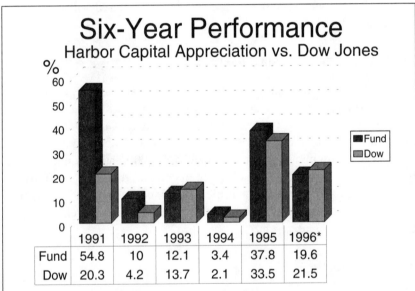

Six-Year Performance
Harbor Capital Appreciation vs. Dow Jones

	1991	1992	1993	1994	1995	1996*
Fund	54.8	10	12.1	3.4	37.8	19.6
Dow	20.3	4.2	13.7	2.1	33.5	21.5

% Annual Total Return
Fund vs. Dow Jones Industrial Avg.

*1996 returns through 11/10/96
(5-year return through 7/96: 153%)

30
T. Rowe Price New America Growth Fund

T. Rowe Price Funds
100 East Pratt Street
Baltimore, MD 21202

Fund manager: John LaPorte
Fund objective: Long-term growth

Toll-free: 800-225-5132
In-state: 410-547-2000
Fax: 410-347-1574

Performance	★ ★ ★
Consistency	★ ★ ★ ★
Fees/Services	★ ★ ★ ★ ★
PRWAX	**12 Points**

The service industry has been one of the biggest growth areas of the U.S. economy in recent years, a trend that's helped power the stellar performance of the New America Growth Fund. The fund invests primarily in stocks of service-related companies such as First Data, United Health-Care, and Olsten.

Over the past ten years, the fund has had an average annual return of 14 percent. A $10,000 investment in the fund ten years ago would now be worth about $37,000.

In selecting stocks for the portfolio, fund manager John LaPorte looks for solid, growing companies with a good balance sheet, strong management, and significant market share in their key sector. The stocks in the portfolio vary in size from small, emerging growth companies to large blue chips.

LaPorte is fairly modest in his trading strategy, with an annual portfolio turnover ratio of 56 percent. The fund stays almost fully invested in stocks most of the time.

Among the types of stocks the fund buys are health care, computer processing, retailers, restaurant chains, insurance and financial services, media, entertainment, energy services, and environmental services. Business services account for about 46 percent of total assets; consumer sevices make up 42 percent, and financial services account for 10 percent. The fund has about 70 stock holdings in all.

PERFORMANCE

The New America Growth Fund has experienced outstanding growth over the past five years. Including dividends and capital gains distributions, the fund has provided a total return for the past five years (through mid-1996) of 152 percent. A $10,000 investment in 1991 would have grown to about $25,000 five years later. Average annual return: 20.4 percent.

CONSISTENCY

The fund has been very consistent, outperforming the Dow Jones Industrial Average four of the five years through 1995 (and it was ahead of the Dow again through the first half of 1996). The fund did suffer a loss of 7.4 percent in 1994. Its biggest gain came in 1991, when it rose 61.9 percent (compared with a 20.3 percent rise in the Dow).

FEES/SERVICES/MANAGEMENT

Like all T. Rowe Price funds, the New America Growth Fund is a true no-load fund—no fee to buy, no fee to sell. It has a very low total annual expense ratio of 1.07 percent (with no 12b-1 fee).

The fund offers all the standard services such as retirement account availability, automatic withdrawal, and automatic checking account deduction. Its minimum initial investment of $2,500 and minimum subsequent investment of $100 are a little higher than average.

John LaPorte has managed the fund since 1985. The T. Rowe Price fund family includes 50 funds and allows shareholders to switch from fund to fund by telephone.

Top Ten Holdings

1. CUC International	6. Comcast
2. United HealthCare	7. Viacom
3. HFS	8. General Nutrition
4. ADT	9. Capital Cities
5. Paging Network	10. First Data

Asset Mix: Common stocks: 97%; Cash/equivalents: 3%.
Total Net Assets: $1.3 billion

Fees

Front-end load	*None*
Redemption fee (max)	*None*
12b-1 fee	*None*
Management fee	0.68%
Other expenses	0.39
Total annual expense	1.07%
Minimum initial investment	$2,500
Minimum subsequent investment	$100

Services

Telephone exchanges	*Yes*
Automatic withdrawal	*Yes*
Automatic checking deduction	*Yes*
Retirement plan/IRA	*Yes*
Instant redemption	*Yes*
Financial statements	*Semiannual*
Income distributions	*Annual*
Capital gains distributions	*Annual*
Portfolio manager—years	12
Number of funds in family	50

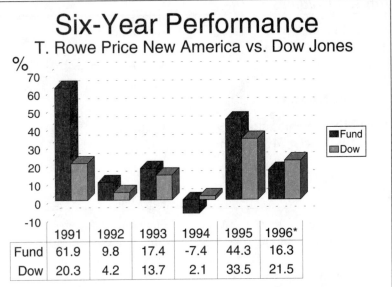

Six-Year Performance
T. Rowe Price New America vs. Dow Jones

	1991	1992	1993	1994	1995	1996*
Fund	61.9	9.8	17.4	-7.4	44.3	16.3
Dow	20.3	4.2	13.7	2.1	33.5	21.5

% Annual Total Return   *1996 returns through 11/10/96
Fund vs. Dow Jones Industrial Avg.   (5-year return through 7/96: 152%)

LONG TERM

31
Strong Schafer Value Fund

Strong Funds
P.O. Box 2936
Milwaukee, WI 53201

Fund manager: David K. Schafer
Fund objective: Long-term growth

Toll-free: 800-368-3863
In-state: 414-359-3400
Fax: 414-359-3947

Performance	★ ★ ★
Consistency	★ ★ ★ ★
Fees/Services	★ ★ ★ ★ ★
SCHVX	**12 Points**

The Strong Schafer Value Fund is a small, no-load growth fund that focuses on bargain stocks. "We're looking for above-average growth selling at a discount to the overall market," says fund manager David Schafer. Schafer looks for stocks with low PE ratios that may have been beaten down by the market and are poised for a rebound.

The fund has moved up about 14 percent per year since its inception in 1985. A $10,000 investment in the fund ten years ago would now be worth about $40,000.

The fund invests primarily in midrange to large capitalization stocks such as Whirlpool, Philip Morris, Kmart, and Federal Express.

Schafer takes a conservative long-term approach. His annual portfolio turnover ratio is 33 percent. "When we buy a stock that we think is a bargain, we're content to wait for the market to realize its value," says Schafer. "That means we generally hold stocks for the long term and keep our portfolio turnover very low."

The fund is well diversified, holding stocks from a broad range of sectors. "We try to maintain an equal weighting of every stock in the portfolio," says Schafer. "That way we don't let our natural enthusiasm for a particular stock influence our diversification strategy. And we tend to remain fully invested because we believe that trying to time the market will decrease rather than increase our return over time."

In all, the fund has about 40 stock holdings. Leading sectors include retail, 10 percent of assets; energy, 10 percent; automotive, 8 percent; banks, 9 percent; and insurance, 8 percent.

PERFORMANCE

The Strong Schafer Value Fund has enjoyed excellent growth over the past five years. Including dividends and capital gains distributions, the fund has provided a total return for the past five years (through mid-1996) of 149 percent. A $10,000 investment in 1991 would have grown to about $25,000 five years later. Average annual return: 20 percent.

CONSISTENCY

The fund has been relatively consistent, outperforming the Dow Jones Industrial Average four of the five years from 1991 through 1995 (but it trailed the Dow through the first half of 1996).

FEES/SERVICES/MANAGEMENT

The Value Fund is a no-load fund, with no fee to buy and no fee to sell. The fund's total annual expense ratio of 1.23 percent (with no 12b-1 fee) compares favorably with other funds.

The fund offers all the standard services such as retirement account availability, automatic withdrawal, and automatic checking account deduction. Its minimum initial investment of $2,500 is a little higher than average, but its minimum subsequent investment of $50 compares favorably with other funds.

David K. Schafer has managed the fund since its inception in 1985. The Strong fund family includes a total of 21 funds and allows shareholders to switch from fund to fund by telephone.

Top Ten Holdings

1. Borg-Warner Automotive
2. Avnet
3. Circuit City Stores
4. May Department Stores
5. General Motors
6. Merrill Lynch
7. PaineWebber Group
8. KetCorp
9. Mellon Bank
10. LaSalle Holdings

Asset Mix: Common stocks: 96%; Cash/equivalents: 4%
Total Net Assets: $333 million

Fees

Front-end load	*None*
Redemption fee	*None*
12b-1 fee	*None*
Management fee	1.00%
Other expenses	0.28
Total annual expense	1.28%
Minimum initial investment	$2,500
Minimum subsequent investment	$50

Services

Telephone exchanges	*Yes*
Automatic withdrawal	*Yes*
Automatic checking deduction	*Yes*
Retirement plan/IRA	*Yes*
Instant redemption	*Yes*
Financial statements	*Quarterly*
Income distributions	*Quarterly*
Capital gains distributions	*Annual*
Portfolio manager—years	12
Number of funds in family	21

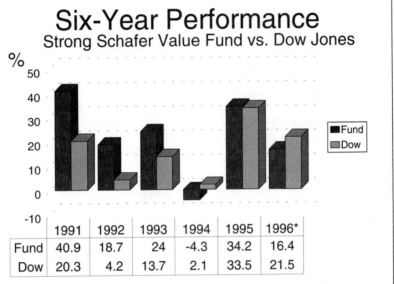

Six-Year Performance
Strong Schafer Value Fund vs. Dow Jones

	1991	1992	1993	1994	1995	1996*
Fund	40.9	18.7	24	-4.3	34.2	16.4
Dow	20.3	4.2	13.7	2.1	33.5	21.5

% Annual Total Return
Fund vs. Dow Jones Industrial Avg.

*1996 returns through 11/10/96
(5-year return through 7/96: 149%)

32
Mairs and Power Growth Fund

Mairs and Power Funds
W-2062 First National Bank Building
St. Paul, MN 55101

Fund manager: George A. Mairs III
Fund objective: Long-term growth

Toll-free: 800-304-7404
In-state: 612-222-8478

Performance	★ ★ ★
Consistency	★ ★ ★ ★
Fees/Services	★ ★ ★ ★ ★
MPGFX	**12 Points**

Opened in 1958, the Mairs and Power Growth Fund is one of the oldest funds in America. But even after all these years, it's still an undiscovered diamond in the rough in the mutual fund industry, with assets under management of just $87 million.

Over the past ten years, the fund has posted average annual returns of about 15 percent per year. A $10,000 investment in the fund ten years ago would now be worth about $39,000.

Fund manager George Mairs III invests primarily in large blue chip stocks, but he also includes some small and midsize stocks in the portfolio. Mairs, who has managed the fund since 1980, looks for companies with reasonably predictable earnings, above-average return on equity, market dominance, and financial strength.

The fund has only about 30 stock holdings, more than half of which were plucked from its own backyard in Minnesota, such as Dayton Hudson, General Mills, Medtronic, and 3M. The fund is big on large cap blue chips, although it also owns some midsize stocks.

Mairs believes strongly in the buy-and-hold approach. His fund is the most conservatively traded fund in the "Best 100," with an annual portfolio turnover ratio of just 4 percent. He stays at least 90 percent invested in stocks most of the time.

While the fund has a solid stake in technology stocks, it is well diversified in other industries as well. The leading industrial sectors include consumer goods, 10 percent; financial, 14 percent; technology, 14 percent; industrial manufacturers, 16 percent; and drugs and medical, 22 percent.

PERFORMANCE

The Mairs and Power Growth Fund has enjoyed strong growth over the past five years. Including dividends and capital gains distributions, the fund has provided a total return for the past five years (through mid-1996) of 143 percent. A $10,000 investment in 1991 would have grown to about $24,000 five years later. Average annual return: 19.4 percent.

CONSISTENCY

The fund has been very consistent, outperforming the Dow Jones Industrial Average four of the five years through 1995 (and it was even with the Dow again through the first half of 1996). The fund has had increases of more than 40 percent twice in the last six years. It was up 42.1 percent in 1991 and 49.3 percent in 1995.

FEES/SERVICES/MANAGEMENT

The Mairs and Power Growth Fund is a true no-load fund—no fee to buy, no fee to sell. The fund's total annual expense ratio of 0.99 percent (with no 12b-1 fee) is very low compared with most other funds.

The fund offers some services such as retirement account availability and automatic withdrawal. Its minimum initial investment of $2,500 and minimum subsequent investment of $100 is a little higher than average.

George A. Mairs III has managed the fund since 1980. The Growth Fund is the only fund offered by Mairs and Power.

Top Ten Holdings

1. Medtronic
2. BMC Industries
3. ADC Telecommunications
4. Pfizer
5. Emerson Electric

6. Norwest
7. The Saint Paul Companies
8. First Bank System
9. Minnesota Mining & Manufacturing (3M)
10. Toro

Asset Mix: Common stocks: 95%; Cash/equivalents: 5%
Total Net Assets: $94 million

Fees

Front-end load	*None*
Redemption fee	*None*
12b-1 fee	*None*
Management fee	0.60%
Other expenses	0.39
Total annual expense	0.99%
Minimum initial investment	$2,500
Minimum subsequent investment	$100

Services

Telephone exchanges	*No*
Automatic withdrawal	*Yes*
Automatic checking deduction	*No*
Retirement plan/IRA	*Yes*
Instant redemption	*No*
Financial statements	*Annual*
Income distributions	*Semiannual*
Capital gains distributions	*Annual*
Portfolio manager—years	17
Number of funds in family	1

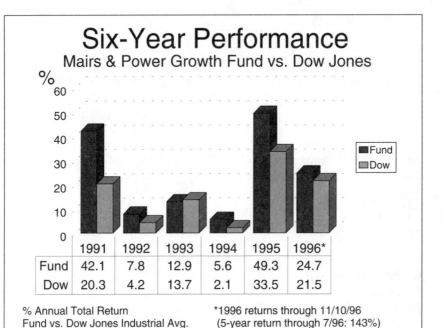

Six-Year Performance
Mairs & Power Growth Fund vs. Dow Jones

	1991	1992	1993	1994	1995	1996*
Fund	42.1	7.8	12.9	5.6	49.3	24.7
Dow	20.3	4.2	13.7	2.1	33.5	21.5

% Annual Total Return   *1996 returns through 11/10/96
Fund vs. Dow Jones Industrial Avg.   (5-year return through 7/96: 143%)

SECTOR

33
Seligman Communications and Information Fund "A"

Seligman Funds
100 Park Avenue
New York, NY 10017

Fund manager: Paul H. Wick
Fund objective: Sector fund

Toll-free: 800-221-2450
In-state: 212-850-1864
Fax: 212-922-5738

Performance	★ ★ ★ ★ ★
Consistency	★ ★ ★ ★
Fees/Services	★ ★ ★
SLMCX	**12 Points**

In this age of information, it's little wonder a mutual fund that specializes in information and communications has become one of the fastest growing investments of the decade. The Seligman Communications and Information Fund has grown about 30.5 percent per year the past five years, and 19.5 percent per year for the past ten years. A $10,000 investment in the fund ten years ago would now be worth about $59,000.

Betting on the right industries has certainly been a key to the fund's lofty performance record, but fund manager Paul Wick's astute buy-and-sell strategy has also helped propel the fund.

"We try to buy panic and sell euphoria," says Wick. "When the public gets too enthusiastic about a sector, we'll often sell out and move into something else."

Wick has invested primarily in small emerging growth stocks in the communications, computer, and semiconductor sectors. "There's always a lot of volatility with small stocks. We just try to recognize the buying opportunities."

Wick takes both a top-down and a bottom-up approach in selecting stocks. He looks at the economy and the most promising sectors, and then he finds stocks that stand to benefit most from those economic trends. "I think we've done a good job of picking not only the right sectors, but the right stocks within those sectors."

Wick is very momentum-oriented in his approach. He wants stocks with rapid growth—in the range of 30 to 60 percent earnings growth per year. He also looks for companies with a lot of cash flow and profit margins of 18 percent or more. "Some of these technology products can hit a sweet spot in the market and really grow at astronomical rates for a while. But their big success usually doesn't last too long." When the growth begins to ebb, Wick bails out.

"When they start reporting disappointing earnings, we get out quickly. It's the cockroach theory—when you see one, there are probably others coming. One thing that has really helped the fund's performance the past few years is that we've gotten better at cutting our losses quickly before they become big losses."

In making buy and sell decisions, Wick looks at more than just numbers on a chart. "We get to know the companies well. I've probably visited 70 percent of the companies in our portfolio. By knowing a company well, [we can] take advantage of volatility in the market. We can recognize buying opportunities, and build a position in the stock when it's at a low moment." To stay on top of the market, Wick is a regular at technology trade shows and conventions. "I also read a tremendous amount, particularly in the trade press—at least 20 different periodicals a month." On top of that, he pages through the stock returns of about 1,300 high tech stocks every day. "We try to stay on top of everything."

In all, the fund has about 80 stock holdings. Wick is fairly moderate in his trading strategy, with an annual portfolio turnover ratio of about 66 percent. The fund's leading industrial sectors include semiconductors, 27 percent; computer hardware and peripherals, 15 percent; computer software, 14 percent; communications infrastructure, 14 percent; and semiconductor capital equipment, 11 percent.

PERFORMANCE

The fund has enjoyed tremendous growth over the past five years. Including dividends and capital gains distributions, the Seligman Communications and Information Fund has provided a total return for the past five years (through mid-1996) of 278 percent. A $10,000 investment in 1991 would have grown to about $38,000 five years later. Average annual return: 30.5 percent.

CONSISTENCY

The fund has been very consistent, outperforming the Dow Jones Industrial Average all five years from 1991 through 1995 (but it trailed the market—with a 5.2 percent decline—through the first half of 1996.) The fund has had gains of more than 30 percent four of the past six years.

FEES/SERVICES/MANAGEMENT

The fund has a front-end load of 4.75 percent and an annual expense ratio of 1.76 percent (including a 0.24 percent 12b-1 fee and a 0.9 percent management fee), which is slightly above average for a front-end load fund.

The fund offers all the standard services such as retirement account availability, automatic withdrawal, and automatic checking account deduction. Its minimum initial investment of $2,500 is a little higher than average, but its minimum subsequent investment of $100 compares favorably with other funds.

Paul Wick has managed the fund since 1989. The Seligman fund family includes 31 funds and allows shareholders to switch from fund to fund by telephone.

Top Ten Holdings

1. EMC
2. Parametric Technology
3. Intel
4. Cisco Systems
5. IntelElectronics for Imaging

6. Oak Technology
7. Xilinx
8. Seagate Technology
9. Altera
10. Synopsys

Asset Mix: Common stocks: 98%; Cash/equivalents: 2%
Total Net Assets: $2.1 billion

Fees

Front-end load	4.75%
Redemption fee	*None*
12b-1 fee	0.24
Management fee	0.90
Other expenses	0.62
Total annual expense	1.76%
Minimum initial investment	$2,500
Minimum subsequent investment	$100

Services

Telephone exchanges	*Yes*
Automatic withdrawal	*Yes*
Automatic checking deduction	*Yes*
Retirement plan/IRA	*Yes*
Instant redemption	*Yes*
Financial statements	*Quarterly*
Income distributions	*Annual*
Capital gains distributions	*Annual*
Portfolio manager—years	8
Number of funds in family	31

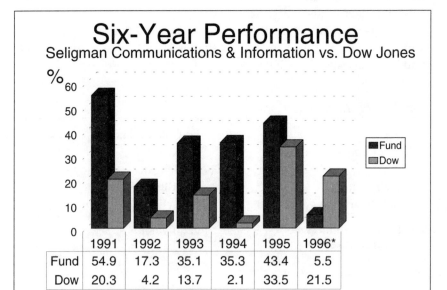

Six-Year Performance
Seligman Communications & Information vs. Dow Jones

	1991	1992	1993	1994	1995	1996*
Fund	54.9	17.3	35.1	35.3	43.4	5.5
Dow	20.3	4.2	13.7	2.1	33.5	21.5

% Annual Total Return
Fund vs. Dow Jones Industrial Avg.

*1996 returns through 11/10/96
(5-year return through 7/96: 278%)

34
John Hancock Freedom Regional Bank Fund

John Hancock Funds
101 Huntington Avenue
Boston, MA 02199-7603

Fund manager: Jim Schmidt
Fund objective: Sector fund

Toll-free: 800-225-5291
In-state: 617-375-1500
Fax: 617-375-1819

Performance	★ ★ ★ ★ ★
Consistency	★ ★ ★ ★
Fees/Services	★ ★ ★
FRBFX	**12 Points**

Banking has been booming over the past few years, and investors in the John Hancock Freedom Regional Bank Fund have cashed in big time on the industry's recovery.

Over the past five years, the Regional Bank Fund has posted an average annual return of 22 percent—a dramatic improvement over its ten-year average annual return of just 12 percent. Like all sector funds, the Freedom Regional Bank Fund can be volatile—especially when interest rates are unstable. The fund suffered a 21 percent decline in 1990, then rebounded in 1991 with a 64 percent gain.

Fund manager Jim Schmidt focuses on undervalued regional banks and thrifts that have good earnings prospects and the potential to merge with or acquire other banks. In all, the fund has shares in nearly 300 banks, thrifts, and other financial institutions throughout the United States. Most are regional banks (43 percent of assets) and thrifts (20 percent), but the fund also owns shares in a number of "super regional" banks (14 percent), such as Banc One, BankAmerica, and First Chicago.

Schmidt takes a very conservative buy-and-hold approach, with a 14 percent annual portfolio turnover ratio.

Recently, Schmidt began allocating more of the fund's assets to California bank stocks. "California has recently emerged from a severe recession, and now employment is growing in all parts of the state," he explains. "Bank investors have an opportunity to benefit from bank consolidation in the state that is similar to the opportunity that existed in the Midwest ten years ago."

PERFORMANCE   ★ ★ ★ ★ ★

The fund has enjoyed outstanding growth over the past five years. Including dividends and capital gains distributions, it has provided a total return for the past five years (through mid-1996) of 234 percent. A $10,000 investment in 1991 would have grown to about $33,000 five years later. Average annual return: 27.3 percent.

CONSISTENCY   ★ ★ ★ ★

The fund has been fairly consistent, outperforming the Dow Jones Industrial Average four of the five years from 1991 to 1995 (although it trailed the Dow through the first half of 1996). The fund has had increases of 47 percent or more three of the past six years.

FEES/SERVICES/MANAGEMENT   ★ ★ ★

The Freedom Regional Bank Fund "A" shares carry a 5 percent front-end load, and a 1.39 percent annual expense ratio. "B" shares have a 5 percent redemption fee that declines 1 percent for each year the investor holds the shares. "B" shares have a much higher annual expense ratio of 2.09 percent.

The fund offers all the standard services such as retirement account availability, automatic withdrawal, and automatic checking account deduction. Its minimum initial investment of $1,000 and minimum subsequent investment of $200 are in line with other funds.

Jim Schmidt has managed the fund since its inception in 1985. John Hancock offers 40 funds and allows shareholders to switch from fund to fund by telephone.

Top Ten Holdings

1. Wells Fargo
2. Greenpoint Financial
3. First of America Bank
4. PNC Bank
5. U.S. Bancorp

6. Bank of New York
7. Corestates Financial
8. Southern National
9. F&M National
10. Fleet Financial Group

Asset Mix: Common stocks: 82%; Preferred stock: 1% ;
Cash/equivalents: 17%
Total Net Assets: $1.7 billion

Fees

Front-end load	5.00%
Redemption fee	*None*
12b-1 fee	0.3
Management fee	0.78
Other expenses	0.31
Total annual expense	1.39%
Minimum initial investment	$1,000
Minimum subsequent investment	$200

Services

Telephone exchanges	*Yes*
Automatic withdrawal	*Yes*
Automatic checking deduction	*Yes*
Retirement plan/IRA	*Yes*
Instant redemption	*Yes*
Financial statements	*Semiannual*
Income distributions	*Quarterly*
Capital gains distributions	*Annual*
Portfolio manager—years	12
Number of funds in family	40

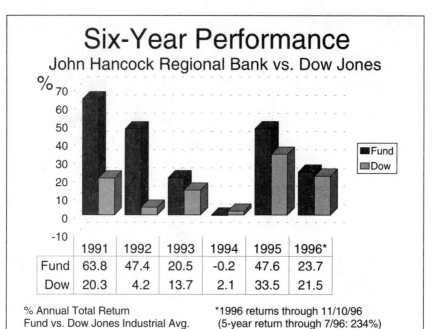

Six-Year Performance
John Hancock Regional Bank vs. Dow Jones

	1991	1992	1993	1994	1995	1996*
Fund	63.8	47.4	20.5	-0.2	47.6	23.7
Dow	20.3	4.2	13.7	2.1	33.5	21.5

% Annual Total Return   *1996 returns through 11/10/96
Fund vs. Dow Jones Industrial Avg.   (5-year return through 7/96: 234%)

35
Fidelity Select Multimedia Portfolio

Fidelity Investments
82 Devonshire Street
Boston, MA 02109

Fund manager: John Porter
Fund objective: Sector fund

Toll-free: 800-544-8888
In-state: 801-534-1910
Fax: 617-476-9753

Performance	★ ★ ★ ★ ★
Consistency	★ ★ ★ ★
Fees/Services	★ ★ ★
FBMPX	**12 Points**

The Multimedia Portfolio takes a major stake in a broad range of media-related companies, including TV and radio broadcasting companies, newspapers, film studios, and cable television. The fund also invests in companies that make products and equipment used in the media industry.

The media business has been on a roll in recent years, helping make the Multimedia Portfolio one of the fastest growing funds in America. Over the past five years, fund shares have grown at an average annual rate of 25 percent, and over the past ten years, the fund has grown at an average annual rate of 17 percent. A $10,000 investment in the fund ten years ago would now be worth about $50,000.

The future of the multimedia industry should be very strong, but the competition is heating up. A new telecommunications law allows phone companies to enter the cable television business, which could shake up the entire industry. It's a business that will continue to go through significant changes in the years ahead.

The fund already has a large position in stocks of telephone service companies (8 percent of assets), and that position could become even greater as the lines blur between telephone services and broadcasting companies. Other key holdings of the fund include newspapers (21 percent of assets), cable TV operators (14 percent), TV and radio communication equipment (12 percent), and periodicals (10 percent).

In all, the fund has about 60 stock holdings. The fund manager takes a fairly active trading approach, with an annual portfolio turnover ratio of 107 percent.

PERFORMANCE

The fund has enjoyed exceptional growth over the past five years. Including dividends and capital gains distributions, the Fidelity Select Multimedia Portfolio has provided a total return for the past five years (through mid-1996) of 205 percent. A $10,000 investment in 1991 would have grown to about $30,500 five years later. Average annual return: 25 percent.

CONSISTENCY

The fund has been very consistent in recent years, outperforming or staying even with the Dow Jones Industrial Average for five consecutive years through 1995 (although it was trailing the Dow through the first half of 1996). The fund can, however, be volatile. In 1990, it dropped 26 percent. Its best years were 1991 and 1993 when it moved up 37.8 percent and 38 percent respectively.

FEES/SERVICES/MANAGEMENT

The fund has a low front-end load of 3 percent and a maximum redemption fee of 0.75 percent, if shares are sold out within 29 days. Otherwise the redemption fee is a flat $7.50.

The fund offers all the standard services such as retirement account availability, automatic withdrawal, and automatic checking account deduction. Its minimum initial investment of $2,500 and minimum subsequent investment of $250 are a little high compared with other funds.

Fund manager John Porter has only been with the fund since 1996. The Fidelity fund family includes about 210 funds.

Top Ten Holdings

1. Meredith
2. Scientific-Atlanta
3. People's Choice TV
4. California Amplifier
5. Times Mirror

6. ADVO-Systems
7. Belo Corp.
8. TCI Group
9. NYNEX
10. DSC Communications

Asset Mix: Common stocks: 95%; Cash/equivalents: 5%
Total Net Assets: $94 million

Fees

Front-end load	3.00%
Redemption fee	$7.50
12b-1 fee	*None*
Management fee	0.61
Other expenses	1.06
Total annual expense	1.67%
Minimum initial investment	$2,500
Minimum subsequent investment	$250

Services

Telephone exchanges	*Yes*
Automatic withdrawal	*Yes*
Automatic checking deduction	*Yes*
Retirement plan/IRA	*Yes*
Instant redemption	*Yes*
Financial statements	*Semiannual*
Income distributions	*Semiannual*
Capital gains distributions	*Semiannual*
Portfolio manager—years	1
Number of funds in family	210

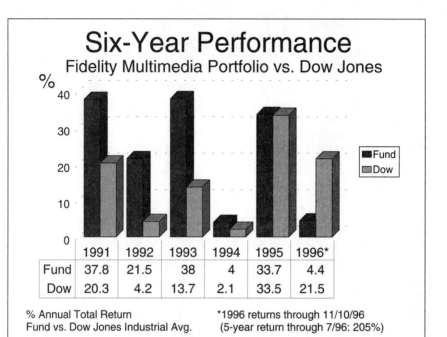

Six-Year Performance
Fidelity Multimedia Portfolio vs. Dow Jones

	1991	1992	1993	1994	1995	1996*
Fund	37.8	21.5	38	4	33.7	4.4
Dow	20.3	4.2	13.7	2.1	33.5	21.5

% Annual Total Return   *1996 returns through 11/10/96
Fund vs. Dow Jones Industrial Avg.   (5-year return through 7/96: 205%)

36
Fidelity Select Software and Computer Services Portfolio

Fidelity Investments
82 Devonshire Street
Boston, MA 02109

Fund manager: John Hurley
Fund objective: Sector fund

Toll-free: 800-544-8888
In-state: 801-534-1910
Fax: 617-476-9753

Performance	★ ★ ★ ★ ★
Consistency	★ ★ ★ ★
Fees/Services	★ ★ ★
FSCSX	**12 Points**

Demand for innovative new computer software has never been stronger. With software applications being developed for a broad range of personal, professional, industrial, and commercial uses, the software industry has been one of the fastest growing areas of the economy the past few years.

The Fidelity Select Software and Computer Services Portfolio has taken advantage of that growth by posting annual returns of more than 30 percent four of the past six years. Over the past ten years, the fund has posted annual average returns of about 18 percent. A $10,000 investment in the fund ten years ago would now be worth about $52,000.

Fund manager John Hurley should have little trouble keeping the fund on its fast track if the computer industry continues to prosper. However, the high tech area has always been subject to wide swings. Hurley can mitigate the volatility of his fund somewhat by combining the more volatile software stocks with the traditionally stable computer services stocks such as Automatic Data Processing and Electronic Data Systems.

Even with the balanced approached, the fund will probably require some patience by investors; it is volatile in the short term with strong long-term potential because of the growth of the software and computer services industries.

The fund is relatively active in its trading policy, with a 164 percent annual portfolio turnover ratio.

The fund holds about 50 stocks, with its heaviest weighting in pre-packaged computer software, which accounts for 33 percent of the assets. Other leading segments include computer services (7.5 percent of assets), CAD/CAM (6 percent), and data processing (5 percent).

PERFORMANCE   ★ ★ ★ ★ ★

The fund has enjoyed exceptional growth over the past five years. Including dividends and capital gains distributions, the Software and Computer Services Portfolio has provided a total return for the past five years (through mid-1996) of 240 percent. A $10,000 investment in 1991 would have grown to about $34,000 five years later. Average annual return: 27.8 percent.

CONSISTENCY   ★ ★ ★ ★

The fund has been very consistent for a sector fund, outperforming the Dow Jones Industrial Average four of the five years through 1995—with increases in excess of 30 percent each of those four years. But the fund trailed the Dow through the first half of 1996.

FEES/SERVICES/MANAGEMENT   ★ ★ ★

The fund has a low front-end load of 3 percent and a maximum redemption fee of 0.75 percent, if shares are sold within 30 days of purchase. Otherwise a $7.50 fee is charged upon redemption. The fund's total annual expense ratio of 1.55 percent (with no 12b-1 fee) is about average among load funds.

The fund offers all the standard services such as retirement account availability, automatic withdrawal, and automatic checking account deduction. Its minimum initial investment of $2,500 and minimum subsequent investment of $250 are a little high compared with other funds.

John Hurley has managed the fund since 1994. The Fidelity fund family includes about 210 funds.

Top Ten Holdings

1. Electronics for Imaging
2. Oracle Systems
3. FileNet
4. SunGard Data Systems
5. Parametric Technology

6. Peoplesoft
7. HBO & Co.
8. Sybase
9. Nintendo Co. Ltd. Ord.
10. General Motors E

Asset Mix: Common stocks: 78%; Preferred stocks: 1.2%; Cash/equivalents: 21%
Total Net Assets: $337.6 million

Fees

Front-end load	3.00%
Redemption fee	$7.50
12b-1 fee	*None*
Management fee	0.61
Other expenses	0.94
Total annual expense	1.55%
Minimum initial investment	$2,500
Minimum subsequent investment	$250

Services

Telephone exchanges	*Yes*
Automatic withdrawal	*Yes*
Automatic checking deduction	*Yes*
Retirement plan/IRA	*Yes*
Instant redemption	*Yes*
Financial statements	*Semiannual*
Income distributions	*Semiannual*
Capital gains distributions	*Semiannual*
Portfolio manager—years	3
Number of funds in family	210

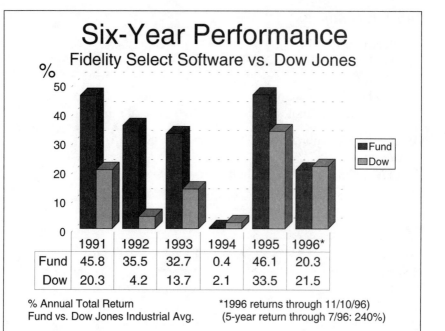

Six-Year Performance
Fidelity Select Software vs. Dow Jones

	1991	1992	1993	1994	1995	1996*
Fund	45.8	35.5	32.7	0.4	46.1	20.3
Dow	20.3	4.2	13.7	2.1	33.5	21.5

% Annual Total Return   *1996 returns through 11/10/96)
Fund vs. Dow Jones Industrial Avg.   (5-year return through 7/96: 240%)

SECTOR

Fidelity Select Financial Services Portfolio

Fidelity Investments
82 Devonshire Street
Boston, MA 02109

Fund manager: Louis Salemy
Fund objective: Sector fund

Toll-free: 800-544-8888
In-state: 801-534-1910
Fax: 617-476-9753

Performance	★ ★ ★ ★ ★
Consistency	★ ★ ★ ★
Fees/Services	★ ★ ★
FIDSX	**12 Points**

The financial services industry has been thriving through the economic boom of the 1990s, helping push the Fidelity Select Financial Services Portfolio through several years of spectacular growth. The fund invests in a wide range of financial services-related industries such as banks, mortgage companies and insurance firms.

The fund, which opened in 1981, has been managed since 1994 by Louis Salemy. The fund's performance the past five years has far exceeded its performance during the late 1980s when interest rates were high and banks were in a slump. In fact, the fund's five-year growth—225 percent—exceeds its ten-year growth of 210 percent.

Salemy attributes much of the fund's recent success to falling interest rates and the rash of mergers and consolidations in the financial services arena.

The fund is relatively small, with only about 35 stock holdings. Most are major institutions such as American Express, Banc One, Beneficial Corp., and Citicorp. The fund maintains a fairly active trading strategy, with an annual portfolio turnover ratio of 107 percent.

The fund is weighted heaviest in stocks of national commercial banks, which make up 32 percent of total assets. Other leading sectors include insurance companies (16.5 percent), federal and federally sponsored credit agencies (11 percent), personal credit institutions (11 percent), and financial services (7 percent).

PERFORMANCE

The fund has enjoyed exceptional growth over the past five years. Including dividends and capital gains distributions, the Fidelity Financial Services Fund has provided a total return for the past five years (through mid-1996) of 225 percent. A $10,000 investment in 1991 would have grown to about $32,000 five years later. Average annual return: 26.6 percent.

CONSISTENCY

The fund has been very consistent recently, outperforming the Dow Jones Industrial Average four of the five years through 1995 (but it trailed the Dow through the first half of 1996). Its best year was in 1991 when it jumped 61.6 percent.

FEES/SERVICES/MANAGEMENT

The fund has a low front-end load of 3 percent and a maximum redemption fee of 0.75 percent if it's sold out within 29 days. Otherwise, shareholders pay a $7.50 redemption fee. Its annual expense ratio of 1.5 percent (with no 12b-1 fee) is about average among all funds.

The fund offers all the standard services such as retirement account availability, automatic withdrawal, and automatic checking account deduction. Its minimum initial investment of $2,500 and minimum subsequent investment of $250 are a little high compared with other funds.

Louis Salemy has managed the fund since 1994. He has been with Fidelity since 1992. The Fidelity fund family includes about 210 funds.

Top Ten Holdings

1. American Express
2. Fleet Financial Group
3. Banc One
4. Beneficial
5. Household International
6. Federal National Mortgage Association
7. Allstate
8. Citicorp
9. Bank of New York
10. Federal Home Loan Mortgage

Asset Mix: Common stocks: 88%; Cash/equivalents: 12%
Total Net Assets: $270 million

Fees

Front-end load	3.00%
Redemption fee	$7.50
12b-1 fee	*None*
Management fee	0.61
Other expenses	0.89
Total annual expense	1.50%
Minimum initial investment	$2,500
Minimum subsequent investment	$250

Services

Telephone exchanges	*Yes*
Automatic withdrawal	*Yes*
Automatic checking deduction	*Yes*
Retirement plan/IRA	*Yes*
Instant redemption	*Yes*
Financial statements	*Semiannual*
Income distributions	*Semiannual*
Capital gains distributions	*Semiannual*
Portfolio manager—years	3
Number of funds in family	210

Six-Year Performance
Fidelity Select Financial Services vs. Dow Jones

	1991	1992	1993	1994	1995	1996*
Fund	61.6	42.8	17.6	-3.7	47.4	28.7
Dow	20.3	4.2	13.7	2.1	33.5	21.5

% Annual Total Return   *1996 returns through 11/10/96)
Fund vs. Dow Jones Industrial Avg.   (5-year return through 7/96: 225%)

SECTOR

38
Fidelity Select Technology Portfolio

Fidelity Investments
82 Devonshire Street
Boston, MA 02109

Fund manager: Adam Hetnarski
Fund objective: Sector fund

Toll-free: 800-544-8888
In-state: 801-534-1910
Fax: 617-476-9753

Performance	★ ★ ★ ★ ★
Consistency	★ ★ ★ ★ ★
Fees/Services	★ ★
FSPTX	**12 Points**

Like other top technology funds, the Fidelity Select Technology Portfolio has been riding the crest of the world's high tech boom. The fund has outperformed the market averages for six straight years.

The Technology Portfolio, which invests in a broad range of technology issues, is a combination of big, well-known companies such as Compaq Computer, IBM, and Digital Equipment, and up-and-coming stocks such as Cisco Systems, Seagate, and Bay Networks. The fund's buying strategy with the larger stocks is to buy when the gross profit margin is high and the stock price is low, based on the PE ratio and other valuation measures. The fund takes a different approach with small stocks, seeking companies with soaring earnings growth.

The fund's trading policy is moderately aggressive, with an annual portfolio turnover ratio of about 100 percent.

The fund has about 175 stock holdings, heavily weighted in the computer sector. Its largest segments include mini- and microcomputers (17 percent of assets), prepackaged computer software (10.5 percent), computers and office equipment (8 percent), and data communications equipment (7 percent).

PERFORMANCE

The fund has enjoyed exceptional growth over the past five years. Including dividends and capital gains distributions, the Fidelity Technology Portfolio has provided a total return for the past five years (through mid-1996) of 201 percent. A $10,000 investment in 1991 would have grown to about $30,000 five years later. Average annual return: 24.7 percent.

CONSISTENCY

The fund has been very consistent, outperforming the Dow Jones Industrial Average for six consecutive years through 1995 (but it trailed the Dow through the first half of 1996). Even in 1990, when the Dow dipped 4.3 percent, the fund posted a 10.5 percent gain. Its biggest gain came in 1991, when it moved up 58.9 percent (compared with a 20.3 percent rise in the Dow).

FEES/SERVICES/MANAGEMENT

The fund has a front-end load of 3 percent and a maximum redemption fee of 0.75 percent if shares are sold off within 30 days. Otherwise, a fee of $7.50 is charged upon redemption. The fund's total annual expense ratio of 1.46 percent (with no 12b-1 fee) is about average among load funds.

The fund offers all the standard services such as retirement account availability, automatic withdrawal, and automatic checking account deduction. Its minimum initial investment of $2,500 and minimum subsequent investment of $250 are a little high compared with other funds.

Adam Hetnarski has managed the fund only since 1996. This is his first assignment as a fund manager at Fidelity. The Fidelity fund family includes 210 funds.

Top Ten Holdings

1. Compaq Computer
2. Digital Equipment
3. Cisco Systems
4. IBM
5. Seagate Technology

6. Dell Computer
7. Symantec
8. Gateway 2000
9. Bay Networks
10. Oracle Systems

Asset Mix: Common stocks: 83%; Cash/equivalents: 17%
Total Net Assets: $483 million

Fees

Front-end load	3.00%
Redemption fee	$7.50
12b-1 fee	None
Management fee	0.61
Other expenses	0.85
Total annual expense	1.46%
Minimum initial investment	$2,500
Minimum subsequent investment	$250

Services

Telephone exchanges	*Yes*
Automatic withdrawal	*Yes*
Automatic checking deduction	*Yes*
Retirement plan/IRA	*Yes*
Instant redemption	*Yes*
Financial statements	*Semiannual*
Income distributions	*Semiannual*
Capital gains distributions	*Semiannual*
Portfolio manager—years	1
Number of funds in family	210

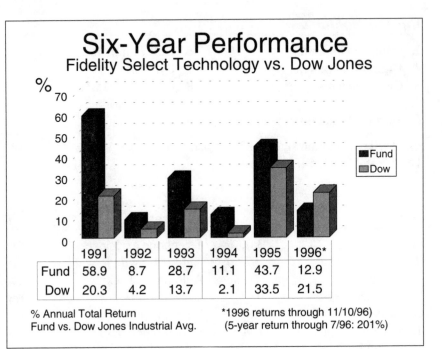

Six-Year Performance
Fidelity Select Technology vs. Dow Jones

	1991	1992	1993	1994	1995	1996*
Fund	58.9	8.7	28.7	11.1	43.7	12.9
Dow	20.3	4.2	13.7	2.1	33.5	21.5

% Annual Total Return   *1996 returns through 11/10/96)
Fund vs. Dow Jones Industrial Avg.   (5-year return through 7/96: 201%)

State Street Research Capital Fund

State Street Funds
One Financial Center
Boston, MA 02111

AGGRESSIVE

Fund manager: Fred Kobrick
Fund objective: Aggressive growth

Toll-free: 800-882-3302
In-state: 617-357-7805
Fax: 617-482-8361

Performance	★ ★ ★ ★ ★
Consistency	★ ★ ★
Fees/Services	★ ★ ★
SCFAX	**11 Points**

Fund manager Fred Kobrick takes a very labor-intensive approach in managing his State Street Research Capital Fund. He gets to know every one of the roughly 120 stocks in the fund's portfolio. He researches, he buys, he follows, he scrutinizes, and if he likes what he sees, he buys more.

"I take a farm system approach," says Kobrick. "If I find a stock that looks interesting, I'll buy a small position in it and watch it to see how the management operates. I'll weed out the ones that don't work out, and buy more of the good ones."

Even after the stock goes up 50 to 100 percent, Kobrick may keep buying. In fact, in many cases, only after a stock makes a large move up does Kobrick jump in and establish a major position. For instance, when computer networking manufacturer Cisco Systems went public at $1.63 a share, Kobrick bought a small position and followed the progress of the company. The stock quickly rose to $3 a share. "We thought the management team executed so well that they actually lengthened their lead over their competition," recalls Kobrick. "That's when we knew it was a great company. We increased our position substantially, and watched it grow more than tenfold to $35 a share before we sold."

Kobrick had a similar experience with Chrysler. He bought the stock at $10 with a target sell price of $20. "But when it hit $20, I had dinner with Lee Iacocca and one of his chief managers. From the discussion, I felt they were still executing well, so we made it the largest position in the fund. It went from $20 to $55 a share."

The fund has posted an average annual return of nearly 16 percent per year over the past ten years. A $10,000 investment in the fund a decade ago would now be worth about $43,000.

In initially selecting stocks for the portfolio, Kobrick says he buys companies "with high earnings growth, compelling valuations relative to the company's growth rate (in other words, fast-growing companies at a fair price), and managements that can execute. We have to really get to know management."

He takes a bottom-up approach. "We're buy-and-sell stock managers. We don't go by themes or trends. We go stock by stock."

In deciding when to sell, Kobrick looks at several specific factors:

- *Target price.* "If it hits our target price based on its valuation, it's a sell."
- *Change in management strategy.* "We'd rather they would experiment with someone else's money."
- *Failure to execute.* "If profit margins are coming down, key personnel are leaving, products are coming out late, costs are getting out of control, or earnings are lower than projected, those are all signs that the management is not executing."

Kobrick is quick to get out of a stock that's not living up to expectations. "We're willing to take lots of little losses, but we won't ride a stock down."

In terms of industrial sectors, the fund is heavily weighted in technology-related stocks. Computer software and services account for 10 percent of the fund's assets, electronics makes up 13 percent, electrical equipment accounts for 11 percent, and retail stocks make up 8 percent.

PERFORMANCE

The fund has enjoyed exceptional growth over the past five years. Including dividends and capital gains distributions, the State Street Research Capital Fund has provided a total return for the past five years (through mid-1996) of 206 percent. A $10,000 investment in 1991 would have grown to about $31,000 five years later. Average annual return: 25.1 percent.

CONSISTENCY

The fund has been fairly consistent, outperforming the Dow Jones Industrial Average three of the five years through 1995 (and again through the first half of 1996). Its biggest gain came in 1991, when it jumped 75.7 percent (compared with a 20.3 percent rise in the Dow).

FEES/SERVICES/MANAGEMENT

The State Street Research Capital Fund "A" has a front-end load of 4.5 percent and a total annual expense ratio of 1.33 percent (including a 0.25 percent 12b-1 fee and a 0.75 percent management fee), which compares favorably with other funds.

The fund offers all the standard services such as retirement account availability, automatic withdrawal, and automatic checking account deduction. Its minimum initial investment of $2,500 is a little high, but the minimum subsequent investment of $50 compares favorably with other funds. (For investors who set up an automatic checking account deduction plan, the minimum initial investment is $1,000.)

Fred Kobrick has managed the fund since 1985. The State Street fund family includes 15 funds and allows shareholders to switch from fund to fund by telephone.

Top Ten Holdings

1. Sunglass Hut Int'l
2. General Electric
3. HFS
4. Gucci Group
5. Philip Morris
6. Halliburton
7. Allstate
8. Northwest Airlines
9. Travelers Group
10. Digital Equipment

Asset Mix: Common stocks: 85%; Corporate bonds: 10%; Cash/equivalents: 5%
Total Net Assets: $80 million

Fees

Front-end load	4.50%
Redemption fee	None
12b-1 fee	0.25
Management fee	0.75
Other expenses	0.33
Total annual expense	1.33%
Minimum initial investment	$2,500
Minimum subsequent investment	$50

Services

Telephone exchanges	*Yes*
Automatic withdrawal	*Yes*
Automatic checking deduction	*Yes*
Retirement plan/IRA	*Yes*
Instant redemption	*Yes*
Financial statements	*Semiannual*
Income distributions	*Annual*
Capital gains distributions	*Annual*
Portfolio manager—years	11
Number of funds in family	15

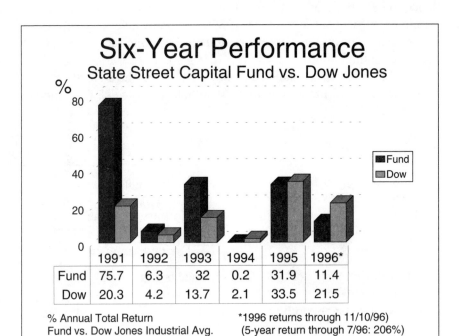

Six-Year Performance
State Street Capital Fund vs. Dow Jones

	1991	1992	1993	1994	1995	1996*
Fund	75.7	6.3	32	0.2	31.9	11.4
Dow	20.3	4.2	13.7	2.1	33.5	21.5

% Annual Total Return
Fund vs. Dow Jones Industrial Avg.

*1996 returns through 11/10/96)
(5-year return through 7/96: 206%)

AGGRESSIVE

40
Delaware Trend Fund "A"

Delaware Group
1818 Market Street
Philadelphia, PA 19103-3682

Fund manager: Edward Antoian
Fund objective: Aggressive growth

Toll-free: 800-523-4640
In-state: 215-988-1050
Fax: 215-988-1044

Performance	★ ★ ★ ★ ★
Consistency	★ ★ ★
Fees/Services	★ ★ ★
DELTX	**11 Points**

The Delaware Trend Fund follows the trends—sometimes to an extreme. When the market was up in 1991, the fund was way up, climbing 74.5 percent. And when the market had another strong run in 1995, the fund had another big year, moving up 42.5 percent. But when the market muddled through poor years in 1990 and 1994, the Trend Fund fell through the floor. It was down 24.6 percent in 1990 and 10 percent in 1994.

For those who can stand the volatility, the Trend Fund may provide outstanding long-term returns. It has moved up, on average, about 24 percent per year the past five years, and 14.5 percent per year over the past ten years. A $10,000 investment in the fund ten years ago would now be worth about $41,000. But this is probably a fund to avoid in a bear market.

The Trend Fund invests in a broad range of small, emerging growth stocks. Fund manager Edward Antoian says, "We strive to benefit from the early phases of a company's life cycle, a period that generally offers the greatest capital appreciation potential." In selecting stocks, Antoian tries to anticipate the effect of social and demographic changes on business and consumer behavior, and he studies each company's operational history, strategic focus, and competitive environment.

He takes a patient approach, holding many stocks for at least two years. He maintains a relatively light trading policy, with an annual portfolio turnover ratio of 64 percent.

The fund has about 170 stock holdings. The leading industry groups include consumer nondurables, 14 percent of assets; business services, 16 percent; consumer services, 16 percent; health care, 13 percent; and technology, 26 percent.

PERFORMANCE

The fund has enjoyed exceptional growth over the past five years. Including dividends and capital gains distributions, the Trend Fund has provided a total return for the past five years (through mid-1996) of 197 percent. A $10,000 investment in 1991 would have grown to about $30,000 five years later. Average annual return: 24.3 percent.

CONSISTENCY

The fund has been fairly consistent, outperforming the Dow Jones Industrial Average four of the five years through 1995 (and again through the first half of 1996). It did have declines of 10 percent in 1994 and 24.6 percent in 1990, so the fund can be volatile. The fund's biggest year was 1991, when it jumped 74.5 percent.

FEES/SERVICES/MANAGEMENT

The fund has a 4.25 percent front-end sales load, and an annual expense ratio of 1.36 percent (including a 0.24 percent 12b-1 fee and a 0.75 percent management fee), which is about average among all funds.

The fund's minimum initial investment of $1,000 and minimum subsequent investment of $100 are comparable with other funds.

Edward Antoian has managed the fund since 1984. The Delaware fund family includes 20 funds and allows shareholders to switch from fund to fund by telephone.

Top Ten Holdings

1. Republic Industries
2. Central Sprinkler
3. Cadence Design Systems
4. Advance Ross
5. Excalibur Technologies

6. Sierra On-Line
7. General Nutrition
8. Gilead Sciences
9. Ascent Entertainment Group
10. Gandalf Technologies

Asset Mix: Common stocks: 93%; Cash/equivalents: 7%
Total Net Assets: $513 million

Fees

Front-end load	4.75%
Redemption fee	*None*
12b-1 fee	0.24
Management fee	0.75
Other expenses	0.37
Total annual expense	1.36%
Minimum initial investment	$1,000
Minimum subsequent investment	$100

Services

Telephone exchanges	*Yes*
Automatic withdrawal	*Yes*
Automatic checking deduction	*Yes*
Retirement plan/IRA	*Yes*
Instant redemption	*Yes*
Financial statements	*Semiannual*
Income distributions	*Semiannual*
Capital gains distributions	*Annual*
Portfolio manager—years	13
Number of funds in family	20

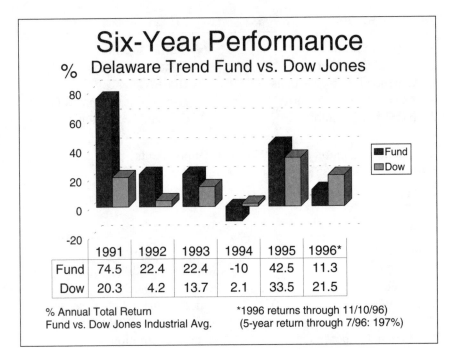

Six-Year Performance
% Delaware Trend Fund vs. Dow Jones

	1991	1992	1993	1994	1995	1996*
Fund	74.5	22.4	22.4	-10	42.5	11.3
Dow	20.3	4.2	13.7	2.1	33.5	21.5

% Annual Total Return
Fund vs. Dow Jones Industrial Avg.

*1996 returns through 11/10/96)
(5-year return through 7/96: 197%)

AGGRESSIVE

41
Van Kampen American Capital Emerging Growth Fund

Van Kampen American Capital
Asset Management, Inc.
2800 Post Oak Blvd.
Houston, TX 77056

Fund manager: Gary M. Lewis
Fund objective: Aggressive growth

Toll-free: 800-421-5666
In-state: 713-933-0500
Fax: 713-622-4832

Performance	★ ★ ★ ★
Consistency	★ ★ ★ ★
Fees/Services	★ ★ ★
ACEGX	**11 Points**

The Van Kampen American Capital Emerging Growth Fund has been a steady performer for more than a quarter of a century. A $10,000 investment in the fund when it opened in 1970 would now be worth about $575,000.

Fund manager Gary Lewis looks for fast-growing small to midsized stocks in a variety of industries. The vast majority of the more than 250 stocks in the portfolio are little-known companies on the upswing, such as Videoserver, Pure Software, and Novadigm.

Lewis looks at several factors in selecting stocks: rising earnings estimates, accelerating growth rates in both revenues and per-share earnings, and rising profit margins. For an aggressive growth fund, the Emerging Growth Fund is fairly aggressive in its trading activity, with a 101 percent annual portfolio turnover ratio.

Broad diversification has been an ongoing objective of the fund, which might be one prime reason the fund has been so consistent over the years. The fund's leading industrial sectors include technology, 31 percent of total assets; health care, 12 percent; finance, 11 percent; consumer distribution, 7 percent; consumer services, 8 percent; and producer manufacturing, 7 percent.

PERFORMANCE

The fund has enjoyed exceptional growth over the past five years. Including dividends and capital gains distributions, the Capital Emerging Growth Fund has provided a total return for the past five years (through mid-1996) of 186 percent. A $10,000 investment in 1991 would have grown to about $29,000 five years later. Average annual return: 23.4 percent.

CONSISTENCY

The fund has been very consistent, outperforming the Dow Jones Industrial Average four of the five years through 1995 (and it was well ahead of the Dow through the first half of 1996). Its biggest gain came in 1991, when it jumped 60.4 percent (compared with a 20.3 percent rise in the Dow).

FEES/SERVICES/MANAGEMENT

The fund has a front-end load of 5.75 percent and a total annual expense ratio of 1.14 percent (including a 0.19 percent 12b-1 fee and a 0.52 percent management fee), which compares favorably with other load fund fees. (The fund also offers "B" shares, which have no front-end load but carry a maximum 5 percent redemption fee and a much higher annual expense ratio of about 2 percent.)

The fund offers all the standard services such as retirement account availability, automatic withdrawal, and automatic checking account deduction. Its minimum initial investment of $500 and minimum subsequent investment of $25 compare very favorably with other funds.

Gary M. Lewis has managed the fund since 1989. The Van Kampen fund family includes 42 funds and allows shareholders to switch from fund to fund by telephone.

Top Ten Holdings

1. Ascend Communications
2. HBO
3. C-Cube Microsystems
4. Sun Microsystems
5. Bank of Boston
6. Cadence Design Systems
7. Cisco Systems
8. Corrections of America
9. Guidant
10. IMC Global

Asset Mix: Common stocks: 92%; Cash/equivalents: 8%
Total Net Assets: $1.15 billion

Fees

Front-end load	5.75%
Redemption fee	*None*
12b-1 fee	0.19
Management fee	0.52
Other expenses	0.43
Total annual expense	1.14%
Minimum initial investment	$500
Minimum subsequent investment	$25

Services

Telephone exchanges	*Yes*
Automatic withdrawal	*Yes*
Automatic checking deduction	*Yes*
Retirement plan/IRA	*Yes*
Instant redemption	*Yes*
Financial statements	*Annual*
Income distributions	*Annual*
Capital gains distributions	*Annual*
Portfolio manager—years	8
Number of funds in family	42

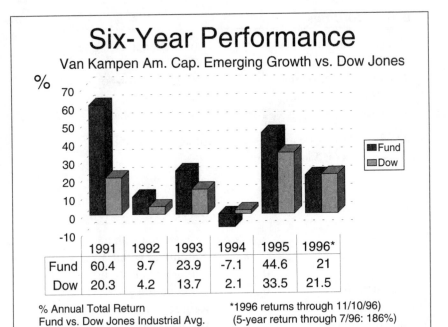

Six-Year Performance
Van Kampen Am. Cap. Emerging Growth vs. Dow Jones

	1991	1992	1993	1994	1995	1996*
Fund	60.4	9.7	23.9	-7.1	44.6	21
Dow	20.3	4.2	13.7	2.1	33.5	21.5

% Annual Total Return   *1996 returns through 11/10/96)
Fund vs. Dow Jones Industrial Avg.   (5-year return through 7/96: 186%)

AGGRESSIVE

42
AIM Constellation Fund

AIM Funds
11 Greenway Plaza, Suite 1919
Houston, TX 77046-1188

Fund managers: Robert Kippes,
Ken Zschappel, Charles Scavone,
Dave Barnard
Fund objective: Aggressive growth

Toll-free: 800-347-4246
In-state: 713-626-1919
Fax: 713-993-9890

Performance	★ ★ ★ ★
Consistency	★ ★ ★ ★
Fees/Services	★ ★ ★
CSTGX	**11 Points**

The aggressive AIM Constellation Fund has continued to keep its share-holders happy by pairing outstanding long-term returns with consistent year-to-year performance. It has outperformed the Dow Jones Industrial Average five of the past six years while providing an average annual return for the past five years of about 23 percent.

The Constellation Fund, which opened in 1976, has provided an average annual return over the past ten years of about 18 percent. A $10,000 investment in the fund ten years ago would now be worth about $52,000.

The fund managers try to load the fund with the fastest-growing stocks available. Earnings momentum is the primary criterion they consider in selecting stocks. They are much more interested in present growth momentum than past history. "The race is not always to the swift, nor the battle to the strong," explained former AIM Constellation Fund comanager Jonathan Schoolar, "but that's the way you have to bet. That's also how we invest. Charts tell you what has happened—not what's going to happen. I hate charts. I've never met a rich technician."

The fund management takes a bottom-up approach (based on a company-by-company evaluation) rather than a top-down approach (which puts the emphasis on the economy and the big picture). "One bad decision in the top-down style can knock you out of the game. Any study will show you that the market makes the bulk of its move in a very short time. If you miss it, you just can't make it up." That's why the fund stays fully invested all the time.

The fund maintains a portfolio of about 300 stocks, selected from hundreds and hundreds of small-, medium- and large-capitalization stocks the fund managers evaluate on an ongoing basis. The portfolio consists of about 40 percent emerging growth stocks, 40 percent medium-size firms, and 20 percent large-capitalization companies. The fund has an annual portfolio turnover ratio of about 45 percent.

One key to the fund's success is the strict sell discipline of the fund managers. Managers emphasize the sell side, quickly unloading stocks that have lost earnings momentum. The fund managers are more concerned with present earnings than future earnings projections. Nor do they try to project sales of a new product. Rather, they wait and see how it does, and then make future projections based on its initial market results.

The AIM Funds were started by Harry Hutzler in 1976. Hutzler, who retired in 1993, began with the Value Line Investment Survey in the 1950s and 1960s. He started the very successful Weingarten Fund in 1969, and then added the AIM Constellation Fund seven years later.

The Constellation Fund portfolio is heavily weighted in computer-related stocks. Leading sectors include computer software, services, networking, and peripherals, 23 percent of assets; semiconductors, 17 percent; medical stocks, 14 percent; and retail, 9 percent.

PERFORMANCE

The fund has enjoyed exceptional growth over the past five years. Including dividends and capital gains distributions, the AIM Constellation Fund has provided a total return for the past five years of 177 percent. A $10,000 investment in 1991 would have grown to about $28,000 five years later. Average annual return: 22.6 percent.

CONSISTENCY

The fund has been very consistent, outperforming the Dow Jones Industrial Average four of the five years from 1991 to 1995 (and again through the first half of 1996). Its biggest gain came in 1991, when it jumped 70.4 percent (compared with a 20.3 percent rise in the Dow).

FEES/SERVICES/MANAGEMENT

The fund has a front-end load of 5.5 percent. Its total annual expense ratio of 1.16 percent (including a 0.3 percent 12b-1 fee and a 0.62 percent management fee) compares favorably with other funds.

The fund offers all the standard services such as retirement account availability, automatic withdrawal, and automatic checking account deduction. Its minimum initial investment of $500 and minimum subsequent investment of $50 compare very favorably with other funds.

Comanagers Robert Kippes and Dave Barnard have been with the fund since 1987, while Ken Zschappel and Charles Scavone have recently been added to the management team. The AIM fund family includes 21 funds. Shareholders may switch freely from fund to fund by telephone.

Top Ten Holdings

1. Parametric Technology
2. Cisco Systems
3. FORE Systems
4. Cardinal Health
5. MBNA
6. HEALTHSOUTH
7. Oracle Systems
8. Service Corp. Int'l
9. Computer Associates
10. Apria Healthcare Group

Asset Mix: Common stocks: 93%; Cash/equivalents: 7%
Total Net Assets: $ 9.2 billion

Fees

Front-end load	5.50%
Redemption fee	*None*
12b-1 fee	0.30
Management fee	0.62
Other expenses	0.24
Total annual expense	1.16%
Minimum initial investment	$500
Minimum subsequent investment	$50

Services

Telephone exchanges	*Yes*
Automatic withdrawal	*Yes*
Automatic checking deduction	*Yes*
Retirement plan/IRA	*Yes*
Instant redemption	*Yes*
Financial statements	*Quarterly*
Income distributions	*Annual*
Capital gains distributions	*Annual*
Portfolio managers—years:	10
Number of funds in family:	21

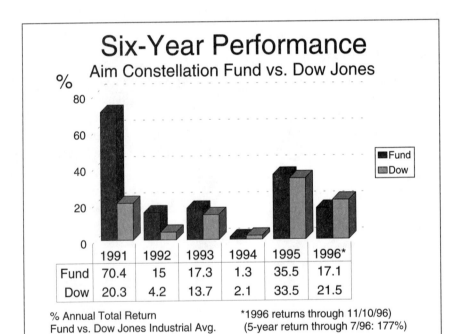

Six-Year Performance
Aim Constellation Fund vs. Dow Jones

	1991	1992	1993	1994	1995	1996*
Fund	70.4	15	17.3	1.3	35.5	17.1
Dow	20.3	4.2	13.7	2.1	33.5	21.5

% Annual Total Return
Fund vs. Dow Jones Industrial Avg.

*1996 returns through 11/10/96)
(5-year return through 7/96: 177%)

LONG TERM

43
Pioneer Capital Growth Fund "A"

Pioneer Funds
60 State Street
Boston, MA 02109

Fund manager: Warren J. Isabelle
Fund objective: Long-term growth

Toll-free: 800-225-6292
In-state: 617-742-7825
Fax: 617-422-4275

Performance	★ ★ ★ ★
Consistency	★ ★ ★ ★
Fees/Services	★ ★ ★
PCGRX	**11 Points**

Pioneer Capital Growth Fund manager Warren J. Isabelle has established a solid, consistent track record by focusing on four types of stocks. Isabelle, who has been fund manager since the fund opened in 1990, looks for the following:

1. *Turnarounds*—companies in a position to rebound
2. *Transitions*—companies adopting their expertise to new market niches
3. *Cyclicals*—companies with unique business cycles with profits that rise and fall in tune with worldwide supply and demand
4. *Emerging companies*—smaller firms with great growth potential.

Since its inception in 1990, fund shares have grown at an average annual rate of 17 percent. A $10,000 investment in the fund when it opened would have grown to about $27,000 six years later.

In all, the fund has about 140 stock holdings, most of which are small and midsized companies. Isabelle takes a fairly conservative buy-and-hold approach, with an annual portfolio turnover ratio of 59 percent.

The fund is diversified across a broad range of industry groups. Its leading sector is consumer nondurables (clothing, textiles, etc.), which accounts for 24 percent of total assets. Other leading segments include technology, 21 percent; services, 16 percent; capital goods, 14 percent; and basic industries, 10 percent.

PERFORMANCE

The fund has experienced excellent growth over the past five years. Including dividends and capital gains distributions, the Pioneer Capital Growth Fund has provided a total return for the past five years (through mid-1996) of 171 percent. A $10,000 investment in 1991 would have grown to about $27,000 five years later. Average annual return: 22.1 percent.

CONSISTENCY

The fund has been fairly consistent, outperforming the Dow Jones Industrial Average four of the five years through 1995 (and it narrowly trailed the Dow through the first half of 1996).

FEES/SERVICES/MANAGEMENT

The fund has a 5.75 percent front-end sales load, and an annual expense ratio of 1.14 percent (including a 0.24 percent 12b-1 fee and a 0.65 percent management fee), which is fairly low compared with most other funds.

The fund offers all the standard services such as retirement account availability, automatic withdrawal, and automatic checking account deduction. Its minimum initial investment of $1,000 and subsequent investment minimum of $50 compares favorably to other funds.

Pioneer was founded in 1928. Warren J. Isabelle has managed the fund since its inception in 1990. The Pioneer fund family includes 18 funds and allows shareholders to switch from fund to fund by telephone.

Top Ten Holdings

1. Toys "R" Us
2. Western National
3. 20th Century Industries
4. IDEON Group
5. Melville
6. Insilco
7. Lone Star Industries
8. Avondale Industries
9. Unisys
10. Teradyne

Asset Mix: Common stocks: 84%; Cash/equivalents: 16%
Total Net Assets: $1.08 billion

Fees

Front-end load	5.75%
Redemption fee	*None*
12b-1 fee	.24
Management fee	0.65
Other expenses	0.25
Total annual expense	1.14%
Minimum initial investment	$1,000
Minimum subsequent investment	$50

Services

Telephone exchanges	*Yes*
Automatic withdrawal	*Yes*
Automatic checking deduction	*Yes*
Retirement plan/IRA	*Yes*
Instant redemption	*Yes*
Financial statements	*Annual*
Income distributions	*Annual*
Capital gains distributions	*Annual*
Portfolio manager—years	7
Number of funds in family	18

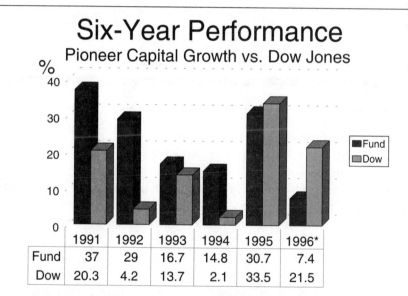

Six-Year Performance
Pioneer Capital Growth vs. Dow Jones

	1991	1992	1993	1994	1995	1996*
Fund	37	29	16.7	14.8	30.7	7.4
Dow	20.3	4.2	13.7	2.1	33.5	21.5

% Annual Total Return
Fund vs. Dow Jones Industrial Avg.

*1996 returns through 11/10/96
(5-year return through 7/96: 171%)

44

MainStay Capital Appreciation Fund "B"

LONG TERM

MainStay Funds
260 Cherry Hill Road
Parsippany, NJ 07054-0421

Fund managers: Rudolph Carryl
  and Edmond Spelman
Fund objective: Long-term growth

Toll-free: 800-522-4202
In-state: 201-331-2000
Fax: 201-331-2593

Performance	★ ★ ★ ★
Consistency	★ ★ ★ ★
Fees/Services	★ ★ ★
MCSCX	**11 Points**

The MainStay Capital Appreciation Fund is a growth fund that concentrates primarily on stocks of fast-growing small to midrange companies, such as 3Com, Amgen, and United Healthcare.

Fund managers Rudolph Carryl and Edmond Spelman focus on companies with "positive growth characteristics, strong management, new products, and other innovations with potential to fuel rapid and sustained earnings growth."

Since the fund opened in 1986, it has grown at an average annual rate of about 14 percent. A $10,000 investment in the fund when it opened would now be worth about $38,000. Most of that growth has come in the past five years when it averaged 22 percent per year.

The managers take a conservative buy-and-hold approach, with an annual portfolio turnover ratio of just 29 percent.

In terms of industrial sectors, the Capital Appreciation Fund has 11 percent of assets in technology stocks, 10 percent in finance, 10 percent in pharmaceuticals, 8 percent in computers and office equipment, and 7 percent in health care.

PERFORMANCE

The fund has enjoyed exceptional growth over the past five years. Including dividends and capital gains distributions, the Capital Appreciation Fund has provided a total return for the past five years (through mid 1996) of 170 percent. A $10,000 investment in the fund five years ago would now be worth $27,000. Average annual return: 22 percent.

CONSISTENCY

The fund has been very consistent, outperforming the Dow Jones Industrial Average four of the past five years through 1995 (although it trailed the Dow through the first half of 1996). Its biggest year was in 1991 when it climbed 68.4 percent.

FEES/SERVICES/MANAGEMENT

The MainStay Capital Appreciation Fund has a 5 percent redemption fee that declines about 1 percent per year as long as you hold the shares (with no fee if you sell after six years).

The fund's total annual expense ratio of 1.69 percent (including a 0.79 percent 12b-1 fee and a management fee of 0.63 percent) is fairly low for a back-end load fund.

The fund offers all the standard services such as retirement account availability, automatic withdrawal, and automatic checking account deduction. Its minimum initial investment of $500 and minimum subsequent investment of $50 compare very favorably with other funds.

Rudolph Carryl and Edmond Spelman have managed the fund since 1991. The MainStay fund family includes 11 funds and allows shareholders to switch freely from fund to fund by telephone.

Top Ten Holdings

1. HFS
2. 3Com
3. GE Capital
4. Amgen
5. Computer Associates Int'l
6. Green Tree Financial
7. SunAmerica
8. ALCO Standard
9. First Interstate Bancorp
10. United Healthcare

Asset Mix: Common stocks: 94%; Cash/equivalents: 6%
Total Net Assets: $990 million

Fees

Front-end load	*None*
Redemption fee	5.00%
12b-1 fee	0.79
Management fee	0.63
Other expenses	0.27
Total annual expense	1.69%
Minimum initial investment	$500
Minimum subsequent investment	$50

Services

Telephone exchanges	*Yes*
Automatic withdrawal	*Yes*
Automatic checking deduction	*Yes*
Retirement plan/IRA	*Yes*
Instant redemption	*Yes*
Financial statements	*Semiannual*
Income distributions	*Quarterly*
Capital gains distributions	*Annual*
Portfolio managers—years	6
Number of funds in family	11

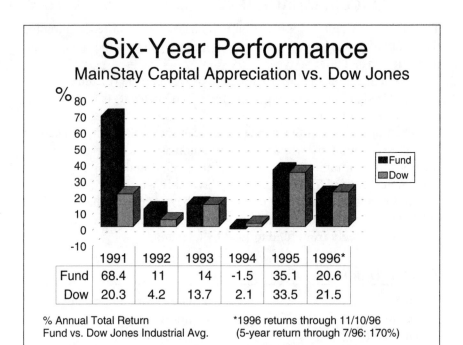

Six-Year Performance
MainStay Capital Appreciation vs. Dow Jones

	1991	1992	1993	1994	1995	1996*
Fund	68.4	11	14	-1.5	35.1	20.6
Dow	20.3	4.2	13.7	2.1	33.5	21.5

% Annual Total Return   *1996 returns through 11/10/96
Fund vs. Dow Jones Industrial Avg.   (5-year return through 7/96: 170%)

AGGRESSIVE

45
Loomis Sayles
Small Cap Fund

Loomis Sayles Funds
One Financial Center
Boston, MA 02111

Fund managers: Jeff Petherick
and Mary Champagne
Fund objective: Aggressive growth

Toll-free: 800-633-3330
In-state: 617-482-2450
Fax: 617-439-0460

Performance	★ ★ ★ ★
Consistency	★ ★
Fees/Services	★ ★ ★ ★ ★
LSSCX	**11 Points**

The Loomis Sayles Small Cap Fund invests in undervalued small emerging growth stocks with strong earnings potential. But as fund manager Jeff Petherick points out, buying the right stocks at the right time is only half the battle.

"We place as much emphasis on the sell decisions as we do on the buy decisions," explains Petherick. Stocks that don't live up to Petherick's expectations are sold and replaced with other good prospects. "We know that one of the greatest threats to a portfolio's performance in the long run is not the difficulty of finding good investments, but in the frequent reluctance to let go of the poor ones. Over the years, this has been one of the main tenets of our investment discipline and is one of the main reasons for our superior investment results."

Petherick and comanager Mary Champagne are very aggressive in their trading strategy, with a 155 percent annual portfolio turnover ratio. The fund, which opened in 1991, has posted annual average returns of 21 percent the past five years.

The fund invests at least 65 percent of its assets in stocks with market capitalizations of under $1 billion. The fund stays 80 to 90 percent invested in stocks most of the time.

In all, the fund has about 100 stock holdings. The portfolio is well diversified across a broad spectrum of industry sectors. Leading sectors include insurance, 7 percent; banks and financial services, 7 percent; health and medical, 11 percent; real estate, 6 percent; and housing and building materials, 4 percent.

PERFORMANCE

The Small Cap Fund has enjoyed outstanding growth over the past five years. Including dividends and capital gains distributions, the fund has provided a total return for the past five years (through mid-1996) of 162 percent. A $10,000 investment in 1991 would have grown to about $26,000 five years later. Average annual return: 21.3 percent.

CONSISTENCY

The fund has been somewhat inconsistent, outperforming the Dow Jones Industrial Average only two of the four years from 1992 through 1995 (and it was ahead of the Dow through the first half of 1996). The fund's biggest gain came in 1991, when it rose 67 percent (compared with a 20.3 percent rise in the Dow). The fund had a loss of 8.3 percent in 1994.

FEES/SERVICES/MANAGEMENT

The Loomis Sayles Small Cap Fund is a true no-load fund—no fee to buy, no fee to sell. The fund's total annual expense ratio of 1.25 percent (with no 12b-1 fee) compares favorably with other no-load funds.

The fund offers all the standard services such as retirement account availability, automatic withdrawal, and automatic checking account deduction. Its minimum initial investment of $2,500 is a little higher than average, but its minimum subsequent investment of $50 compares favorably with other funds.

Jeff Petherick has managed the fund since its inception in 1991. Comanager Mary Champagne joined the fund in 1995. The Loomis Sayles fund family includes ten funds and allows shareholders to switch from fund to fund by telephone.

Top Ten Holdings

1. Sofamor-Danek Group
2. Seitel
3. Reinsurance Group of America
4. Chateau Properties
5. Vintage Petroleum

6. Community Health Systems
7. Toro
8. Allied Group
9. Whittaker
10. Gelman Sciences

Asset Mix: Common stocks: 87%; Cash/equivalents: 13%
Total Net Assets: $1.1 billion

Fees

Front-end load	*None*
Redemption fee	*None*
12b-1 fee	*None*
Management fee	1.00%
Other expenses	0.25
Total annual expense	1.25%
Minimum initial investment	$2,500
Minimum subsequent investment	$50

Services

Telephone exchanges	*Yes*
Automatic withdrawal	*Yes*
Automatic checking deduction	*Yes*
Retirement plan/IRA	*Yes*
Instant redemption	*Yes*
Financial statements	*Annual*
Income distributions	*Annual*
Capital gains distributions	*Annual*
Portfolio manager—years	6
Number of funds in family	10

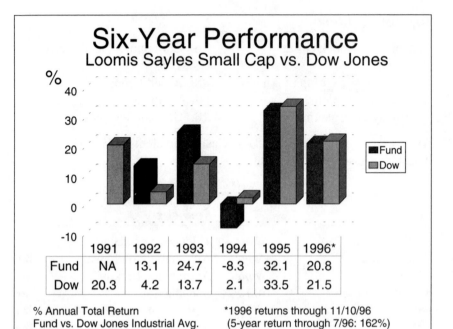

Six-Year Performance
Loomis Sayles Small Cap vs. Dow Jones

	1991	1992	1993	1994	1995	1996*
Fund	NA	13.1	24.7	-8.3	32.1	20.8
Dow	20.3	4.2	13.7	2.1	33.5	21.5

% Annual Total Return   *1996 returns through 11/10/96
Fund vs. Dow Jones Industrial Avg.   (5-year return through 7/96: 162%)

AGGRESSIVE

46

Evergreen Aggressive Growth Fund

Evergreen Asset Management Corp.
2500 Westchester Avenue
Purchase, NY 10577

Fund manager: Harold J. Ireland
Fund objective: Aggressive growth

Toll-free: 800-235-0064
In-state: 914-694-2020
Fax: 914-641-2277

Performance	★ ★ ★ ★
Consistency	★ ★ ★ ★
Fees/Services	★ ★ ★
EAGAX	**11 Points**

Evergreen Aggressive Growth Fund manager Harold Ireland maintains one of the smallest portfolios in the mutual fund industry, with only about 30 stock holdings. So when he bets big on a stock, he better get it right, or be prepared to pay the consequences.

Ireland's strategy has produced some short-term volatility—and a 9 percent drop in 1994—but over the long term the fund has provided shareholders with solid returns. During the past ten years, the fund has grown at an average annual rate of 13 percent. A $10,000 investment in the fund 10 years ago would now be worth about $33,000.

Formerly called the ABT Emerging Growth Fund, the fund invests primarily in young emerging growth companies that Wall Street has yet to discover.

Momentum is an important element for Ireland. He wants stocks of companies with annual sales and earnings growth rates of 40 percent or more—the fastest-growing segment of the market. He also prefers stocks with at least $100 million in annual sales, return on equity of at least 20 percent, low debt, proven leadership in its industry (or in a niche within a market), proven management experience, and insider ownership.

The fund takes a regional approach, selecting most of its stocks from Florida and the Southeastern United States. Ireland takes a conservative buy-and-hold strategy, with an annual portfolio turnover ratio of just 31 percent. The fund stays nearly 100 percent invested in stocks most of the time.

Most of the stocks in the fund are concentrated in a few fast-growing industrial sectors, including health care, 21 percent of assets; specialty retail, 21 percent; business services, 20 percent; and technology, 12 percent.

PERFORMANCE

The fund has enjoyed excellent growth over the past five years. Including dividends and capital gains distributions, the Evergreen Aggressive Growth Fund has provided a total return for the five-year period (through mid-1996) of 160 percent. A $10,000 investment in 1991 would have grown to about $26,000 five years later. Average annual return: 21.1 percent.

CONSISTENCY

The fund has been very consistent, outperforming the Dow Jones Industrial Average four of the five years from 1991 through 1995 (and it was virtually even with the Dow through the first half of 1996). The fund's biggest gain was in 1991, when it jumped 77.2 percent (compared with a 20.3 percent gain for the Dow).

FEES/SERVICES/MANAGEMENT

The fund has a front-end sales load of 4.75 percent. Its total annual expense ratio of 1.47 percent (including a 0.75 percent 12b-1 fee and a 0.6 percent management fee) is about average among load funds.

The fund offers all the standard services such as retirement account availability, automatic withdrawal, and automatic checking account deduction. Its minimum initial investment of $1,000 and minimum subsequent investment of $100 are in line with other funds.

Harold Ireland has managed the fund since its inception in 1983. The Evergreen fund family includes 30 funds and allows shareholders to switch from fund to fund by telephone.

Top Ten Holdings

1. Cisco Systems	6. Atmel
2. Apac Teleservices	7. Mylan Laboratories
3. Republic Industries	8. Green Tree Financial
4. Parametric Technology	9. Office Depot
5. Medtronic	10. First Data

Asset Mix: Common stocks: 99%; Cash/equivalents: 1%
Total Net Assets: $91 million

Fees

Front-end load	4.75%
Redemption fee	*None*
12b-1 fee	0.75%
Management fee	0.60%
Other expenses	0.12%
Total annual expense	1.47%
Minimum initial investment	$1,000
Minimum subsequent investment	$100

Services

Telephone exchanges	*Yes*
Automatic withdrawal	*Yes*
Automatic checking deduction	*Yes*
Retirement plan/IRA	*Yes*
Instant redemption	*Yes*
Financial statements	*Semiannual*
Income distributions	*Annual*
Capital gains distributions	*Annual*
Portfolio manager—years	14
Number of funds in family	30

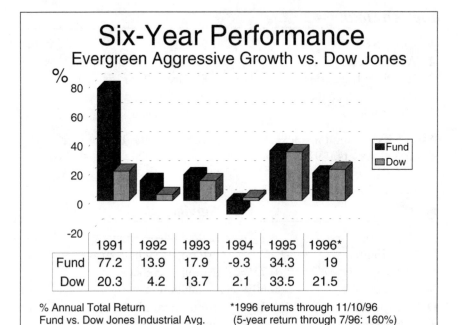

Six-Year Performance
Evergreen Aggressive Growth vs. Dow Jones

	1991	1992	1993	1994	1995	1996*
Fund	77.2	13.9	17.9	-9.3	34.3	19
Dow	20.3	4.2	13.7	2.1	33.5	21.5

% Annual Total Return
Fund vs. Dow Jones Industrial Avg.

*1996 returns through 11/10/96
(5-year return through 7/96: 160%)

MFS Value Fund

MFS Family of Funds
500 Boylston Street
Boston, MA 02116-3741

LONG TERM

Fund manager: John F. Brennan
Fund objective: Long-term growth

Toll-free: 800-637-2929
In-state: 617-954-5000
Fax: 617-954-6617

Performance	★ ★ ★ ★
Consistency	★ ★ ★ ★
Fees/Services	★ ★ ★
MVLFX	**11 Points**

MFS Value Fund manager John Brennan tries to cash in on the hard luck, down-and-out corporate cast-offs that he believes are headed for a turnaround. The fund invests in several types of "value" stocks, including restructured companies, those emering from bankruptcy, and companies with strong growth potential that are trading at a low price relative to the market.

Over the past ten years, the fund has posted a 14 percent average annual return. A $10,000 investment in the fund ten years ago would have grown to about $37,000.

The fund invests primarily in medium- to large-capitalization stocks such as Nike, Philip Morris, and Southwest Airlines.

Brennan takes a fairly aggressive trading approach, with an annual portfolio turnover ratio of 109 percent. In all, the fund has about 90 stock holdings. The fund has a fair representation of foreign stocks, which account for about 11 percent of total assets.

The fund is well diversified across a broad range of industry sectors. Leading sectors include entertainment, 11 percent; financial, 8 percent; consumer goods and services, 7 percent; computer software, 5 percent; and automotive, 5 percent. The fund stays almost fully invested in stocks most of the time.

PERFORMANCE

The fund has enjoyed superior growth over the past five years. Including dividends and capital gains distributions, the MFS Value Fund has provided a total return for the past five years (through mid-1996) of 160 percent. A $10,000 investment in 1991 would have grown to about $26,000 five years later. Average annual return: 21 percent.

CONSISTENCY

The fund has been fairly consistent, outperforming the Dow Jones Industrial Average four of the five years through 1995 (and the fund was about even with the Dow through the first half of 1996). The fund's biggest year was 1995 when it jumped 44.2 percent.

FEES/SERVICES/MANAGEMENT

The fund has a 5.75 percent front-end sales load, and an annual expense ratio of 1.35 percent (including a 0.25 percent 12b-1 fee and a 0.75 percent management fee), which is well in line with other funds.

The fund offers all the standard services such as retirement account availability, automatic withdrawal and automatic checking account deduction. Its minimum initial investment of $1,000 and subsequent investment minimum of $50 compares favorably to other funds.

John Brennan Jr. has managed the fund since 1991. The MFS fund family includes 33 funds and allows shareholders to switch from fund to fund by telephone.

Top Ten Holdings

1. Harrah's Entertainment
2. Tyco International
3. First Interstate Bancorp
4. Promus
5. BMC Software
6. Federal Home Loan Mortgage Corp.
7. Harvard Industries
8. Showboat
9. Loral
10. Wisconsin Central Transport

Asset Mix: Common stocks: 89%; Bonds: 1%; Cash/equivalents: 10%
Total Net Assets: $323 million

Fees

Front-end load	5.75%
Redemption fee	*None*
12b-1 fee	0.25
Management fee	0.75
Other expenses	0.35
Total annual expense	1.35%
Minimum initial investment	$1,000
Minimum subsequent investment	$50

Services

Telephone exchanges	*Yes*
Automatic withdrawal	*Yes*
Automatic checking deduction	*Yes*
Retirement plan/IRA	*Yes*
Instant redemption	*Yes*
Financial statements	*Annual*
Income distributions	*Annual*
Capital gains distributions	*Annual*
Portfolio manager—years	6
Number of funds in family	33

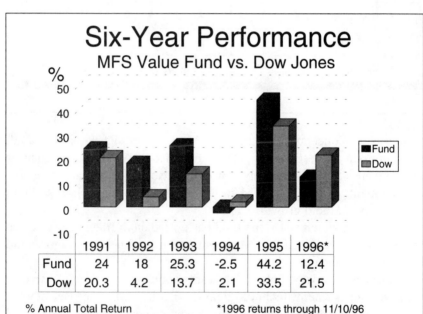

Six-Year Performance
MFS Value Fund vs. Dow Jones

	1991	1992	1993	1994	1995	1996*
Fund	24	18	25.3	-2.5	44.2	12.4
Dow	20.3	4.2	13.7	2.1	33.5	21.5

% Annual Total Return
Fund vs. Dow Jones Industrial Avg.

*1996 returns through 11/10/96
(5-year return through 7/96: 160%)

48
United New
Concepts Fund "A"

AGGRESSIVE

United Group
6300 Lamar Avenue
Shawnee Mission, KS 66201-9217

Fund manager: Mark Seferovich
Fund objective: Aggressive growth

Toll-free: 800-366-5465
In-state: 913-236-2000
Fax: 913-236-1595

Performance	★ ★ ★ ★
Consistency	★ ★ ★ ★
Fees/Services	★ ★ ★
UNECX	**11 Points**

United New Concepts Fund manager Mark Seferovich looks for small companies on the verge of big growth. Founded in 1983, the fund focuses on companies that are relatively new or unseasoned, in the early stages of development, or are positioned in new or emerging industries with an opportunity for rapid growth.

Over the past ten years, the fund has posted an average annual return of 13.1 percent. A $10,000 investment in the fund ten years ago would now be worth about $34,000.

In selecting stocks, Seferovich wants companies with aggressive or creative management, technological or specialized expertise, new or unique products or services, entry into new or emerging industries, and special situations arising out of government priorities and programs. Seferovich takes a fairly conservative buy-and-hold approach, with a very modest annual portfolio turnover ratio of just 28 percent.

At times, the fund may buy stocks on margin or invest in options or futures in order to bolster the return of the fund. (However, those investments can also put the fund at risk for larger losses.)

The fund is very heavily weighted in consumer and technology stocks. Technology issues account for about 50 percent of the portfolio, consumer stocks make up 22 percent, and basic industries account for about 3 percent.

PERFORMANCE

The fund has enjoyed stellar growth over the past five years. Including dividends and capital gains distributions, the United New Concepts Fund has provided a total return for the past five years of 157 percent. A $10,000 investment in 1991 would have grown to about $26,000 five years later. Average annual return: 20.8 percent.

CONSISTENCY

The fund has been fairly consistent, outperforming the Dow Jones Industrial Average four of the five years through 1995 (but it trailed the Dow through the first half of 1996). Its biggest gain came in 1991, when it soared 88 percent (compared with a 20.3 percent rise in the Dow).

FEES/SERVICES/MANAGEMENT

The fund has a front-end load of 5.75 percent. Its total annual expense ratio of 1.24 percent (including a 0.13 percent 12b-1 fee and a 0.77 percent management fee) compares favorably with other funds.

The fund offers most of the standard mutual fund services such as retirement account availability, automatic withdrawal, and automatic checking account deduction, but it does not offer instant telephone redemption or switching between funds by phone. Its minimum initial investment of $500 and minimum subsequent investment of $1 compare very favorably with other funds.

Mark Seferovich has managed the fund since 1989. The United Group fund family includes 17 funds. United is part of Waddell & Reed, a financial planning subsidiary of Torchmark.

Top Ten Holdings

1. America Online	6. United HealthCare
2. Cisco Systems	7. CUC International
3. Parametric Technology	8. Harley-Davidson
4. Ascend Communications	9. MFS Communications
5. Omnicare	10. Fastenal

Asset Mix: Common stocks: 78%; Cash/equivalents: 22%
Total Net Assets: $557 million

Fees

Front-end load	5.75%
Redemption fee	*None*
12b-1 fee	0.13
Management fee	0.77
Other expenses	0.34
Total annual expense	1.24%
Minimum initial investment	$500
Minimum subsequent investment	$1

Services

Telephone exchanges	*No*
Automatic withdrawal	*Yes*
Automatic checking deduction	*Yes*
Retirement plan/IRA	*Yes*
Instant redemption	*Yes*
Financial statements	*Semiannual*
Income distributions	*Annual*
Capital gains distributions	*Annual*
Portfolio manager—years	8
Number of funds in family	17

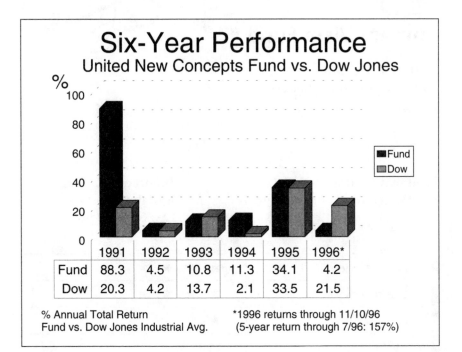

Six-Year Performance
United New Concepts Fund vs. Dow Jones

	1991	1992	1993	1994	1995	1996*
Fund	88.3	4.5	10.8	11.3	34.1	4.2
Dow	20.3	4.2	13.7	2.1	33.5	21.5

% Annual Total Return   *1996 returns through 11/10/96
Fund vs. Dow Jones Industrial Avg.   (5-year return through 7/96: 157%)

49

Putnam Vista Fund "A"

LONG TERM

Putnam Mutual Funds
One Post Office Square
Boston, MA 02109

Fund manager: Jennifer Silver
Fund objective: Long-term growth

Toll-free: 800-225-1581
In-state: 617-292-1000
Fax: 617-760-5869

Performance	★ ★ ★ ★
Consistency	★ ★ ★ ★
Fees/Services	★ ★ ★
PVISX	**11 Points**

The Putnam Vista Fund has the flexibility to invest in companies from a broad vista of industry groups. And while its primary focus is midsized stocks such as Silicon Graphics, Safety-Kleen, and Equifax, the fund may also invest in small emerging companies and major multibillion dollar blue chips. Typically, its stock holdings range in size from $300 million to $3 billion in market capitalization.

Over the past ten years, the fund has provided an average annual return of about 15 percent. A $10,000 investment in the fund ten years ago would now be worth about $41,000.

In selecting stocks for the portfolio, fund manager Jennifer Silver considers several factors such as the company's financial strength, competitive position, and projected future earnings. In all, the fund has about 100 stock holdings. The fund manager is fairly aggressive in her trading policies, with an annual turnover ratio of 115 percent.

Like many of the top-performing mutual funds, the Vista Fund has been heavily weighted in high tech stocks, but it also has a solid selection of companies from other industries. Business services account for about 11 percent of total assets, retail stocks make up another 11 percent, and banks account for 8 percent of assets. Other leading sectors include telecommunications, 10 percent; computer products, 5 percent; and electronics and electrical equipment, 8 percent.

The fund stays almost fully invested in stocks most of the time.

PERFORMANCE

The fund has enjoyed outstanding growth over the past five years. Including dividends and capital gains distributions, the Putnam Vista Fund has provided a total return for the past five years (through mid-1996) of 156 percent. A $10,000 investment in 1991 would have grown to about $26,000 five years later. Average annual return: 20.7 percent.

CONSISTENCY

The fund has been very consistent, outperforming the Dow Jones Industrial Average four of the five years from 1991 through 1995 (and again through the first half of 1996). The fund did have a loss of 3.8 percent in 1994.

FEES/SERVICES/MANAGEMENT

The fund has a front-end load of 5.75 percent. Its total annual expense ratio of 1.07 percent (including a 0.25 percent 12b-1 fee and a 0.60 percent management fee) compares favorably with other funds.

The fund offers all the standard services such as retirement account availability, automatic withdrawal, and automatic checking account deduction. Its minimum initial investment of $500 and minimum subsequent investment of $50 compare very favorably with other funds.

Jennifer Silver has managed the fund since 1991. The Putnam fund family includes 77 funds and allows shareholders to switch from fund to fund by telephone.

Top Ten Holdings

1. HFS
2. 3Com
3. America Online
4. Parametric Technology
5. Paychex

6. Mentor
7. Bank of Boston
8. U.S. Filter
9. General Nutrition
10. Boston Scientific

Asset Mix: Common stocks: 94%; Cash/equivalents: 6%
Total Net Assets: $1.2 billion

Fees

Front-end load	5.75%
Redemption fee	*None*
12b-1 fee	0.25
Management fee	0.60
Other expenses	0.22
Total annual expense	1.07%
Minimum initial investment	$500
Minimum subsequent investment	$50

Services

Telephone exchanges	*Yes*
Automatic withdrawal	*Yes*
Automatic checking deduction	*Yes*
Retirement plan/IRA	*Yes*
Instant redemption	*Yes*
Financial statements	*Semiannual*
Income distributions	*Annual*
Capital gains distributions	*Annual*
Portfolio manager—years	6
Number of funds in family	77

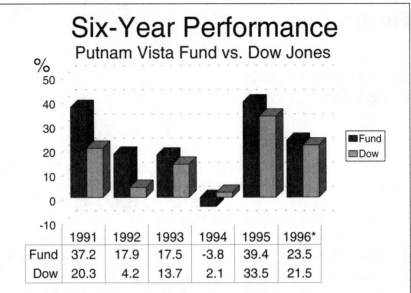

Six-Year Performance
Putnam Vista Fund vs. Dow Jones

	1991	1992	1993	1994	1995	1996*
Fund	37.2	17.9	17.5	-3.8	39.4	23.5
Dow	20.3	4.2	13.7	2.1	33.5	21.5

% Annual Total Return
Fund vs. Dow Jones Industrial Avg.

*1996 returns through 11/10/96
(5-year return through 7/96: 156%)

50
Fidelity Contrafund

Fidelity Investments
82 Devonshire Street
Boston, MA 02109

LONG TERM

Fund manager: William Danoff
Fund objective: Long-term growth

Toll-free: 800-544-8888
In-state: 801-534-1910
Fax: 617-476-9753

Performance	★ ★ ★
Consistency	★ ★ ★ ★
Fees/Services	★ ★ ★ ★
FCNTX	**11 Points**

The Contrafund's long-term success is a testament to the popular Wall Street adage "Every dog has its day." The fund is stocked with plodding giants with disappointing pasts such as Caterpillar, General Motors, and Burlington Northern. But fund manager William Danoff's ability to buy those types of stocks just as they're turning the corner has helped make the Contrafund one of the top large stock funds in the country.

The name "Contrafund" refers to the contrarian nature of the fund's philosophy. "We like down-and-out stocks that are getting better," Danoff explains. But he does not consider himself a value investor. "A value investor is someone who tries to buy for 50 cents an asset that's worth $1. We want to buy an asset worth $1 today that will be worth $2 to $3 in a year or two, and we want to buy it as cheaply as possible."

While value investors may jump on a stock when they think it is bottoming out, Danoff prefers to wait for a favorable uptick. "I'd rather buy a stock on the way up—after it has turned the corner."

The fund also invests in small growth stocks. "We like rapid growers—stocks that are growing at 40 percent-plus per year—and turnaround stocks," says Danoff.

The Contrafund is one of the nation's largest funds, with assets of nearly $20 billion. Managing the fund—which now has more than 700 stocks in the portfolio—may become increasingly difficult because of its size. It has grown about twentyfold since 1991 when it had assets of about $1 billion. But so far, Danoff has managed to keep the fund on track. It was up 36 percent in 1995, and up another 9 percent through the first half of 1996.

Introduced in 1967, the fund has enjoyed exceptional long-term growth. Over the past ten years, the fund has averaged a return of about 18 percent per year. A $10,000 investment in the fund ten years ago would now be worth about $54,000.

Danoff is particularly interested in companies with improving fundamentals that are selling at a reasonable price. In scouting out turnaround stocks, he is drawn to companies that have shown a sudden jump in earnings or sales. "I look for significant earnings increases, like a 50 percent increase. Then I look for why it had that increase. Maybe it just sold off a division that's been losing money, maybe it's a new product, or new management. Sometimes, it's part of an industrywide growth trend. I'm looking for some sort of spark that will lead to accelerating earnings." If he finds that spark, he'll add the stock to his portfolio.

For example, Danoff bought IBM after it had plunged from a high of over $150 a share to under $50 a share because he saw evidence of a legitimate turnaround. The company had new management, improving earnings, and a huge cost-cutting program designed to trim billions of dollars in expenses from the balance sheet.

Danoff will sell a stock for a couple of reasons—if the company loses momentum or if the stock price gets too high. "A stock that was a good buy at $20 may not be as attractive at $35," he explains. "I'll also sell when the growth slows and the fundamentals begin to deteriorate. That may mean the competition in its industry is up, or it could mean its sales are declining, or its profit margins are dropping. I'm constantly pruning out companies with deteriorating fundamentals."

The fund invests in a broad mix of small-, mid- and large-cap stocks across a diverse range of industries. Its largest industrial sectors include finance, 17 percent of assets; technology, 12 percent; energy, 10 percent; and durables, 6 percent.

PERFORMANCE

The fund has enjoyed exceptional growth over the past five years. Including dividends and capital gains distributions, the Contrafund has provided a total return for the past five years (through mid-1996) of 154 percent. A $10,000 investment in 1991 would have grown to about $25,000 five years later. Average annual return: 20.5 percent.

CONSISTENCY

The fund has been very consistent, outperforming the Dow Jones Industrial Average four of the five years through 1995 (but it trailed the Dow through the first half of 1996). Its best year was 1991, when it climbed 54.9 percent (compared with a 20.3 percent rise in the Dow).

FEES/SERVICES/MANAGEMENT

The fund has a low front-end load of 3 percent. Its total annual expense ratio of 0.98 percent (with no 12b-1 fee) compares very favorably with other funds.

The fund offers all the standard services such as retirement account availability, automatic withdrawal, and automatic checking account deduction. Its minimum initial investment of $2,500 and minimum subsequent investment of $250 are a little high compared with other funds.

Will Danoff has managed the fund since 1990. He has been a Fidelity Fund manager since 1986. The Fidelity fund family includes about 210 funds.

Top Ten Holdings

1. Chrysler	6. Caterpillar
2. General Motors	7. Household International
3. Schlumberger Ltd.	8. Travelers
4. Canon	9. Boeing
5. Burlington Northern Santa Fe	10. Federal National Mortgage Association

Asset Mix: Common stocks: 83%; U.S. Treasury obligations: 10%; Repurchase agreements: 7%
Total Net Assets: $19.5 billion

Fees

Front-end load	3.00%
Redemption fee	*None*
12b-1 fee	*None*
Management fee	0.71
Other expenses	0.27
Total annual expense	0.98%
Minimum initial investment	$2,500
Minimum subsequent investment	$250

Services

Telephone exchanges	*Yes*
Automatic withdrawal	*Yes*
Automatic checking deduction	*Yes*
Retirement plan/IRA	*Yes*
Instant redemption	*Yes*
Financial statements	*Semiannual*
Income distributions	*Annual*
Capital gains distributions	*Annual*
Portfolio manager—years	7
Number of funds in family	210

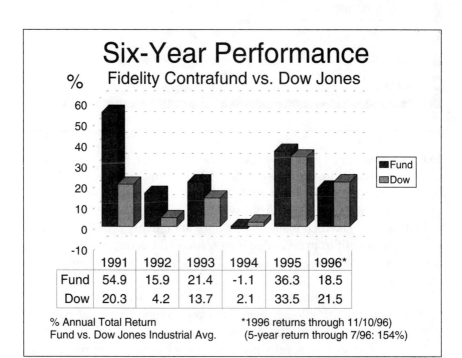

Six-Year Performance
Fidelity Contrafund vs. Dow Jones

	1991	1992	1993	1994	1995	1996*
Fund	54.9	15.9	21.4	-1.1	36.3	18.5
Dow	20.3	4.2	13.7	2.1	33.5	21.5

% Annual Total Return
Fund vs. Dow Jones Industrial Avg.

*1996 returns through 11/10/96)
(5-year return through 7/96: 154%)

51

Acorn Fund

AGGRESSIVE

Wanger Asset Management
227 West Monroe Street, #3000
Chicago, IL 60606

Fund managers: Ralph Wanger,
  Charles P. McQuaid, Terence M. Hogan
Fund objective: Aggressive growth

Toll-free: 800-922-6769
In-state: 312-634-9200
Fax: 312-634-0016

Performance	★ ★ ★
Consistency	★ ★ ★
Fees/Services	★ ★ ★ ★ ★
ACRNX	**11 Points**

In the 27 years since Ralph Wanger opened his Acorn Fund, he has made a lot of investors a lot of money. A $10,000 investment in the small stock growth fund when it opened in 1970 would now be worth about $500,000.

The Acorn Fund invests in a diverse cross-section of small emerging growth stocks. The fund managers look for attractively priced companies that should benefit from favorable long-term social, economic, or political trends. About 20 percent of the fund's assets are invested in foreign stocks.

The fund management takes a long-term approach, buying stocks with the intention of holding them for several years. Its annual portfolio turnover ratio is a very low 29 percent.

The fund stays almost fully invested in stocks most of the time. In all, the fund has more than 300 stock holdings.

Among its leading industrial segments are communications and information, 21 percent of assets; health care, 11 percent; finance, 15 percent; and consumer goods and services, 11.5 percent.

PERFORMANCE

The fund has experienced outstanding growth over the past five years. Including dividends and capital gains distributions, the Acorn Fund has provided a total return for the past five years (through mid-1996) of 153 percent. A $10,000 investment in 1991 would have grown to $25,000 five years later. Average annual return: 20.4 percent.

CONSISTENCY

The fund has been fairly consistent, outperforming the Dow Jones Industrial Average three of the five years through 1995 (and it was outpacing the Dow through the first half of 1996). The fund's worst recent year was 1994 when it dropped 7.5 percent. Its best year was 1991 when it jumped 47.4 percent.

FEES/SERVICES/MANAGEMENT

The Acorn Fund is a true no-load—no fee to buy, no fee to sell. Its annual expense ratio of 57 percent (with no 12b-1 fee) is very low compared with other funds.

The fund offers all the standard services such as retirement account availability, automatic withdrawal, and automatic checking account deduction. Its minimum initial investment of $1,000 and minimum subsequent investment of $100 is in line with other funds.

Ralph Wanger has managed the fund since its inception in 1970. He receives help from Charles P. McQuaid and Terence M. Hogan, who serve as comanagers of the fund. Acorn offers only one other fund, the Acorn International Fund.

Top Ten Holdings

1. Thermo Electron
2. Newell
3. ADVANTA
4. Harley-Davidson
5. Solectron
6. Liberty Media
7. Carnival
8. First USA
9. Tele-Comms TCI Group
10. Lincare Holdings

Asset Mix: Common stocks: 96%; Cash/equivalents: 4%
Total Net Assets: $2.8 billion

Fees

Front-end load	*None*
Redemption fee	*None*
12b-1 fee	*None*
Management fee	0.47%
Other expenses	0.10
Total annual expense	0.57%
Minimum initial investment	$1,000
Minimum subsequent investment	$100

Services

Telephone exchanges	*Yes*
Automatic withdrawal	*Yes*
Automatic checking deduction	*Yes*
Retirement plan/IRA	*Yes*
Instant redemption	*Yes*
Financial statements	*Annual*
Income distributions	*Semiannual*
Capital gains distributions	*Annual*
Portfolio manager—years	27
Number of funds in family	2

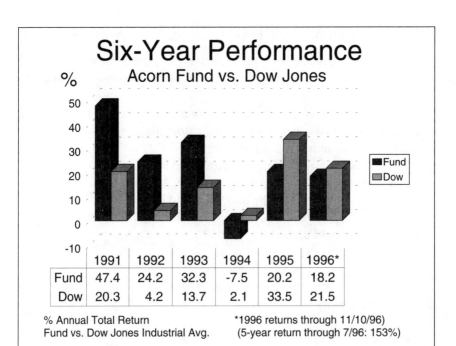

Six-Year Performance
Acorn Fund vs. Dow Jones

	1991	1992	1993	1994	1995	1996*
Fund	47.4	24.2	32.3	-7.5	20.2	18.2
Dow	20.3	4.2	13.7	2.1	33.5	21.5

% Annual Total Return
Fund vs. Dow Jones Industrial Avg.

*1996 returns through 11/10/96)
(5-year return through 7/96: 153%)

AGGRESSIVE

Twentieth Century
Ultra Investors

Twentieth Century Family of Funds
4500 Main Street
Kansas City, MO 64141-6200

Fund managers: Christopher Boyd, James Stowers III, Derek Felske
Fund objective: Aggressive growth

Toll-free: 800-345-2021
In-state: 816-531-5575
Fax: 816-340-4753

Performance	★ ★ ★
Consistency	★ ★ ★
Fees/Services	★ ★ ★ ★ ★
TWCUX	**11 Points**

Momentum is the key force behind the rapid growth of the Twentieth Century Ultra Investors Fund. "We like to find stocks that have business momentum," says fund comanager Christopher Boyd. "We look for earnings and revenue acceleration."

With more than $17 billion in assets in the fund, Boyd and comanagers James Stowers III and Derek Felske must take a broad approach in selecting stocks for the fund. They maintain a portfolio of about 175 medium- and large-cap stocks. "We're not as concerned about the size of the company as we are the momentum of the business," explains Boyd. "We're just trying to put the best growth stocks in the portfolio."

The Ultra Investors Fund has been one of the nation's top-performing funds over the past decade. The fund has posted an average annual return of about 18 percent per year over the past ten years. A $10,000 investment in the fund a decade ago would now be worth about $53,000.

The fund managers try to keep the fund on the upswing through close and continuous scrutiny of their holdings. They examine every stock in the portfolio each week to make sure the companies are still on an upward trend. They also keep their eye on a prospects list of 20 to 30 other stocks that could find their way into the portfolio when some of the fund's stock holdings begin to weaken.

The portfolio selection process is very much a team effort. In addition to the three fund managers, a team of financial analysts constantly pore over the financial records of hundreds of companies to uncover viable prospects for the portfolio. Their selections are then passed on to a team of three investment analysts who investigate the companies further, including personal interviews with each company's top managers. Once they have made their assessment, the analysts pass their list on to the three fund managers. "We're the ones who are ultimately responsible for what gets into the portfolio," says Boyd.

In analyzing a stock's momentum, Boyd believes it is important to assess the company's ongoing success before it actually makes it into the company's financial report. "By then it's too late [to buy the stock]. We look at things like orders and backlog that may have an effect on future earnings reports."

Boyd and his comanagers don't always go strictly by the numbers in uncovering hot stock prospects. "Sometimes it's just companies we happen to come across. In 1990, my wife and my sister kept talking about the Gap stores. The stores were packed, and sales were great. That Christmas, it seemed like half of our gifts were from the Gap." Boyd bought some Gap stock for the fund, and watched it rise from $11 a share in 1990 to $50 in 1992. "Then my wife went back to the Gap stores, and felt that the selection was poor and the stores were empty. We looked at the numbers and found that same-store sales were starting to slow down, so we sold out at $50." The stock quickly dropped to about $30 per share.

With their growth-oriented approach, the Ultra fund managers pay less attention to PE ratios and other factors that value investors thrive on. "We're more interested in the direction and sustainability of the growth rate than in PEs and other value factors. But we're always aware of the PE. A high PE stock that is starting to lose growth momentum can spell trouble."

Generally speaking, the fund stays almost fully invested in stocks at all times. The fund has a fairly aggressive annual portfolio turnover ratio of 87 percent. The fund is heavily weighted in technology stocks. Computer products and services account for 37 percent of the fund's assets; communications manufacturing and service companies make up 12 percent; health care and medical make up 17 percent; and banking and financial services account for 9 percent.

PERFORMANCE

The fund has enjoyed outstanding growth over the past five years. It has provided a total return over the past five years (through mid-1996) of 151 percent. A $10,000 investment in 1991 would have grown to $25,000 five years later. Average annual return: 20.2 percent.

CONSISTENCY

The fund has been fairly consistent, outperforming the Dow Jones Industrial Average three of the five years from 1991 through 1995 (but it trailed the Dow through the first half of 1996). Its biggest gain came in 1991, when it jumped 81.4 percent (compared with a 20.3 percent rise in the Dow).

FEES/SERVICES/MANAGEMENT

Like all Twentieth Century funds, the Ultra Investors Fund is a true no-load fund—no fee to buy, no fee to sell. The fund has a very low total annual expense ratio of 1.0 percent (with no 12b-1 fee).

The fund offers all the standard services such as retirement account availability, automatic withdrawal, and automatic checking account deduction.

The fund requires a minimum initial investment of $2,500 and a minimum subsequent investment of $50.

The fund has been team-managed since 1981. The Twentieth Century fund family includes 23 funds and allows shareholders to switch from fund to fund by telephone.

Top Ten Holdings

1. Cisco Systems	6. Pfizer
2. Sun Microsystems	7. Citicorp
3. Ascend Communications	8. Johnson & Johnson
4. U.S. Robotics	9. Amgen
5. Merck	10. 3Com

Asset Mix: Common stocks: 99%; Cash/equivalents: 1%
Total Net Assets: $17.4 billion

Fees

Front-end load	*None*
Redemption fee	*None*
12b-1 fee	*None*
Management fee	1.00%
Other expenses	*None*
Total annual expense	1.00%
Minimum initial investment	$2,500
Minimum subsequent investment	$50

Services

Telephone exchanges	*Yes*
Automatic withdrawal	*Yes*
Automatic checking deduction	*Yes*
Retirement plan/IRA	*Yes*
Instant redemption	*Yes*
Financial statements	*Semiannual*
Income distributions	*Annual*
Capital gains distributions	*Annual*
Portfolio managers—years	16
Number of funds in family	23

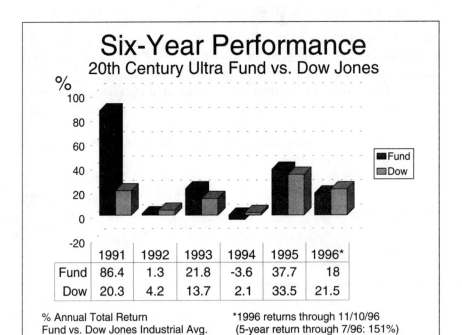

Six-Year Performance
20th Century Ultra Fund vs. Dow Jones

	1991	1992	1993	1994	1995	1996*
Fund	86.4	1.3	21.8	-3.6	37.7	18
Dow	20.3	4.2	13.7	2.1	33.5	21.5

% Annual Total Return
Fund vs. Dow Jones Industrial Avg.

*1996 returns through 11/10/96
(5-year return through 7/96: 151%)

53
AIM Value Fund "A"

AIM Funds
11 Greenway Plaza, Suite 1919
Houston, TX 77046

Fund managers: Claude Cody IV
and Joel Dobberpuhl
Fund objective: Long-term growth

Toll-free: 800-347-4246
In-state: 713-626-1919
Fax: 713-993-9890

Performance	★ ★ ★
Consistency	★ ★ ★ ★ ★
Fees/Services	★ ★ ★
AVLFX	**11 Points**

AIM Value Fund managers Claude Cody and Joel Dobberpuhl have compiled a record of consistent performance by uncovering undervalued stocks with strong turnaround potential. They closely monitor undervalued stocks, looking for signs of earnings improvement. When they find a company that appears to be on the verge of renewed profitability, they add the stock to their portfolio.

The Value Fund has enjoyed exceptional long-term success, especially for a fund that is not considered an aggressive growth fund. Over the past ten years, the fund has posted an average annual return of 17 percent. A $10,000 investment in the fund ten years ago would now be worth about $49,000.

The Value Fund portfolio consists of about 50 percent medium-sized stocks (up to $2 billion in market capitalization) and 50 percent large-capitalization companies. In all, the fund portfolio includes nearly 200 stocks. About 7 percent of its holdings are in foreign issues. The fund managers are fairly aggressive in their trading approach, with an annual portfolio turnover ratio of 125 percent.

The fund is heavily weighted in high tech stocks. Computer stocks make up about 20 percent of the portfolio, medical stocks account for 8 percent, and telecommunications companies make up 4 percent. Other leading segments include finance and insurance (6 percent), banking (2 percent), and tobacco (4 percent).

PERFORMANCE

The fund has enjoyed exceptional growth over the past five years. Including dividends and capital gains distributions, the AIM Value Fund has provided a total return for the past five years (through mid-1996) of 152 percent. A $10,000 investment in 1991 would have grown to about $25,000 five years later. Average annual return: 20.3 percent.

CONSISTENCY

The fund has been very consistent, outperforming the Dow Jones Industrial Average every year of the five-year period through 1995 (although it trailed the Dow through the first half of 1996). The fund's biggest gain came in 1991, when it rose 43.5 percent (compared with a 20.3 percent rise in the Dow).

FEES/SERVICES/MANAGEMENT

The fund has a front-end load of 5.5 percent. Its total annual expense ratio of 1.12 percent (including a 0.25 percent 12b-1 fee and a 0.62 percent management fee) compares favorably with other funds.

The fund offers all the standard services such as retirement account availability, automatic withdrawal, and automatic checking account deduction. Its minimum initial investment of $500 and minimum subsequent investment of $50 compare very favorably with other funds.

Claude Cody IV and Joel Dobberpuhl have managed the fund since 1992. The AIM fund family includes 21 funds and allows shareholders to switch freely from fund to fund by telephone.

Top Ten Holdings

1. Philip Morris	6. Aetna Life & Casualty
2. Ciba-Geigy AG	7. Baxter International
3. Ameritech	8. MFS Communications
4. Unicom	9. British Gas
5. Schering-Plough	10. American Electric Power

Asset Mix: Common stocks: 71%; Cash/equivalents: 29%
Total Net Assets: $7.52 billion

Fees

Front-end load	5.50%
Redemption fee	*None*
12b-1 fee	0.25
Management fee	0.62
Other expenses	0.25
Total annual expense	1.12%
Minimum initial investment	$500
Minimum subsequent investment	$50

Services

Telephone exchanges	*Yes*
Automatic withdrawal	*Yes*
Automatic checking deduction	*Yes*
Retirement plan/IRA	*Yes*
Instant redemption	*Yes*
Financial statements	*Quarterly*
Income distributions	*Annual*
Capital gains distributions	*Annual*
Portfolio managers—years	5
Number of funds in family	21

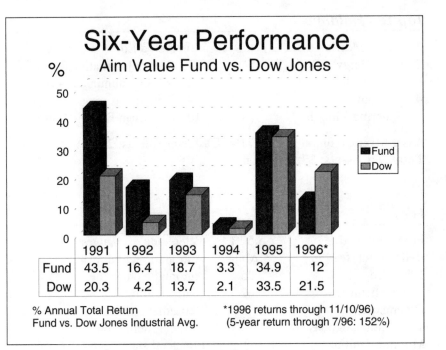

Six-Year Performance
Aim Value Fund vs. Dow Jones

	1991	1992	1993	1994	1995	1996*
Fund	43.5	16.4	18.7	3.3	34.9	12
Dow	20.3	4.2	13.7	2.1	33.5	21.5

% Annual Total Return   *1996 returns through 11/10/96)
Fund vs. Dow Jones Industrial Avg.   (5-year return through 7/96: 152%)

AGGRESSIVE

54

Fidelity Emerging Growth Fund

Fidelity Investments
82 Devonshire Street
Boston, MA 02109

Fund manager: Lawrence Greenburg
Fund objective: Aggressive growth

Toll-free: 800-544-8888
In-state: 801-534-1910
Fax: 617-476-9743

Performance	★ ★ ★ ★
Consistency	★ ★ ★ ★
Fees/Services	★ ★ ★
FDEGX	**11 Points**

The Fidelity Emerging Growth Fund has the flexibility to diversify across a broad range of industrial sectors. But, like many of the best funds of the 1990s, this fund's portfolio roster reads very much like a high tech sector fund.

Fund manager Lawrence Greenburg has invested nearly 70 percent of the fund's assets in technology and health-related stocks. (Retail and wholesale stocks account for about 10 percent and utilities make up 8 percent.)

The objective of the fund is to invest at least 65 percent of its assets in small, emerging stocks that "are in the developing stage of their life cycle, and offer the potential for accelerated growth." But the median market capitaliztion of the companies in the fund is about $4 billion—so this is not exactly a small stock fund. The fund has investments in a number of larger high tech companies such as Microsoft and Oracle that continue to have strong growth prospects. It also has a fair share of foreign stock holdings.

The fund, which opened in 1990, has experienced outstanding performance the past five years, with an average annual return of about 20 percent. The fund has nearly 250 stock holdings in the portfolio. Greenburg pursues a fairly active trading strategy with a 102 percent annual portfolio turnover ratio.

PERFORMANCE

The fund has enjoyed exceptional growth over the past five years. Including dividends and capital gains distributions, the Emerging Growth Fund has provided a total return for the past five years (through mid-1996) of 163 percent. A $10,000 investment in 1991 would have grown to about $26,000 five years later. Average annual return: 21.3 percent.

CONSISTENCY

The fund has been very consistent recently, outperforming the Dow Jones Industrial Average four of the five years through 1995 (and it was ahead of the Dow through the first half of 1996). Its best year was in 1991 when it jumped 67.1 percent.

FEES/SERVICES/MANAGEMENT

The fund has a low front-end load of 3 percent and a maximum redemption fee of 0.75 percent if it's sold out within 29 days. Its low annual expense ratio of 1.1 percent (with no 12b-1 fee) compares favorably with other funds.

The fund offers all the standard services such as retirement account availability, automatic withdrawal, and automatic checking account deduction. Its minimum initial investment of $2,500 and minimum subsequent investment of $250 are a little high compared with other funds.

Lawrence Greenburg has managed the fund since October 1993. He has been with Fidelity since 1986. The Fidelity fund family includes about 210 funds.

Top Ten Holdings

1. Oracle
2. Cisco Systems
3. Microsoft
4. AirTouch Communications
5. DSC Communications
6. 3Com
7. Compaq Computer
8. Nokia (ADR)
9. Silicon Graphics
10. Vanguard Cellular Systems

Asset Mix: Common stocks: 82%; Cash/equivalents: 18%
Total Net Assets: $1.8 billion

Fees

Front-end load	3.00%
Redemption fee (max)	0.75%
12b-1 fee	*None*
Management fee	0.76%
Other expenses	0.34%
Total annual expense	1.10%
Minimum initial investment	$2,500
Minimum subsequent investment	$250

Services

Telephone exchanges	*Yes*
Automatic withdrawal	*Yes*
Automatic checking deduction	*Yes*
Retirement plan/IRA	*Yes*
Instant redemption	*Yes*
Financial statements	*Semiannual*
Income distributions	*Annual*
Capital gains distributions	*Annual*
Portfolio manager—years	3
Number of funds in family	210

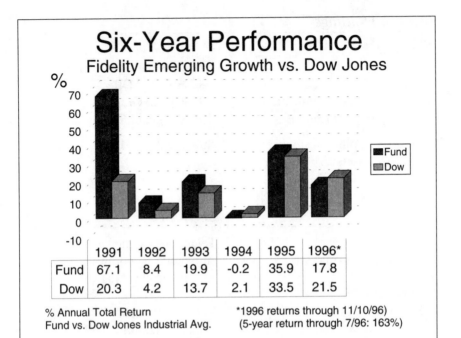

Six-Year Performance
Fidelity Emerging Growth vs. Dow Jones

	1991	1992	1993	1994	1995	1996*
Fund	67.1	8.4	19.9	-0.2	35.9	17.8
Dow	20.3	4.2	13.7	2.1	33.5	21.5

% Annual Total Return   *1996 returns through 11/10/96)
Fund vs. Dow Jones Industrial Avg.   (5-year return through 7/96: 163%)

LONG TERM

55
Neuberger & Berman
Focus Fund

Neuberger & Berman Group
605 Third Avenue, 2nd Floor
New York, NY 10158-0006

Fund managers: Kent Simons
and Lawrence Marx III
Fund objective: Long-term growth

Toll-free: 800-877-9700
In-state: 212-476-8800
Fax: 212-476-8944

Performance	★ ★
Consistency	★ ★ ★ ★
Fees/Services	★ ★ ★ ★ ★
NBSSX	**11 Points**

Neuberger & Berman Focus Fund managers Kent Simons and Larry Marx rarely ever get excited about a stock until the rest of the investment world gives up on it. "When Wall Street stops looking at a stock, that's when we start looking," says Marx.

The Focus Fund invests in undervalued stocks with solid financial strength and proven management. Simons and Marx like to ferret out industries that are out of favor on Wall Street, and invest in the strongest companies within those industries. "When Wall Street gives up on an industry, it punishes all companies indiscriminately—the good and the bad," explains Marx. "Over time, the market may recognize that it had overreacted and may bid up the prices of the healthy stocks that it had once punished incorrectly."

Opened in 1955, the Focus Fund is one of the oldest mutual funds in America. Since inception, it has grown at a rate of about 12 percent per year. A $10,000 investment in the fund when it opened in 1955 would now be worth about $1.1 million. Over the past ten years, the fund has grown at a rate of about 14 percent per year.

Most of the fund's approximately 75 stock holdings are large-capital-ization blue chip stocks such as Citicorp, Chrysler, and Wells Fargo. The fund is heavily weighted in financial stocks, which account for 33 percent of total assets. Other leading sectors include technology, 21 percent; heavy industry, 13 percent; health care, 10 percent; and automotive, 6 percent.

The fund managers take a conservative buy-and-hold approach, with an annual portfolio turnover ratio of 36 percent.

PERFORMANCE

The Focus Fund has experienced solid growth over the past five years. Including dividends and capital gains distributions, the fund has provided a total return for the past five years (through mid-1996) of 128 percent. A $10,000 investment in 1991 would have grown to about $23,000 five years later. Average annual return: 18 percent.

CONSISTENCY

The fund has been very consistent, outperforming the Dow Jones Indus-trial Average four of the five years through 1995 (but it trailed the Dow through the first half of 1996).

FEES/SERVICES/MANAGEMENT

Like all Neuberger & Berman funds, the Focus Fund is a true no-load fund—no fee to buy, no fee to sell. It has a very low total annual expense ratio of just 0.92 percent (with no 12b-1 fee).

The fund offers all the standard services such as retirement account availability, automatic withdrawal, and automatic checking account deduction. Its minimum initial investment of $1,000 and minimum subse-quent investment of $100 is in line with other funds.

Kent Simons and Larry Marx both began managing the fund in 1988. The Neuberger & Berman fund family includes 14 funds and allows shareholders to switch from fund to fund by telephone.

Top Ten Holdings

1. Citicorp
2. Chrysler
3. Federal National Mortgage Association
4. Foundation Health
5. Neiman-Marcus Group
6. Compaq Computer
7. Federal Home Loan Mortgage Corp.
8. Travelers Group
9. General Motors
10. AT&T

Asset Mix: Common stocks: 99%; Cash/equivalents: 1%
Total Net Assets: $1.2 billion

Fees

Front-end load	*None*
Redemption fee	*None*
12b-1 fee	*None*
Management fee	0.79%
Other expenses	0.13%
Total annual expense	0.92%
Minimum initial investment	$1,000
Minimum subsequent investment	$100

Services

Telephone exchanges	*Yes*
Automatic withdrawal	*Yes*
Automatic checking deduction	*Yes*
Retirement plan/IRA	*Yes*
Instant redemption	*Yes*
Financial statements	*Annual*
Income distributions	*Annual*
Capital gains distributions	*Annual*
Portfolio managers—years	9
Number of funds in family	14

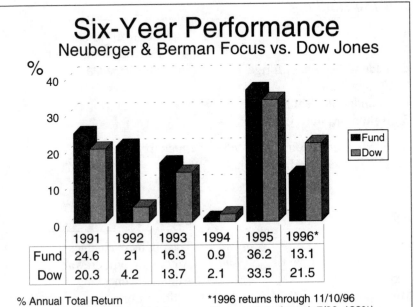

Six-Year Performance
Neuberger & Berman Focus vs. Dow Jones

	1991	1992	1993	1994	1995	1996*
Fund	24.6	21	16.3	0.9	36.2	13.1
Dow	20.3	4.2	13.7	2.1	33.5	21.5

% Annual Total Return
Fund vs. Dow Jones Industrial Avg.

*1996 returns through 11/10/96
(5-year return through 7/96: 128%)

Founders Frontier Fund

AGGRESSIVE

Founders Funds
Founders Financial Center
2930 East Third Avenue
Denver, CO 80206

Fund manager: Michael Haines
Fund objective: Aggressive growth

Toll-free: 800-525-2440
In-state: 303-394-4404
Fax: 303-394-4021

Performance	★ ★
Consistency	★ ★ ★ ★
Fees/Services	★ ★ ★ ★ ★
FOUNX	**11 Points**

The Founders Frontier Fund invests primarily in small to midsized companies with annual revenue in the range of $200 million to $1 billion. Most of its stock holdings are in U.S. companies, although fund manager Michael Haines keeps about 10 percent of the fund's assets invested in foreign stocks.

Since its inception in 1987, the fund has had average annual rate of return of about 20 percent. A $10,000 investment in the fund when it opened would now be worth about $50,000.

As with most of the leading small-stock funds, the Frontier Fund is heavily weighted in technology stocks. Computer-related companies account for 15 percent of the fund's assets, health care and medical make up about 13 percent, and telecommunications account for about 8 percent. In all, the fund has about 90 stock holdings.

Haines takes a bottom-up approach in selecting stocks, looking for well-managed young companies that offer superior earnings growth potential. He is fairly conservative in his trading approach, with a 92 percent annual portfolio turnover ratio.

PERFORMANCE

The Founders Frontier Fund has posted solid returns over the past five years. Including dividends and capital gains distributions, the fund has provided a total return for the past five years (through mid-1996) of 127 percent. A $10,000 investment in 1991 would have grown to about $23,000 five years later. Average annual return: 17.9 percent.

CONSISTENCY

The fund has been very consistent, outperforming the Dow Jones Industrial Average four of the five years through 1995 (and it narrowly trailed the Dow through the first half of 1996). The fund's biggest gain came in 1991, when it rose 49.3 percent (compared with a 20.3 percent rise in the Dow).

FEES/SERVICES/MANAGEMENT

The Founders Frontier Fund is a true no-load fund—no fee to buy, no fee to sell. The fund's total annual expense ratio of 1.57 percent (including a 0.25 percent 12b-1 fee and a 0.97 percent management fee) is in line with other no-load funds.

The fund offers all the standard services such as retirement account availability, automatic withdrawal and automatic checking account deduction. Its minimum initial investment of $1,000 and minimum subsequent investment of $100 compare favorably with other funds.

Michael Haines has managed the fund since 1987. The Founders fund family includes 11 funds and allows shareholders to switch from fund to fund by telephone.

Top Ten Holdings

1. Maxim Integrated Products
2. International Rectifier
3. HBO
4. Midlantic
5. Jones Apparel Group
6. Input/Output
7. HealthCare COMPARE
8. Viking Office Products
9. Frontier
10. Oakwood Homes

Asset Mix: Common stocks: 82%; Cash/equivalents: 18%
Total Net Assets: $382 million

Fees

Front-end load	*None*
Redemption fee (max)	*None*
12b-1 fee	0.25%
Management fee	0.97
Other expenses	0.35
Total annual expense	1.57%
Minimum initial investment	$1,000
Minimum subsequent investment	$100

Services

Telephone exchanges	*Yes*
Automatic withdrawal	*Yes*
Automatic checking deduction	*Yes*
Retirement plan/IRA	*Yes*
Instant redemption	*Yes*
Financial statements	*Annual*
Income distributions	*Annual*
Capital gains distributions	Annual
Portfolio manager—years	10
Number of funds in family	11

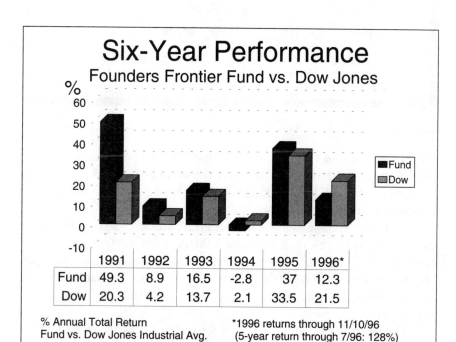

Six-Year Performance
Founders Frontier Fund vs. Dow Jones

	1991	1992	1993	1994	1995	1996*
Fund	49.3	8.9	16.5	-2.8	37	12.3
Dow	20.3	4.2	13.7	2.1	33.5	21.5

% Annual Total Return
Fund vs. Dow Jones Industrial Avg.

*1996 returns through 11/10/96
(5-year return through 7/96: 128%)

57
T. Rowe Price OTC Fund

AGGRESSIVE

T. Rowe Price Funds
100 East Pratt Street
Baltimore, MD 21202

Fund manager: Gregory A. McCrickard
Fund objective: Aggressive growth

Toll-free: 800-225-5132
In-state: 410-547-2000
Fax: 410-347-1574

Performance	★ ★
Consistency	★ ★ ★ ★
Fees/Services	★ ★ ★ ★ ★
OTCFX	**11 Points**

As its name implies, the T. Rowe Price OTC Fund invests in small, emerging stocks that are traded over-the-counter or on the NASDAQ over-the-counter exchange. On average, the stocks in the fund have market capitalizations of about $400 million.

The fund has done much better over the past five years—when small stocks were surging—than it has over the past ten. Its five-year growth rate is about 19 percent per year, whereas its ten-year growth rate is just 10 percent per year. A $10,000 investment in the fund 10 years ago would now be worth about $26,000 (compared to $24,000 if invested just five years ago).

Fund manager Greg McCrickard looks for companies with veteran management, solid business franchises, sound financials, and proven ability to deliver increasing earnings. He invests in both "value" stocks—those trading at a discount to the market relative to their book value or earnings—and growth companies—those with strong growth momentum.

McCrickard takes a fairly modest trading approach, with an annual portfolio turnover ratio of 58 percent. The fund stays about 80 to 95 percent invested in the market all the time.

In all, the fund has about 100 stock holdings. Leading sectors include consumer nondurables, 19 percent of assets; financial, 16 percent; business services, 16 percent; consumer services, 8 percent; and technology, 8 percent.

PERFORMANCE

The OTC Fund has experienced strong growth over the past five years. Including dividends and capital gains distributions, the fund has provided a total return for the past five years (through mid-1996) of 137 percent. A $10,000 investment in 1991 would have grown to about $24,000 five years later. Average annual return: 18.9 percent.

CONSISTENCY

The fund has been very consistent, outperforming the Dow Jones Industrial Average four of the five years through 1995 (and it was ahead of the Dow again through the first half of 1996). The fund's biggest gain came in 1991, when it rose 38.6 percent (compared with a 20.3 percent rise in the Dow).

FEES/SERVICES/MANAGEMENT

Like all T. Rowe Price funds, the OTC Fund is a true no-load fund—no fee to buy, no fee to sell. It has a low total annual expense ratio of 1.11 percent (with no 12b-1 fee).

The fund offers all the standard services such as retirement account availability, automatic withdrawal, and automatic checking account deduction. Its minimum initial investment of $2,500 and minimum subsequent investment of $100 are a little higher than average.

Greg McCrickard has managed the fund since 1992. The T. Rowe Price fund family includes 50 funds and allows shareholders to switch from fund to fund by telephone.

Top Ten Holdings

1. Richfood Holdings
2. Orthodontic Centers of America
3. Selective Insurance
4. Insituform Technologies
5. Weatherford Enterra

6. Holophane
7. Electro Rent
8. Collective Bancorp
9. JP Foodservice
10. Glacier Bancorp

Asset Mix: Common stocks: 91%; Cash/equivalents: 9%
Total Net Assets: $291 million

Fees

Front-end load	*None*
Redemption fee	*None*
12b-1 fee	*None*
Management fee	0.79%
Other expenses	0.32
Total annual expense	1.11%
Minimum initial investment	$2,500
Minimum subsequent investment	$100

Services

Telephone exchanges	*Yes*
Automatic withdrawal	*Yes*
Automatic checking deduction	*Yes*
Retirement plan/IRA	*Yes*
Instant redemption	*Yes*
Financial statements	*Semiannual*
Income distributions	*Annual*
Capital gains distributions	*Annual*
Portfolio manager—years	5
Number of funds in family	50

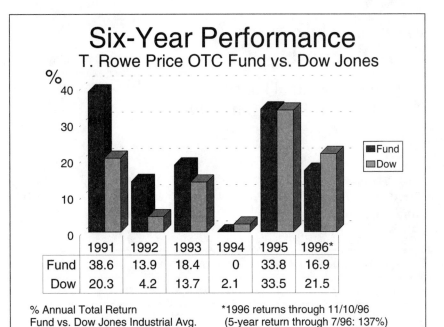

Six-Year Performance
T. Rowe Price OTC Fund vs. Dow Jones

	1991	1992	1993	1994	1995	1996*
Fund	38.6	13.9	18.4	0	33.8	16.9
Dow	20.3	4.2	13.7	2.1	33.5	21.5

% Annual Total Return
Fund vs. Dow Jones Industrial Avg.

*1996 returns through 11/10/96
(5-year return through 7/96: 137%)

58

William Blair
Growth Fund

William Blair Mutual Funds
222 W. Adams Street, 34th Floor
Chicago, IL 60606

Fund managers: Rocky Barber
  and Mark Fuller III
Fund objective: Long-term growth

Toll-free: 800-742-7272
In-state: 312-364-8000
Fax: 312-236-1497

Performance	★ ★
Consistency	★ ★ ★ ★
Fees/Services	★ ★ ★ ★ ★
WBGSX	**11 Points**

The William Blair Growth Fund has been around since 1946 and it continues to prove its worth today. Its steady performance, low fees, and broad range of services make this a very attractive fund for investors.

The fund has outperformed the Dow Jones Industrial Average six of the past seven years, and even when it trailed the Dow in 1995, it still posted a very respectable 29.1 percent gain.

Over the past ten years, the fund has produced an average annual return of about 14 percent per year. A $10,000 investment in the fund ten years ago would now be worth about $37,000.

The fund invests in a blend of large, medium and small capitalization stocks, including well-known blue chip stocks such as Pepsico, Microsoft, and Home Depot, and high-flying emerging companies such as First Data, AirTouch Communications, and Whole Foods Market. Fund managers Rocky Barber and Mark Fuller like stocks that have averaged 15 to 20 percent in annual earnings growth over the past five to ten years. The fund maintains a modest portfolio turnover ratio of 32 percent.

The fund stays fully invested in the market most of the time. It has about 65 stock holdings, concentrated in fast-growing industries. Leading sectors include applied technology, 20 percent of assets; retail, 17 percent; financial services, 10 percent; medical-related, 10 percent; technology, 8 percent; distribution, 8 percent; industrial products, 8 percent; and consumer services and products, 6 percent.

PERFORMANCE

The William Blair Growth Fund has posted strong growth over the past five years. Including dividends and capital gains distributions, the fund has provided a total return for the past five years (through mid-1996) of 137 percent. A $10,000 investment in 1991 would have grown to about $24,000 five years later. Average annual return: 18.8 percent.

CONSISTENCY

The fund has been very consistent, outperforming the Dow Jones Industrial Average four of the five years from 1991 through 1995 (and it was about even with the Dow through the first half of 1996). The fund's biggest gain came in 1991, when it rose 44.4 percent (compared with a 20.3 percent rise in the Dow).

FEES/SERVICES/MANAGEMENT

The Growth Fund is a true no-load fund—no fee to buy and no fee to sell. It has a very low total annual expense ratio of just 0.65 percent (with no 12b-1 fee).

The fund offers all the standard services such as retirement account availability, automatic withdrawal, and automatic checking account deduction. Its minimum initial investment of $5,000 and minimum subsequent investment of $250 are quite a bit higher than most other funds.

Fund mangers Rocky Barber and Mark Fuller have managed the fund since 1993. Barber has been a fund manager with William Blair since 1986, following nine years as a portfolio manager with Alliance Capital. Fuller has been with William Blair since 1983. The William Blair fund family includes three funds and allows shareholders to switch from fund to fund by telephone.

Top Ten Holdings

1. First Data
2. Home Depot
3. Alco Standard
4. Microsoft
5. AirTouch Communications
6. State Street Boston
7. Elan (ADR)
8. SmithKline Beecham (ADR)
9. Automatic Data Processing
10. Cardinal Health

Asset Mix: Common stocks: 97%; Cash/equivalents: 3%
Total Net Assets: $450 million

Fees

Front-end load	*None*
Redemption fee	*None*
12b-1 fee	*None*
Management fee	0.75%
Other expenses	0.12
Total annual expense	0.87%
Minimum initial investment	$5,000
Minimum subsequent investment	$250

Services

Telephone exchanges	*Yes*
Automatic withdrawal	*Yes*
Automatic checking deduction	*Yes*
Retirement plan/IRA	*Yes*
Instant redemption	*Yes*
Financial statements	*Semiannual*
Income distributions	*Semiannual*
Capital gains distributions	*Annual*
Portfolio managers—years	4
Number of funds in family	3

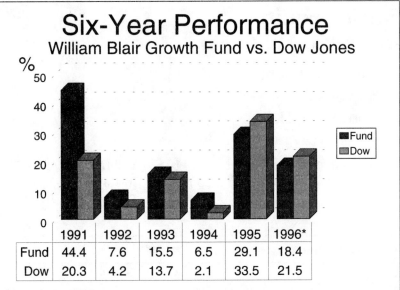

Six-Year Performance
William Blair Growth Fund vs. Dow Jones

	1991	1992	1993	1994	1995	1996*
Fund	44.4	7.6	15.5	6.5	29.1	18.4
Dow	20.3	4.2	13.7	2.1	33.5	21.5

% Annual Total Return   *1996 returns through 11/10/96
Fund vs. Dow Jones Industrial Avg.   (5-year return through 7/96: 137%)

59
Fidelity Equity Income II Fund

GROWTH

Fidelity Investments
82 Devonshire Street
Boston, MA 02109

Fund manager: Brian Posner
Fund objective: Growth and income

Toll-free: 800-544-8888
In-state: 801-534-1910
Fax: 617-476-9753

Performance	★ ★
Consistency	★ ★ ★ ★
Fees/Services	★ ★ ★ ★ ★
FEQTX	**11 Points**

Because of its focus on major corporations that pay dividends, the Fidelity Equity Income II Fund has not achieved the same level of growth recently that many of the small-stock funds have enjoyed. But it has provided solid growth and a steady stream of income for its shareholders.

Since its inception in 1990, the fund has grown at an average annual rate of 21 percent. A $10,000 investment in the fund in 1990 would have grown to about $31,000 six years later. The fund pays an annual yield of about 1.6 percent.

Fund manager Brian Posner invests most of the fund's assets in stocks of major manufacturers, energy companies, and financial institutions that pay good dividends, such as Philip Morris, American Express, and British Petroleum.

Posner looks for growing companies that are trading at relatively low prices. "This means companies that are not only trading at low price-to-earnings and price-to-cash-flow ratios, but also are providing their own-ers—the shareholders—relatively attractive, if not improving, returns on assets, equity, and capital."

The fund stays about 80 percent invested in stocks most of the time, with most of the balance going into bonds and money market investments. About 12 percent of the fund's assets are invested in foreign securities.

Posner maintains a fairly conservative trading practice, with an annual portfolio turnover ratio of 45 percent.

The Equity Income II Fund is one of the largest funds in the Fidelity family with $13 billion in assets and nearly 250 stock holdings. The fund's leading industrial sectors include finance, 15 percent of assets; energy, 14 percent; retail and wholesale, 8 percent; chemicals and plastics, 7 percent; and technology, 5 percent.

PERFORMANCE

The Fidelity Equity Income II Fund has experienced solid growth over the past five years. Including dividends and capital gains distributions, the fund has provided a total return for the past five years (through mid-1996) of 135 percent. A $10,000 investment in 1991 would have grown to about $23,250 five years later. Average annual return: 18.6 percent.

CONSISTENCY

The fund has been relatively consistent, outperforming the Dow Jones Industrial Average four of the five years through 1995 (but it trailed the Dow through the first half of 1996). The fund's biggest gain came in 1991, when it rose 46.6 percent (compared with a 20.3 percent rise in the Dow).

FEES/SERVICES/MANAGEMENT

The Fidelity Equity Income II Fund is a true no-load fund—no fee to buy, no fee to sell. And it has a very low annual expense ratio of just 0.76 percent (with no 12b-1 fee).

The fund offers all the standard services such as retirement account availability, automatic withdrawal, and automatic checking account deduction. Its minimum initial investment of $2,500 and minimum subsequent investment of $250 are a little high compared with other funds.

Brian Posner has managed the fund since 1992. He joined Fidelity in 1987. The Fidelity fund family includes about 210 funds.

Top Ten Holdings

1. American Express	6. Philip Morris
2. British Petroleum	7. NYNEX
3. E.I. du Pont de Nemours	8. Great Lakes Chemical
4. Schlumberger	9. Allstate
5. Federal National Mortgage Association	10. Wal-Mart

Asset Mix: Common stocks: 84%; Cash/equivalents: 16%
Total Net Assets: $14.3 billion

Fees

Front-end load	*None*
Redemption fee	*None*
12b-1 fee	*None*
Management fee	0.51%
Other expenses	0.25
Total annual expense	0.76%
Minimum initial investment	$2,500
Minimum subsequent investment	$250

Services

Telephone exchanges	*Yes*
Automatic withdrawal	*Yes*
Automatic checking deduction	*Yes*
Retirement plan/IRA	*Yes*
Instant redemption	*Yes*
Financial statements	*Annual*
Income distributions	*Quarterly*
Capital gains distributions	*Semiannual*
Portfolio manager—years	5
Number of funds in family	210

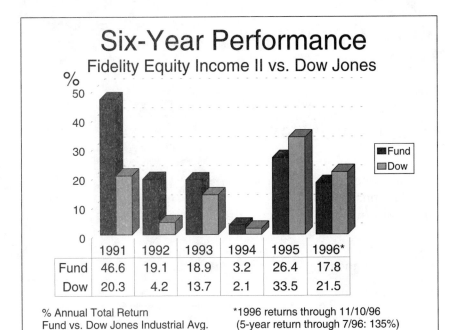

Six-Year Performance
Fidelity Equity Income II vs. Dow Jones

	1991	1992	1993	1994	1995	1996*
Fund	46.6	19.1	18.9	3.2	26.4	17.8
Dow	20.3	4.2	13.7	2.1	33.5	21.5

% Annual Total Return
Fund vs. Dow Jones Industrial Avg.

*1996 returns through 11/10/96
(5-year return through 7/96: 135%)

60
Strong Opportunity Fund

LONG TERM

Strong Funds
P.O. Box 2936
Milwaukee, WI 53201-2936

Fund managers: Richard Weiss
and Marina Carlson
Fund objective: Long-term growth

Toll-free: 800-368-3863
In-state: 414-359-3400
Fax: 414-359-3947

Performance	★ ★
Consistency	★ ★ ★ ★
Fees/Services	★ ★ ★ ★ ★
SOPFX	**11 Points**

The Strong Opportunity Fund invests primarily in midsized growth companies that fund managers Richard Weiss and Marina Carlson consider to be "underresearched by Wall Street analysts and undervalued by the market."

Over the past ten years, the fund has had an average annual return of about 15 percent. A $10,000 investment in the fund ten years ago would now be worth about $56,000.

In addition to its U.S. stocks, the fund holds stocks from 12 other countries. About 13 percent of its stock holdings are from outside the United States. In all, the fund has about 125 stocks across a diverse range of industries. Leading sectors include retail, 10 percent of assets; telecommunications, 6 percent; electronics, 7 percent; health-related, 9 percent; and media, 8 percent.

In selecting stocks for the portfolio, Weiss and Carlson look for companies with fundamental value or growth potential that is not yet reflected in the stock price. They like companies that have not become widely recognized by other analysts or by the financial press. In researching stock prospects, the managers may visit the companies and talk with the corporate managers.

The fund generally stays 70 percent to 90 percent invested in stocks. The managers take a fairly aggressive buy-and-sell approach, with a 97 percent annual portfolio turnover ratio.

PERFORMANCE

The Strong Opportunity Fund has experienced solid growth over the past five years. Including dividends and capital gains distributions, the fund has provided a total return for the past five years (through mid-1996) of 134 percent. A $10,000 investment in 1991 would have grown to about $23,000 five years later. Average annual return: 18.5 percent.

CONSISTENCY

The fund has been relatively consistent, outperforming the Dow Jones Industrial Average four of the five years through 1995 (but it trailed the Dow through the first half of 1996).

FEES/SERVICES/MANAGEMENT

Like all Strong funds, the Opportunity Fund is a true no-load fund—no fee to buy, no fee to sell. The fund's total annual expense ratio of 1.3 percent (with no 12b-1 fee) is in line with other funds.

The fund offers all the standard services such as retirement account availability, automatic withdrawal, and automatic checking account deduction. Its minimum initial investment of $2,500 is a little higher than average, but its minimum subsequent investment of $50 compares favorably with other funds.

Robert Weiss has managed the fund since 1991. Marina Carlson joined the fund as comanager in 1993. The Strong fund family includes 21 funds and allows shareholders to switch from fund to fund by telephone.

Top Ten Holdings

1. U.S. Surgical	6. Seagate Technology
2. Stop & Shop	7. Petroleum Geo-Services
3. Toys "R" Us	8. Arrow Electronics
4. Whitman	9. Teledyne
5. U.S. West Media Group	10. Kroger

Asset Mix: Common stocks: 88%; Cash/equivalents: 12%
Total Net Assets: $1.6 billion

Fees

Front-end load	*None*
Redemption fee	*None*
12b-1 fee	*None*
Management fee	1.00%
Other expenses	0.30
Total annual expense	1.30%
Minimum initial investment	$1,000
Minimum subsequent investment	$50

Services

Telephone exchanges	*Yes*
Automatic withdrawal	*Yes*
Automatic checking deduction	*Yes*
Retirement plan/IRA	*Yes*
Instant redemption	*Yes*
Financial statements	*Annual*
Income distributions	*Annual*
Capital gains distributions	*Annual*
Portfolio manager—years	6
Number of funds in family	21

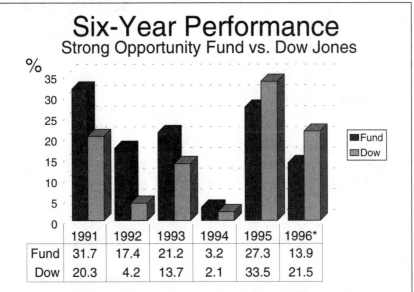

Six-Year Performance
Strong Opportunity Fund vs. Dow Jones

	1991	1992	1993	1994	1995	1996*
Fund	31.7	17.4	21.2	3.2	27.3	13.9
Dow	20.3	4.2	13.7	2.1	33.5	21.5

% Annual Total Return   *1996 returns through 11/10/96
Fund vs. Dow Jones Industrial Avg. (5-year return through 7/96: 134%)

61

Fidelity Value Fund

Fidelity Investments
82 Devonshire Street
Boston, MA 02109

LONG TERM

Fund manager: Richard Fentin
Fund objective: Long-term growth

Toll-free: 800-544-8888
In-state: 801-534-1910
Fax: 617-476-9753

Performance	★ ★ ★
Consistency	★ ★ ★ ★
Fees/Services	★ ★ ★ ★
FDVLX	**11 Points**

The Fidelity Value Fund specializes in undervalued stocks that appear poised for a run-up. Most of its leading holdings are large well-known companies such as Philip Morris, American Express, Citicorp, and British Petroleum.

The fund has enjoyed strong growth the past five years after a lackluster period in the late 1980s. While its five-year average annual return is about 19 percent, its ten-year average annual return is just 13 percent. A $10,000 investment in the fund ten years ago would now be worth about $35,000.

The objective of the fund is to invest in companies with valuable fixed assets, or stocks that appear to be undervalued based on the company's assets, earnings, or growth potential. Fund manager Richard Fentin also looks for companies that have recently changed management and seem to be on the verge of a rebound in earnings.

The fund, which has about 200 stock holdings, maintains a fairly active trading policy, with an annual portfolio turnover ratio of 125 percent.

The Value Fund is not high tech-oriented. Its leading industrial segment is financial stocks, which account for about 19 percent of assets.

Other leading sectors include energy, 8 percent; nondurables (foods, tobacco, household products), 8 percent; utilities, 7 percent; and health, 6.5 percent.

PERFORMANCE

The fund has enjoyed outstanding growth over the past five years. Including dividends and capital gains distributions, the Fidelity Value Fund has provided a total return for the past five years (through mid-1996) of 141 percent. A $10,000 investment in 1991 would have grown to about $24,000 five years later. Average annual return: 19 percent.

CONSISTENCY

The fund has been fairly consistent recently, outperforming the Dow Jones Industrial Average four of the five years through 1995 (and was trailing the Dow by about 2 percent through the first half of 1996). The fund has had gains of more than 20 percent four of the past six years.

FEES/SERVICES/MANAGEMENT

The Fidelity Value Fund is a true no-load fund—no fees to buy or sell shares of the fund. It also has a very low annual expense ratio of 0.97 percent (with no 12b-1 fee).

The fund offers all the standard services such as retirement account availability, automatic withdrawal, and automatic checking account deduction. Its minimum initial investment of $2,500 and minimum subsequent investment of $250 are a little high compared with other funds.

Fund manager Richard Fentin has only been with the fund since 1996. Formerly the manager of the Fidelity Puritan Fund, Fentin has been with Fidelity since 1979. The Fidelity fund family includes about 210 funds.

Top Ten Holdings

1. Philip Morris	6. Citicorp
2. Federal National Mortgage Association	7. British Petroleum
	8. United Technologies
3. American Express	9. Bell South
4. NYNEX	10. Burlington Northern Santa Fe
5. Schlumberger	

Asset Mix: Common stocks: 92%; Cash/equivalents: 8%
Total Net Assets: $6.6 billion

Fees

Front-end load	*None*
Redemption fee	*None*
12b-1 fee	*None*
Management fee	0.70%
Other expenses	0.27
Total annual expense	0.97%
Minimum initial investment	$2,500
Minimum subsequent investment	$250

Services

Telephone exchanges	*Yes*
Automatic withdrawal	*Yes*
Automatic checking deduction	*Yes*
Retirement plan/IRA	*Yes*
Instant redemption	*Yes*
Financial statements	*Semiannual*
Income distributions	*Annual*
Capital gains distributions	*Annual*
Portfolio manager—years	1
Number of funds in family	210

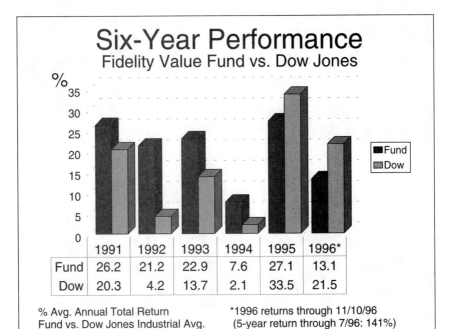

Six-Year Performance
Fidelity Value Fund vs. Dow Jones

	1991	1992	1993	1994	1995	1996*
Fund	26.2	21.2	22.9	7.6	27.1	13.1
Dow	20.3	4.2	13.7	2.1	33.5	21.5

% Avg. Annual Total Return
Fund vs. Dow Jones Industrial Avg.

*1996 returns through 11/10/96
(5-year return through 7/96: 141%)

62

John Hancock Global Technology Fund

SECTOR

John Hancock Funds
101 Huntington Avenue
Boston, MA 02199-7603

Fund managers: Barry Gordon
and Mark Klee
Fund objective: Sector fund

Toll-free: 800-225-5291
In-state: 617-375-1500
Fax: 617-375-1819

Performance	★ ★ ★ ★
Consistency	★ ★ ★ ★ ★
Fees/Services	★ ★
NTTFX	**11 Points**

You can't question the success of the John Hancock Global Technology Fund. It's been an outstanding fund for a number of years.

But the name's got to go.

To call this fund "Global" is like calling Fargo cosmopolitan. Scan the fund's top 10 holdings and you won't find a single stock from outside North America. Its foreign holdings, in fact, recently ebbed to just 10 percent of total assets—and much of that was in foreign phone services such as Telefonos de Mexico and Hong Kong Telecommunications.

Over the past ten years, the fund has posted average annual returns of about 12 percent. A $10,000 investment in the fund ten years ago would now be worth about $31,000.

In all, the fund has about 50 stocks holdings. Its leading industrial segments are computer software, which accounts for 24 percent of total assets; electronics, 20 percent; telecommunications, 11 percent; and computer services, 10 percent.

Fund managers Barry Gordon and Mark Klee take a fairly conservative trading approach, with a 70 percent annual portfolio turnover ratio.

The managers take a top-down stock selection approach, first identifying the fastest-growing sectors of the technology area, then ferreting out the most promising stocks within that sector.

PERFORMANCE

The fund has enjoyed excellent growth over the past five years. Including dividends and capital gains distributions, the Global Technology Fund has provided a total return for the past five years (through mid-1996) of 174 percent. A $10,000 investment in 1991 would have grown to about $37,000 five years later. Average annual return: 22.4 percent.

CONSISTENCY

The fund has been very consistent, outperforming the Dow Jones Industrial Average each of the past five years through 1995 (but it trailed the Dow through the first half of 1996). The fund's biggest year was 1995, when it jumped 46.5 percent.

FEES/SERVICES/MANAGEMENT

The fund charges a 5 percent front-end load. Its total annual expense ratio of 1.67 percent (including a 0.3 percent 12b-1 fee and a 0.82 percent management fee) is a little high for a front-end load fund. Its minimum initial investment of $1,000 and minimum subsequent investment of $1 compare favorably with other funds.

The fund offers all the standard services such as retirement account availability, automatic withdrawal, and automatic checking account deduction. However, the fund loses a point on one service issue. We made three calls to the company service line to request an annual report, and each time they sent us a prospectus, but no annual. After the fourth call, the company finally sent a report, but it was more than a year old, and it was a semiannual, not an annual.

The management team of Barry Gordon and Mark Klee have been with the fund since 1983. John Hancock offers 40 funds and allows shareholders to switch from fund to fund by telephone.

Top Ten Holdings

1. Computer Associates Int'l	6. Microsoft
2. UAL	7. United Technologies
3. Thermo Electron	8. AMR
4. Parametric Technology	9. Newbridge Network
5. Adaptec	10. Oracle

Asset Mix: Common stocks: 86%; Cash/equivalents: 14%
Total Net Assets: $171 million

Fees

Front-end load	5.00%
Redemption fee	*None*
12b-1 fee	0.30%
Management fee	0.82
Other expenses	0.55
Total annual expense	1.67%
Minimum initial investment	$1,000
Minimum subsequent investment	$1

Services

Telephone exchanges	*Yes*
Automatic withdrawal	*Yes*
Automatic checking deduction	*Yes*
Retirement plan/IRA	*Yes*
Instant redemption	*Yes*
Financial statements	*Semiannual*
Income distributions	*Annual*
Capital gains distributions	*Annual*
Portfolio managers—years	14
Number of funds in family	40

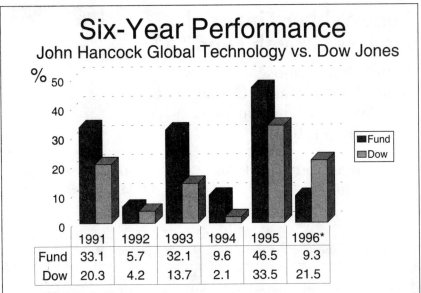

Six-Year Performance
John Hancock Global Technology vs. Dow Jones

	1991	1992	1993	1994	1995	1996*
Fund	33.1	5.7	32.1	9.6	46.5	9.3
Dow	20.3	4.2	13.7	2.1	33.5	21.5

% Annual Total Return
Fund vs. Dow Jones Industrial Avg.

*1996 returns through 11/10/96
(5-year return through 7/96: 174%)

63

PaineWebber Financial Services Growth Fund "A"

SECTOR

PaineWebber Funds
Mutual Funds Finance Department
1285 Avenue of the Americas
New York, NY 10019

Fund manager: Karen Levy Finkel
Fund objective: Sector fund

Toll-free: 800-647-1568
In-state: 201-902-7341
Fax: 212-713-4715

Performance	★ ★ ★ ★ ★
Consistency	★ ★ ★
Fees/Services	★ ★ ★
PREAX	**11 Points**

The banking business has been booming in recent years, which is one key reason the PaineWebber Regional Financial Growth Fund has soared 192 percent the past five years. Founded in 1986, the fund invests in a variety of regional banks, insurance companies, money centers, and other financial institutions.

Over the past ten years, the fund has had an average annual return of about 15 percent. A $10,000 investment in the fund ten years ago would now be worth about $40,000.

Fund manager Karen Levy Finkel has sifted out many of the most successful banks from each region of the country. The Bank of New York, BayBanks in Massachusetts, Florida's Barnett Banks, and Minnesota-based Norwest Bank are among approximately 75 top-tier regional bank and financial stocks that make up the fund's $64 million portfolio.

Finkel takes a buy-and-hold approach, with a very low 14 percent annual portfolio turnover ratio.

The fund focuses on stocks of banks that are located in geographic regions experiencing strong growth, are well managed and currently providing above-average returns on assets and shareholder equity, and are expanding into new services or geographic areas.

Eastern banks account for 17 percent of the fund's assets; Southern banks make up 10 percent; Midwestern banks make up 15 percent; and Western banks account for 11 percent. Financial services companies make up about 14 percent of the portfolio. The fund also invests in insurance companies and money center banks.

PERFORMANCE

The Financial Services Growth Fund has enjoyed exceptional growth over the past five years. Including dividends and capital gains distributions, the fund has provided a total return for the past five years of 192 percent. A $10,000 investment in 1991 would have grown to about $29,000 five years later. Average annual return: 23.9 percent.

CONSISTENCY

Like many sector funds, the Regional Financial Growth Fund has been somewhat volatile, trailing the Dow Jones Industrial Average three of the five years from 1991 through 1995 (and it was trailing the Dow through the first half of 1996). Its biggest gain came in 1991, when it jumped 65.5 percent (compared with a 20.3 percent rise in the Dow).

FEES/SERVICES/MANAGEMENT

The Regional Financial Growth Fund "A" has a front-end load of 4.5 percent. Its total annual expense ratio of 1.45 percent (including a 0.25 percent 12b-1 fee and a 0.70 percent management fee) is about average among load funds. The fund is also offered in "B" shares, which carry a 5 percent redemption fee that drops to zero over six years. But "B" shares carry a much higher 2.22 percent annual expense ratio.

The fund offers most of the standard mutual fund services such as retirement account availability, automatic withdrawal, and automatic checking account deduction. Its minimum initial investment of $1,000 and minimum subsequent investment of $100 are in line with other funds.

Karen Levy Finkel has managed the fund since its inception in 1986. The PaineWebber fund family includes 64 funds.

Top Ten Holdings

1. First Empire State
2. Norwest
3. Bank of New York
4. Zions Bancorp
5. Chemical Banking

6. CCB Financial
7. Federal National Mortgage Association
8. Mercantile Bancorp
9. Marshall & Ilsley
10. Citicorp

Asset Mix: Common stocks: 83%; Cash/equivalents: 17%
Total Net Assets: $64 million

Fees

Front-end load	4.50%
Redemption fee	*None*
12b-1 fee	0.25
Management fee	0.70
Other expenses	0.50
Total annual expense	1.45%
Minimum initial investment	$1000
Minimum subsequent investment	$100

Services

Telephone exchanges	*No*
Automatic withdrawal	*Yes*
Automatic checking deduction	*Yes*
Retirement plan	*Yes*
Instant redemption	*Yes*
Financial statements	*Semiannual*
Income distributions	*Annual*
Capital gains distributions	*Annual*
Portfolio manager—years	11
Number of funds in family	64

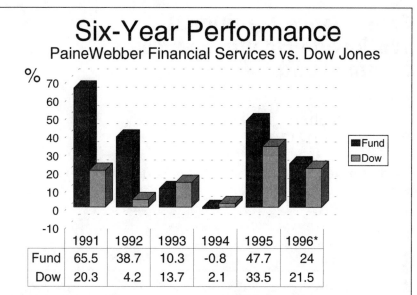

Six-Year Performance
PaineWebber Financial Services vs. Dow Jones

	1991	1992	1993	1994	1995	1996*
Fund	65.5	38.7	10.3	-0.8	47.7	24
Dow	20.3	4.2	13.7	2.1	33.5	21.5

% Annual Total Return
Fund vs. Dow Jones Industrial Avg.

*1996 returns through 11/10/96
(5-year return through 7/96: 192%)

64

Eaton Vance Traditional Worldwide Health Science Income Fund

SECTOR

Eaton Vance Group
24 Federal Street, 5th Floor
Boston, MA 02110

Fund manager: Samuel D. Isaly
Fund objective: Sector fund

Toll-free: 800-225-6265
In-state: 617-482-8260
Fax: 617-542-8672

Performance	★ ★ ★ ★
Consistency	★ ★ ★
Fees/Services	★ ★ ★ ★
MRIFX	**11 Points**

Fund manager Samuel Isaly scours the globe in search of the world's top emerging medical stocks. Foreign stocks account for well over half of the fund's total assets. Formerly the Capstone Medical Research Investment trust, the fund was purchased in 1996 by Eaton Vance.

Most of the fund's assets are in little-known emerging stocks such as Cyto Therapeutics, Procept, and SangStat Medical. Pfizer and Warner-Lambert are the only household names among the roughly 30 stocks in the portfolio.

Opened in 1985, the Health Science Income Fund has about 41 percent of its assets in North American stocks. Outside the United States, the fund's greatest concentration of assets is in stocks from the Far East, which account for about 34 percent of assets. Its European holdings account for about 29 percent of assets.

The fund invests in several types of medical stocks: pharmaceuticals, biotechnology companies, medical and dental equipment manufacturers and suppliers, hospital suppliers, hospital management companies, nursing centers, and diagnostic centers. In selecting stocks for the fund, Isaly considers several factors. He looks at the usual financial considerations such as revenue, earnings, and dividend growth, and he examines the company's commitment to research and development, with a bias toward companies that invest heavily in R&D.

Over the past ten years, the fund has posted an average annual return of about 15 percent. A $10,000 investment in the fund ten years ago would now be worth about $42,000.

Isaly takes a long-term investment approach. The fund has a modest annual portfolio turnover ratio of about 45%.

PERFORMANCE

The fund has enjoyed exceptional growth over the past five years. Including dividends and capital gains distributions, the Health Science Income Fund has provided a total return for the past five years (through mid-1996) of 186 percent. A $10,000 investment in 1991 would have grown to about $29,000 five years later. Average annual return: 23.4 percent.

CONSISTENCY

The fund has been a bit inconsistent, trailing the Dow Jones Industrial Average two of the five years from 1991 to 1995 (but it was well ahead of the Dow through the first half of 1996). The fund had a 6.4 percent decline in 1994, but bounced back with a huge 61.2 percent increase in 1995.

FEES/SERVICES/MANAGEMENT

This is a true no-load fund—no fee to buy and no fee to sell. However, it still has an inordinately high annual expense ratio of 2.44 percent (including a 0.25 percent 12b-1 fee and a 1.25 percent management fee).

The fund offers all the standard services such as retirement account availability, automatic withdrawal, and automatic checking account deduction. Its minimum initial investment of $200, and $50 minimum subsequent investment, compare very favorably with other funds.

Samuel Isaly has managed the fund since 1989. The Eaton Vance fund family includes about 35 funds and allows shareholders to switch from fund to fund by telephone.

Top Ten Holdings

1. Ares-Serono	6. Takeda Chemical Industries
2. Altana AG	7. Taisho Pharmaceutical
3. Banyu Pharmaceutical	8. Vertex Pharmaceutical
4. Sandoz AG	9. Sankyo
5. Teikoku Hormone	10. Warner-Lambert

Asset Mix: Common stock: 100%
Total Net Assets: $47 million

Fees

Front-end load	*None*
Redemption fee	*None*
12b-1 fee	0.25%
Management fee	1.25
Other expenses	0.94
Total annual expense	2.44%
Minimum initial investment	$200
Minimum subsequent investment	$1

Services

Telephone exchanges	*Yes*
Automatic withdrawal	*Yes*
Automatic checking deduction	*Yes*
Retirement plan/IRA	*Yes*
Instant redemption	*Yes*
Financial statements	*Semiannual*
Income distributions	*Annual*
Capital gains distributions	*Annual*
Portfolio manager—years	8
Number of funds in family	5

Six-Year Performance
Eaton Vance Worldwide Health vs. Dow Jones

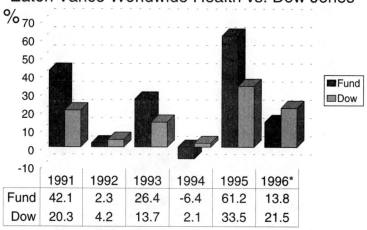

	1991	1992	1993	1994	1995	1996*
Fund	42.1	2.3	26.4	-6.4	61.2	13.8
Dow	20.3	4.2	13.7	2.1	33.5	21.5

% Annual Total Return   *1996 returns through 11/10/96)
Fund vs. Dow Jones Industrial Avg.   (5-year return through 7/96: 186%)

65

Fidelity Select Telecommunications Portfolio

SECTOR

Fidelity Investments
82 Devonshire Street
Boston, MA 02109

Fund manager: David Felman
Fund objective: Sector fund

Toll-free: 800-544-8888
In-state: 801-534-1910
Fax: 617-476-9753

Performance	★ ★ ★ ★
Consistency	★ ★ ★
Fees/Services	★ ★ ★ ★
FSTCX	**11 Points**

Telecommunications has been one of the hottest industries worldwide for the past several years—and it has also been one of the hottest sectors on Wall Street. The Fidelity Select Telecommunications Portfolio, which invests in communications-related stocks around the world, has ridden the crest of the telecommunications tidal wave.

Over the past ten years, the fund has posted an average annual return of 18 percent. A $10,000 investment in the fund ten years ago would now be worth about $53,000.

The fund invests both in service companies such as AT&T and Sprint and communications equipment manufacturers such as Cabletron and Cisco Systems.

The telecommunications industry continues to be a volatile but growing sector. Fierce competition in the cellular phone business, for instance, has severely cut profits. "No one knows for sure who's going to buy whom, who's going to build what, or where prices are going to end up," explains fund manager David Felman. "On the other hand, there's a strong sense of growth and opportunity pervading the industry. To take just one example, demand for phone service continues to grow as consumers see the need for more than one phone line."

The dominant segment within the Telecommunications Fund is the telephone services industry, which accounts for 54 percent of assets. Other leading areas are data communications equipment, 6 percent; cellular and communication services, 4 percent; and computer services, 3 percent.

In all, the fund has about 75 stock holdings, many of which are foreign phone companies. Felman maintains a fairly active trading policy, with an annual portfolio turnover ratio of 107 percent.

PERFORMANCE

The fund has enjoyed exceptional growth over the past five years. Including dividends and capital gains distributions, the Fidelity Select Telecommunications Portfolio has provided a total return for the past five years (through mid-1996) of 160 percent. A $10,000 investment in 1991 would have grown to $26,000 five years later. Average annual return: 21 percent.

CONSISTENCY

The fund has been consistent for a sector fund, outperforming the Dow Jones Industrial Average four of the five years through 1995 (although it trailed the Dow through the first half of 1996). Its biggest year was 1991 when it moved up 59 percent.

FEES/SERVICES/MANAGEMENT

The fund has a low front-end load of 3 percent and a maximum redemption fee of 0.75 percent, if shares are sold within 30 days of purchase. Otherwise a $7.50 fee is charged upon redemption. The fund's total annual expense ratio of 1.55 percent (with no 12b-1 fee) is about average among load funds.

The fund offers all the standard services such as retirement account availability, automatic withdrawal, and automatic checking account deduction. Its minimum initial investment of $2,500 and minimum subsequent investment of $250 are a little high compared with other funds. David Felman has managed the fund since 1994. The Fidelity fund family includes about 210 funds.

Top Ten Holdings

1. Cisco Systems
2. Frontier
3. GTE
4. Bell South
5. Ameritech

6. NYNEX
7. WorldCom
8. LCI International
9. AT&T
10. HBO

Asset Mix: Common stocks: 78%; Preferred stocks: 3%
Cash/equivalents: 19%
Total Net Assets: $468 million

Fees

Front-end load	3.00%
Redemption fee	$7.50
12b-1 fee	*None*
Management fee	0.61
Other expenses	0.94
Total annual expense	1.55%
Minimum initial investment	$2,500
Minimum subsequent investment	$250

Services

Telephone exchanges	*Yes*
Automatic withdrawal	*Yes*
Automatic checking deduction	*Yes*
Retirement plan/IRA	*Yes*
Instant redemption	*Yes*
Financial statements	*Semiannual*
Income distributions	*Semiannual*
Capital gains distributions	*Semiannual*
Portfolio manager—years	3
Number of funds in family	210

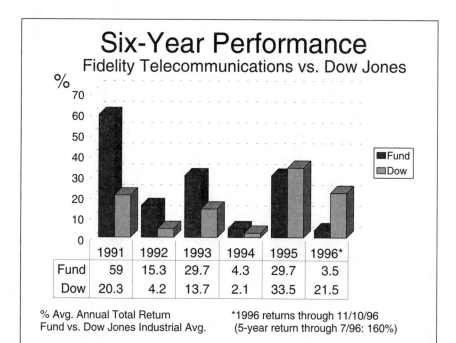

Six-Year Performance
Fidelity Telecommunications vs. Dow Jones

	1991	1992	1993	1994	1995	1996*
Fund	59	15.3	29.7	4.3	29.7	3.5
Dow	20.3	4.2	13.7	2.1	33.5	21.5

% Avg. Annual Total Return
Fund vs. Dow Jones Industrial Avg.

*1996 returns through 11/10/96
(5-year return through 7/96: 160%)

66
Fidelity Select Regional Banks Portfolio

SECTOR

Fidelity Investments
82 Devonshire Street
Boston, MA 02109

Fund manager: Remy Trafelet
Fund objective: Sector fund

Toll-free: 800-544-8888
In-state: 801-534-1910
Fax: 617-476-9753

Performance	★ ★ ★ ★ ★
Consistency	★ ★ ★
Fees/Services	★ ★ ★
FSRBX	**11 Points**

The volatile regional bank stock sector has been on a strong run through the 1990s. A robust economy and relatively low interest rates have been good for business at banks throughout the United States. And that's been good news for investors of the Fidelity Select Regional Banks Portfolio, which has posted returns of more than 40 percent two of the past five years.

New fund manager Remy Trafelet, who joined the fund in January 1996, also attributes some of the growth in the banking sector to consolidations, cost-cutting measures, and share buy-back programs.

Trafelet said he expects the fee-based services banks now offer, such as mutual funds, securities clearing, and order ticket processing, to continue to boost bank stock prices.

Introduced in 1986, the fund has posted average annual returns of about 16 percent over the past ten years. A $10,000 investment in the fund ten years ago would now be worth about $35,000.

The fund invests in large and midsize regional banks throughout the country, as well as companies involved in discount brokerage, leasing, and insurance. Its highest concentration of holdings is in the Northeast (25 percent of assets), the Midwest (20 percent), and the West (16 percent).

The fund manager is fairly aggressive in his trading approach, with an annual portfolio turnover ratio of 106 percent.

PERFORMANCE

The fund has enjoyed tremendous returns over the past five years. Including dividends and capital gains distributions, the Regional Bank Fund has provided a total return for the past five years (through mid-1996) of 237 percent. A $10,000 investment in 1991 would have grown to about $34,000 five years later. Average annual return: 27.5 percent.

CONSISTENCY

The fund has been somewhat inconsistent (which is typical of sector funds). It trailed the Dow Jones Industrial Average two of the five years from 1991 through 1995 (and again through the first half of 1996). Its worst year was 1990, when it dropped 20.6 percent, but it bounced back the next year with a 65.7 percent gain.

FEES/SERVICES/MANAGEMENT

The fund has a low front-end load of 3 percent and a maximum redemption fee of 0.75 percent if it's sold out within 30 days. Otherwise a fee of $7.50 is imposed upon sale. The fund's annual expense ratio of 1.47 percent (with no 12b-1 fee) is about average among load funds.

The fund offers all the standard services such as retirement account availability, automatic withdrawal, and automatic checking account deduction. Its minimum initial investment of $2,500 and minimum subsequent investment of $250 are a little high compared with other funds.

Fund manager Remy Trafelet has been with the fund only since 1996. This is his first assignment as a fund manager with Fidelity, although he has been with the company since 1992. The Fidelity fund family includes 210 funds.

Top Ten Holdings

1. Fleet Financial Group
2. BankAmerica
3. Bank of New York
4. Chemical Banking
5. American Express
6. Household International
7. First Bank System
8. Boatmen's Bancshares
9. Chase Manhattan
10. Citicorp

Asset Mix: Common stocks: 92%; Cash/equivalents: 8%
Total Net Assets: $315 million

Fees

Front-end load	3.00%
Redemption fee (max)	$7.50
12b-1 fee	*None*
Management fee	0.61
Other expenses	0.86
Total annual expense	1.47%
Minimum initial investment	$2,500
Minimum subsequent investment	$250

Services

Telephone exchanges	*Yes*
Automatic withdrawal	*Yes*
Automatic checking deduction	*Yes*
Retirement plan/IRA	*Yes*
Instant redemption	*Yes*
Financial statements	*Semiannual*
Income distributions	*Semiannual*
Capital gains distributions	*Semiannual*
Portfolio manager—years	1
Number of funds in family	210

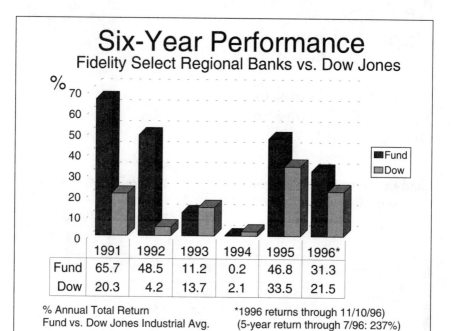

Six-Year Performance
Fidelity Select Regional Banks vs. Dow Jones

	1991	1992	1993	1994	1995	1996*
Fund	65.7	48.5	11.2	0.2	46.8	31.3
Dow	20.3	4.2	13.7	2.1	33.5	21.5

% Annual Total Return
Fund vs. Dow Jones Industrial Avg.

*1996 returns through 11/10/96)
(5-year return through 7/96: 237%)

67

Oppenheimer Discovery Fund "A"

GROWTH

Oppenheimer Funds, Inc.
3410 South Galena Street
Denver, CO 80231

Fund manager: Jay W. Tracey III
Fund objective: Growth and income

Toll-free: 800-525-7048
In-state: 303-671-3200
Fax: 303-743-4269

Performance	★ ★ ★ ★
Consistency	★ ★ ★
Fees/Services	★ ★ ★
OPOCX	**10 Points**

Oppenheimer Discovery Fund manager Jay W. Tracey III specializes in discovering very small, young companies that haven't yet drawn the attention of Wall Street. The vast majority of the fund's 180 stock holdings are little-known, over-the-counter stocks such as Ostech, MedCath, and Rocky Mountain Chocolate Factory.

Tracey takes a bottom-up approach, focusing on individual companies rather than broad industries. "We believe that to invest successfully in the small-cap market, it is better to identify very good individual companies that have carved out a unique market niche, rather than bet on broad industry sectors," explains Tracey. "Our primary focus is on a company and its management; then, only after that careful analysis do we look for anything on the economic horizon that might have either a negative or positive impact."

Since its inception in 1986, the fund has had an average annual return of about 17.5 percent. A $10,000 investment in the fund in 1986 would have grown to about $50,000 ten years later.

The fund manager is fairly aggressive in his trading policy, with an annual portfolio turnover ratio of 83 percent. The fund stays almost fully invested in the market most of the time.

The fund is loaded with technology stocks. Leading sectors include computer software and hardware, 14 percent; health and medical, 20 percent; retail specialty, 12 percent; and telecommunications, 9 percent.

PERFORMANCE

The fund has enjoyed exceptional growth over the past five years. Including dividends and capital gains distributions, the Discovery Fund has provided a total return for the past five years (through mid-1996) of 178 percent. A $10,000 investment in 1991 would have grown to about $28,000 five years later. Average annual return: 22.7 percent.

CONSISTENCY

The fund has outperformed the Dow Jones Industrial Average four of the five years through 1995 (and again through the first half of 1996). But it has also had wide swings over the years, dipping 15 percent in 1990, soaring 72 percent in 1991, and dropping 11 percent in 1994.

FEES/SERVICES/MANAGEMENT

The fund has a 5.75 percent front-end sales load, and an annual expense ratio of 1.33 percent (including a 0.24 percent 12b-1 fee and a 0.71 percent management fee), which is about average among all funds.

The fund offers all the standard services such as retirement account availability, automatic withdrawal, and automatic checking account deduction. Its minimum initial investment of $1,000 and subsequent investment minimum of $25 compare favorably to other funds.

Jay W. Tracey III has managed the fund since 1991. The Oppenheimer family includes 44 funds and allows shareholders to switch from fund to fund by telephone.

Top Ten Holdings

1. Omnicare
2. Tommy Hilfiger
3. Watson Pharmaceuticals
4. LCI International
5. United Waste Systems
6. PhyCor
7. Sunglass Hut Int'l
8. HBO
9. JP Foodservice
10. Glenayre Technologies

Asset Mix: Common stocks: 89%; Preferred stocks: 1%;
Cash/equivalents: 10%
Total Net Assets: $1.1 billion

Fees

Front-end load	5.75%
Redemption fee	*None*
12b-1 fee	0.24
Management fee	0.71
Other expenses	0.38
Total annual expense	1.33%
Minimum initial investment	$1,000
Minimum subsequent investment	$25

Services

Telephone exchanges	*Yes*
Automatic withdrawal	*Yes*
Automatic checking deduction	*Yes*
Retirement plan/IRA	*Yes*
Instant redemption	*Yes*
Financial statements	*Annual*
Income distributions	*Annual*
Capital gains distributions	*Annual*
Portfolio manager—years	6
Number of funds in family	44

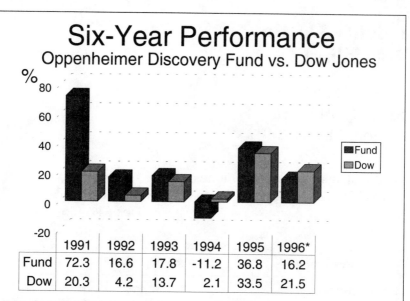

Six-Year Performance
Oppenheimer Discovery Fund vs. Dow Jones

	1991	1992	1993	1994	1995	1996*
Fund	72.3	16.6	17.8	-11.2	36.8	16.2
Dow	20.3	4.2	13.7	2.1	33.5	21.5

% Annual Total Return
Fund vs. Dow Jones Industrial Avg.

*1996 returns through 11/10/96
(5-year return through 7/96: 178%)

68

Fidelity Destiny Portfolio I

LONG TERM

Fidelity Investments
82 Devonshire Street
Boston, MA 02109

Fund manager: George Vanderheiden
Fund objective: Long-term growth

Toll-free: 800-522-7297
In-state: 801-534-1910
Fax: 617-476-9753

Performance	★ ★ ★
Consistency	★ ★ ★ ★ ★
Fees/Services	★ ★
FDESX	**10 Points**

Fidelity Destiny Portfolio manager George Vanderheiden likes to buy stocks when no one else wants them. "It can be lonely to buy when you don't have much company, but that's when you get the best values. I like to buy stocks when most of the risk has already been squeezed out." Vanderheiden, who has managed the Destiny Fund since 1980, has been with Fidelity since 1971. The Destiny I Portfolio (and its clone, Destiny II) invest in major blue chip companies with strong earnings growth that are selling at an attractive price.

"Wall Street lives on perception," says Vanderheiden. Sometimes those perceptions are responsible for pushing the price of stocks of certain industries beyond reasonable levels. "I try to avoid fads. When the cellular industry got hot a few years ago, I didn't know how to value those stocks. They had no earnings." Instead of buying what Wall Street was buying, Vanderheiden bought the British cellular company Vodafone. "It had good earnings, and was the cheapest stock in the group. It's been a great stock.

"A lot of money has been lost in fad stocks, and a lot of money has been made in some very dull stocks."

Vanderheiden sells at the first sign of trouble. "As soon as I see the first crack, I get out. I want to sell my mistakes quickly. For instance, if I buy a stock thinking the company's new concept will do well, and it doesn't work out, I'll sell. Usually the first piece of bad news is not the last piece of bad news."

Vanderheiden is well aware that not all of his picks are going to go up, so he tries to build the largest positions in the stocks he believes have the best long-term promise. "You want to make sure you've put a lot of assets in your 'home run' stocks. I could have a 30–70 win-loss record with my stock picks, but still do fabulously if I have the mass of my assets in the good stocks."

He is fairly modest in his trading activity, with a 55 percent annual portfolio turnover ratio. His top sectors are finance, 17 percent of assets; technology, 9 percent; durables, 8 percent; energy, 8 percent; and nondurables, 7 percent.

Vanderheiden, who has long been one of the most well-respected fund managers in the business, has put together the following top ten list of investment tips (reprinted with permission):

Ten Commandments for Reaching Financial Heaven

1. *Thou shalt avoid the BIG loss.* When you buy a stock, don't be blinded by the upside potential and ignore the downside risk. Moderate gains every year are better than big gains and big losses. Remember, if you start with $100 and you're up 50 percent one year and down 50 percent the next, you're left with only $75. (Corollary: There is no limit to how bad things can get.)
2. *Thou shalt develop conviction in your ideas.* Write down your reasons for buying a stock and if a stock goes down for a temporary or unrelated reason, you won't be panicked out of it. (Corollary: Where all think alike, no one thinks very much.)
3. *Thou shalt invest with the person.* The business world is full of successful managers and proven moneymakers, and you can become their partners for the mere price of a stock. Stan Gault is a talented, GE-trained manager who helped turn Rubbermaid into a premier growth company. The day he announced he was joining Goodyear, its stock went from $25 to $29. It never saw $29 again, and went straight to $75 over the next nine months. (Corollary: Trust everyone, but cut the cards.)

4. *Thou shalt honor pricing power.* Pricing power is the ability of companies to raise their prices well in excess of their costs or inflation. Companies with improving pricing power are stocks to own, and companies with deteriorating pricing power are stocks to sell. (Corollary: The price of a dinner varies inversely with the amount of light.)

5. *Thou shalt respect the force of government action.* As a government directs the full force of its resources at an objective, invest *with* the objective, not counter to it. When the U.S. government entered the space race in 1957, it launched a great technology bull market that lasted for over a decade. The advent of Medicare in 1964 launched a multiyear bull market in health care stocks. (Corollary: Government expands to absorb revenue and then some.)

6. *Thou shalt recognize fear and greed in yourselves and in others, and act accordingly.* Someone once said, "The stock market is only distantly related to economics; it is a function of fear, apprehension, and greed, all superimposed on a business cycle." The more gut-wrenching a decision, the bigger the potential for capital gains. (Corollary: The chief cause of problems is solutions.)

7. *Thou shalt learn how to live with uncertainty and failure.* The only certainty about the stock market is that there is none. Every successful investor constantly makes mistakes. Don't be afraid of failure. While Babe Ruth had 714 homers, he also had 1,330 strikeouts. (Corollary: The person who can smile when things fail has thought of someone else to blame.)

8. *Thou shalt avoid investment bias.* A good stock can be found anywhere, whether it is a cyclical, growth stock, value stock, or high-yielder. (Corollary: A bird in the hand is safer than overhead.)

9. *Thou shalt not be frozen by inertia when events change.* Most investors don't recognize turning points and wrongly stay on their existing course after the dynamics have clearly changed. After the Allies attacked Iraq January 16, 1991, the market surged 115 points instead of going down as everyone expected. Something changed, and the market moved up more than 700 points over the next two years. (Corollary: When in charge, ponder. When in trouble, delegate. When in doubt, mumble.)

10. *Thou shalt have patience.* Start with modest expectations about your stocks and be prepared to be patient. In 1919, Coca-Cola went public and gave 5,000 shares of its stock (worth $110,000) as part of the underwriting fee to the two underwriters, J.P. Morgan

Bank and the Trust Company of Georgia (now SunTrust Banks). J.P. Morgan sold its stock, but SunTrust kept its original shares. After years of growth and stock splits, it now amounts to 24 million shares worth $900 million. (Corollary: Friends may come and go, but enemies accumulate.)

Final rule: As George Bernard Shaw wrote, "There are no golden rules." In other words, once you think you've found the key to the market, someone always comes along and changes the lock. Successful investing requires imagination, independent thinking, patience, and a touch of contrariness, rather than a mechanistic following of rules.

PERFORMANCE

The fund has enjoyed excellent growth over the past five years. Including dividends and capital gains distributions, the Destiny Fund has provided a total return for the past five years (through mid-1996) of 153 percent. A $10,000 investment in Destiny I in 1991 would have grown to about $25,000 five years later. Average annual return: 20.4 percent.

CONSISTENCY

The Destiny Fund has been very consistent, outperforming the Dow Jones Industrial Average five consecutive years through 1995 (but it trailed the Dow through the first half of 1996).

FEES/SERVICES/MANAGEMENT

To buy the Fidelity Destiny Fund (I or II)—or even to get information on the fund—you must go through a stockbroker. The fund has a very complicated fee structure. The plan calls for investors to make automatic monthly contributions to the plan, varying from $50 a month to $10,000 a month. The more you contribute, the lower the sales fee. The maximum fee is a very steep 8.67 percent. The fund has a total annual expense ratio of 0.68 percent (with no 12b-1 fee).

The fund offers most of the standard services such as retirement account availability, automatic withdrawal, and automatic checking account deduction.

George Vanderheiden has managed the fund since 1980. The Fidelity fund family includes 210 funds.

Top Ten Holdings

1. Federal National Mortgage
   Association
2. Philip Morris
3. General Motors
4. Fleet Financial Group
5. Compaq Computer

6. Royal Dutch Petroleum
7. Vodafone Group PLC (ADR)
8. Federal Home Loan
   Mortgage Corp.
9. Columbia/HCA Healthcare
10. E.I. du Pont de Nemours

Asset Mix: Common stocks: 81%; Corporate bonds: 15%;
Cash/equivalents: 4%
Total Net Assets: $4.3 billion

Fees

Front-end load (max)	8.67%
Redemption fee (max)	$2.50
12b-1 fee	*None*
Management fee	0.65
Other expenses	0.03
Total annual expense	0.68%
Minimum initial investment	$50/mo.
Minimum subsequent investment	$50/mo.

Services

Telephone exchanges	*No*
Automatic withdrawal	*Yes*
Automatic checking deduction	*Yes*
Retirement plan/IRA	*Yes*
Instant redemption	*Yes*
Financial statements	*Semiannual*
Income distributions	*Annual*
Capital gains distributions	*Annual*
Portfolio manager—years	16
Number of funds in family	210

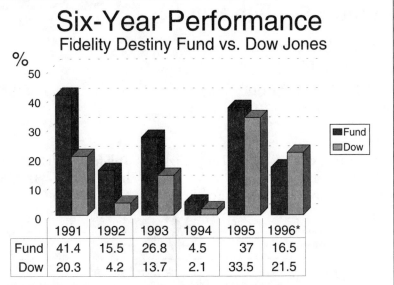

Six-Year Performance
Fidelity Destiny Fund vs. Dow Jones

	1991	1992	1993	1994	1995	1996*
Fund	41.4	15.5	26.8	4.5	37	16.5
Dow	20.3	4.2	13.7	2.1	33.5	21.5

% Annual Total Return
Fund vs. Dow Jones Industrial Avg.

*1996 returns through 11/10/96
(5-year return through 7/96: 153%)

69

Mentor Growth Fund

LONG TERM

Mentor Investment Group
Riverfront Plaza
901 East Byrd Street
Richmond, VA 23211

Fund managers: Ted Price, Linda Ziglar,   **Toll-free:** 800-869-6042
   Jeff Drummond, Ed Rick   **In-state:** 804-782-3754
Fund objective: Long-term growth   **Fax:** 804-782-6604

Performance	★ ★ ★
Consistency	★ ★ ★ ★
Fees/Services	★ ★ ★
MGRTX	**10 Points**

The Mentor Growth Fund invests primarily in little-known small and midsized stocks that the fund managers believe have the potential for strong, consistent earnings growth.

The fund management team, led by Ted Price, with the fund since its inception in 1985, looks at several criteria in selecting stocks. They want companies with emerging leadership in rapidly growing industries, with strong market share, proprietary products and services, and product leadership in niche markets. Most of the stocks in the Mentor Growth portfolio have market capitalizations of under $500 million.

Since its inception in 1985, the fund has grown at an average annual rate of about 14 percent. Its ten-year average annual growth rate is just 12 percent. A $10,000 investment in the fund ten years ago would now be worth about $32,000.

The fund managers take a fairly conservative trading approach, with an annual portfolio turnover ratio of 70 percent. The fund managers are quick to unload stocks at the first sign of trouble. They sell when quarterly earnings come in below expectations, when companies have unfavorable changes, and when the price drops dramatically relative to the market.

They also sell when a stock grows so quickly that it reaches an over-weighted position in the portfolio.

In all, the fund has about 100 stock holdings. The fund is heavily weighted in technology stocks, which account for 23 percent of total assets (primarily computer and communications stocks). Other leading sectors include health, 27 percent; consumer cyclicals, 15 percent; and financial, 8 percent. The fund stays almost fully invested in stocks most of the time.

PERFORMANCE

The fund has enjoyed excellent growth over the past five years. Including dividends and capital gains distributions, the Mentor Growth Fund has provided a total return for the past five years (through mid-1996) of 151 percent. A $10,000 investment in 1991 would have grown to about $25,000 five years later. Average annual return: 20.2 percent.

CONSISTENCY

The fund has been very consistent, outperforming the Dow Jones Industrial Average four of the five years from 1991 through 1995 (and again through the first half of 1996). The fund's biggest year was 1991 when it moved up 50.3 percent.

FEES/SERVICES/MANAGEMENT

The Mentor Growth Fund "A" shares have a front-end load of 5.75 percent. Its total annual expense ratio of 1.32 percent (with no 12b-1 fee) is well in line with other funds. The "B" shares have a 4 percent redemption fee (but no front-end load), and a much higher annual expense ratio of 2.08 percent.

The fund offers all the usual mutual fund services such as retirement account availability, automatic withdrawal, and automatic checking account deduction. Its minimum initial investment of $1,000 and minimum subsequent investment of $100 are in line with other funds.

Ted Price has managed the fund since its inception in 1985. He is now part of a management team that includes Linda Ziglar, Jeff Drummond, and Ed Rick. The Mentor fund family includes nine funds and allows shareholders to switch from fund to fund by telephone.

Top Ten Holdings

1. Career Horizons
2. Markel Corporation
3. Worldcom
4. Frontier Corp.
5. Accustaff

6. Regal Cinemas
7. Apple South
8. Health Management Associates
9. Medcath
10. Healthsource

Asset Mix: Common stocks: 89%; Cash/equivalents: 11%
Total Net Assets: $360 million

Fees

Front-end load	5.75%
Redemption fee	*None*
12b-1 fee	*None*
Management fee	0.70
Other expenses	0.37
Total annual expense	1.32%
Minimum initial investment	$1,000
Minimum subsequent investment	$100

Services

Telephone exchanges	*Yes*
Automatic withdrawal	*Yes*
Automatic checking deduction	*Yes*
Retirement plan/IRA	*Yes*
Instant redemption	*Yes*
Financial statements	*Semiannual*
Income distributions	*Annual*
Capital gains distributions	*Annual*
Portfolio manager—years	12
Number of funds in family	9

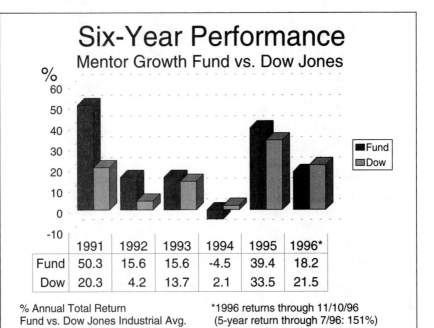

Six-Year Performance
Mentor Growth Fund vs. Dow Jones

	1991	1992	1993	1994	1995	1996*
Fund	50.3	15.6	15.6	-4.5	39.4	18.2
Dow	20.3	4.2	13.7	2.1	33.5	21.5

% Annual Total Return   *1996 returns through 11/10/96
Fund vs. Dow Jones Industrial Avg.   (5-year return through 7/96: 151%)

70

Piper Emerging Growth Fund

AGGRESSIVE

Piper Funds, Inc.
Piper Jaffray Tower
222 S. Ninth Street
Minneapolis, MN 55402

Fund manager: Sandra Shrewsbury
Fund objective: Aggressive growth

Toll-free: 800-866-7778
In-state: 612-342-6402
Fax: 612-342-1624

Performance	★ ★ ★
Consistency	★ ★ ★ ★
Fees/Services	★ ★ ★
PJEGX	**10 Points**

The Piper Emerging Growth Fund takes a distinctively regional approach, investing at least 65 percent of its assets in small to midsized companies with headquarters in states where Piper Jaffray has offices. In fact, recently the fund's top three holdings were Green Tree Financial, TCF Financial, and ADC Telecommunications—all of which are Minneapolis-based companies in Piper's backyard.

Fund manager Sandra Shrewsbury focuses on companies with annual revenues between $10 million and $1 billion, and market capitalizations between $250 million and $4 billion. The fund may also invest in some larger companies whose rates of earnings growth are expected to accelerate because of special factors such as new management, new products, changes in consumer demand, or changes in economic circumstances.

Opened in 1990, the Emerging Growth Fund has grown at an average annual rate of about 19 percent. A $10,000 investment in the fund at its inception in 1990 would have grown to about $29,000 six years later.

The fund is well-diversified across a wide range of industry groups. The leading sector is technology, which accounts for 18 percent of total assets. Other leading sectors include health care, 17 percent; finance, 12 percent; consumer services, 9 percent; and retail, 7 percent.

In all, the fund has about 80 stock holdings. It remains at least 90 percent invested in common stocks most of the time. The fund manager maintains a fairly conservative trading policy, with an annual portfolio turnover ratio of just 33 percent.

PERFORMANCE

The fund has enjoyed excellent growth over the past five years. Including dividends and capital gains distributions, the Piper Emerging Growth Fund has provided a total return for the past five years (through mid-1996) of 148 percent. A $10,000 investment in 1991 would have grown to about $25,000 five years later. Average annual return: 19.9 percent.

CONSISTENCY

The fund has been very consistent, outperforming the Dow Jones Industrial Average four of the five years from 1991 through 1995 (and again through the first half of 1996). The fund did have a 4.9 percent loss in 1994. Its biggest year was 1991 when it jumped 65.6 percent.

FEES/SERVICES/MANAGEMENT

The fund has a 4 percent front-end sales load, and an annual expense ratio of 1.24 percent (including a 0.32 percent 12b-1 fee and a 0.7 percent management fee), which is about average among load funds.

The fund offers all the standard services such as retirement account availability, automatic withdrawal, and automatic checking account deduction. Its minimum initial investment of $250 and subsequent investment minimum of $1 are very low compared with most other funds.

Sandra Shrewsbury has managed the fund since 1990. The Piper fund family includes 15 funds and allows shareholders to switch from fund to fund by telephone.

Top Ten Holdings

1. TCF Financial
2. Green Tree Financial
3. Thermo Electron
4. Medaphis
5. Tommy Hilfiger

6. Frontier
7. Infinity Broadcasting
8. WorldCom
9. Stewart Enterprises
10. Corporate Express

Asset Mix: Common stocks: 94%; Cash/equivalents: 6%
Total Net Assets: $296 million

Fees

Front-end load	4%
Redemption fee	*None*
12b-1 fee	0.32
Management fee	0.70
Other expenses	0.22
Total annual expense	1.24%
Minimum initial investment	$250
Minimum subsequent investment	$1

Services

Telephone exchanges	*Yes*
Automatic withdrawal	*Yes*
Automatic checking deduction	*Yes*
Retirement plan/IRA	*Yes*
Instant redemption	*Yes*
Financial statements	*Annual*
Income distributions	*Annual*
Capital gains distributions	*Annual*
Portfolio managers—years	7
Number of funds in family	15

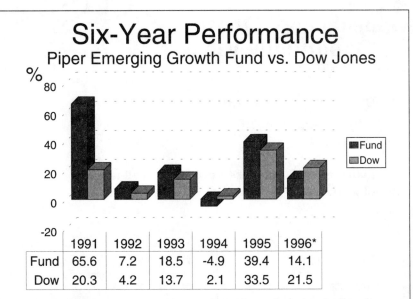

Six-Year Performance
Piper Emerging Growth Fund vs. Dow Jones

	1991	1992	1993	1994	1995	1996*
Fund	65.6	7.2	18.5	-4.9	39.4	14.1
Dow	20.3	4.2	13.7	2.1	33.5	21.5

% Annual Total Return
Fund vs. Dow Jones Industrial Avg.

*1996 returns through 11/10/96
(5-year return through 7/96: 148%)

71

Oppenheimer Quest for Opportunity Value Fund "A"

LONG TERM

Oppenheimer Funds, Inc.
3410 South Galena Street
Denver, CO 80231

Fund manager: Richard Glasebrook III
Fund objective: Long-term growth

Toll-free: 800-525-7048
In-state: 303-671-3200
Fax: 303-743-2808

Performance	★ ★ ★
Consistency	★ ★ ★ ★
Fees/Services	★ ★ ★
QVOPX	**10 Points**

As names go, this one fills the letterhead: the Oppenheimer Quest for Opportunity Value Fund "A." It also fills the bottom line. Since its inception in 1988, the OpQueOpVal Fund has been one of the nation's top performing funds, with an average annual return of 18 percent.

Fund manager Richard Glasebrook III has a different view of value than most investment managers. Standard procedure on Wall Street is to evaluate a stock's value based primarily on earnings and sales growth, but Glasebrook peers a bit deeper into the balance sheet to study the company's cash flow and return on capital. He prefers companies that have a high return on invested capital and that have a strong enough grip on their market niche to sustain that same level of return well into the future.

The portfolio consists of about 35 large capitalization stocks such as Wells Fargo, Union Pacific, and McDonnell Douglas. The portfolio has a decidedly low-tech feel. Banking and financial stocks make up 24 percent of assets, minerals and oil and gas account for 11 percent, paper makes up 7 percent, and aerospace accounts for 9 percent.

Glasebrook takes a conservative trading approach, with an annual portfolio turnover ratio of 42 percent. The fund generally stays heavily invested in stocks, although it recently had 20 percent of assets in short-term corporate notes.

PERFORMANCE

The fund has experienced strong growth over the past five years. Including dividends and capital gains distributions, the Opportunity Fund has provided a total return for the past five years (through mid-1996) of 145 percent. A $10,000 investment five years ago would have grown to about $24,500. Average annual return: 18.6 percent.

CONSISTENCY

The Opportunity Fund has been very consistent, outperforming the Dow Jones Industrial Average four of the five years from 1991 through 1995 (but it narrowly trailed the Dow through the first half of 1996). Its biggest year was 1991, when it jumped 51.4 percent (compared with a 20.3 percent rise in the Dow).

FEES/SERVICES/MANAGEMENT

The fund has a front-end load of 5.75 percent. Its total annual expense ratio of 1.69 percent (including a 0.5 percent 12b-1 fee and a 1 percent management fee) is about in line with most other funds.

The fund offers all the standard services such as retirement account availability, automatic withdrawal, and automatic checking account deduction. Its minimum initial investment of $1,000 and minimum subsequent investment of $250 compare well with most other funds.

Richard Glasebrook III has managed the fund since 1991. The Oppenheimer fund family includes 44 funds and allows shareholders to switch from fund to fund by telephone.

Top Ten Holdings

1. Wells Fargo
2. McDonnell Douglas
3. Federal Home Loan Mortgage Corp.
4. E.I. duPont de Nemours
5. Tenneco
6. Freeport-McMoRan/Gold B
7. Citicorp
8. Union Pacific
9. Countrywide Credit Industry
10. Intel

Asset Mix: Common stocks: 87%; Cash/equivalents: 13%
Total Net Assets: $559 million

Fees

Front-end load	5.75%
Redemption fee	*None*
12b-1 fee	0.50
Management fee	1.00
Other expenses	0.19
Total annual expense	1.69%
Minimum initial investment	$1,000
Minimum subsequent investment	$250

Services

Telephone exchanges	*Yes*
Automatic withdrawal	*Yes*
Automatic checking deduction	*Yes*
Retirement plan/IRA	*Yes*
Instant redemption	*Yes*
Financial statements	*Annual*
Income distributions	*Annual*
Capital gains distributions	*Annual*
Portfolio manager	6
Number of funds in family	44

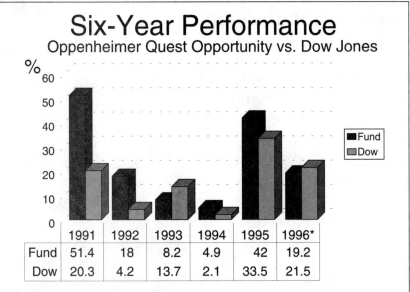

Six-Year Performance
Oppenheimer Quest Opportunity vs. Dow Jones

	1991	1992	1993	1994	1995	1996*
Fund	51.4	18	8.2	4.9	42	19.2
Dow	20.3	4.2	13.7	2.1	33.5	21.5

% Annual Total Return
Fund vs. Dow Jones Industrial Avg.

*1996 returns through 11/10/96
(5-year return through 7/96: 145%)

72

Guardian Park Avenue Fund "A"

LONG TERM

Guardian Investor Services Corporation
201 Park Avenue South
New York, NY 10003

Fund manager: Charles E. Albers
Fund objective: Long-term growth

Toll-free: 800-221-3253
In-state: 212-598-8000
Fax: 212-353-1845

Performance	★ ★ ★
Consistency	★ ★ ★ ★
Fees/Services	★ ★ ★
GPAFX	**10 Points**

Since 1972, fund manager Charles Albers has been leading the Guardian Park Avenue Fund through a quarter century of solid, steady returns. It ranks as one of the nation's top ten performing funds over the past 15 years.

Since 1972, the fund has had an average annual return of about 15 percent. A $10,000 investment in the fund in 1972 would now be worth about $330,000.

The fund invests in large blue-chip growth companies such as AT&T, Merck, Philip Morris, and Exxon. Albers uses a combination bottom-up and top-down approach. The bottom-up approach helps him select top stocks by using his own stock scoring system to ferret out the best values relative to the market. With his top-down strategy, Albers studies the market to determine the most attractive industry sectors, and to decide the proper allocation between large and small stocks.

Albers takes a fairly aggressive trading approach, with a 78 percent annual portfolio turnover ratio. The fund stays almost fully invested in stocks most of the time.

The fund's leading sectors include utilities, 9 percent of assets; energy, 11 percent; financial, 19 percent; industrial cyclicals, 14 percent; and technology, 18 percent.

PERFORMANCE

The fund has enjoyed exceptional growth over the past five years. Including dividends and capital gains distributions, the Guardian Park Avenue Fund has provided a total return for the past five years (through mid-1996) of 144 percent. A $10,000 investment in 1991 would have grown to about $24,000 five years later. Average annual return: 19.5 percent.

CONSISTENCY

The fund has been fairly consistent, outperforming the Dow Jones Industrial Average four of the five years through 1995 (and it narrowly trailed the Dow through the first half of 1996). The fund has had gains of 20 percent or more four of the past five years.

FEES/SERVICES/MANAGEMENT

The fund has a front-end load of 4.5 percent, and a very low total annual expense ratio of 0.81 percent (with no 12b-1 fee).

The fund offers all the usual mutual fund services such as retirement account availability, automatic withdrawal, and automatic checking account deduction. Its minimum initial investment of $1,000 and minimum subsequent investment of $100 are in line with other funds.

Charles Albers has managed the fund since its inception in 1972. The Guardian fund family includes seven funds and allows shareholders to switch from fund to fund by telephone.

Top Ten Holdings

1. Merck
2. AT&T
3. Philip Morris
4. Johnson & Johnson
5. Exxon

6. McDonnell Douglas
7. Green Tree Financial
8. Computer Associates International
9. PepsiCo
10. Bristol-Myers Squibb

Asset Mix: Common stocks: 93%; Cash/equivalents: 7%
Total Net Assets: $1.1 billion

Fees

Front-end load	4.50%
Redemption fee	*None*
12b-1 fee	*None*
Management fee	0.50
Other expenses	0.31
Total annual expense	0.81%
Minimum initial investment	$1,000
Minimum subsequent investment	$100

Services

Telephone exchanges	*Yes*
Automatic withdrawal	*Yes*
Automatic checking deduction	*Yes*
Retirement plan/IRA	*Yes*
Instant redemption	*Yes*
Financial statements	*Quarterly*
Income distributions	*Semiannual*
Capital gains distributions	*Annual*
Portfolio manager—years	25
Number of funds in family	7

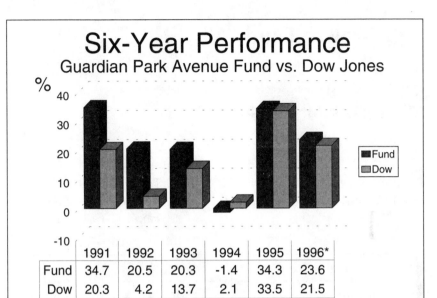

Six-Year Performance
Guardian Park Avenue Fund vs. Dow Jones

	1991	1992	1993	1994	1995	1996*
Fund	34.7	20.5	20.3	-1.4	34.3	23.6
Dow	20.3	4.2	13.7	2.1	33.5	21.5

% Annual Total Return
Fund vs. Dow Jones Industrial Avg.

*1996 returns through 11/10/96
(5-year return through 7/96: 144%)

73

IDS Growth Fund "A"

LONG TERM

IDS Group
IDS Tower 10
Minneapolis, MN 55440-0010

Fund manager: Mitzi Malevich
Fund objective: Long-term growth

Toll-free: 800-328-8300
In-state: 612-671-3733
Fax: 612-671-5113

Performance	★ ★ ★
Consistency	★ ★ ★ ★
Fees/Services	★ ★ ★
INIDX	**10 Points**

IDS Growth Fund manager Mitzi Malevich believes in searching for growth company by company—not by industry. But she keeps finding growth in the same place—technology. "I keep nearly all of the portfolio invested in stocks, concentrating on rapidly growing companies, with minimal regard for type of business," she explains. "As has been the case for some time, many of those companies fall into the technology group; therefore, usually the fund owns a substantial amount of technology stocks."

Although there are still a few nontech names in the portfolio—such as Coke, Deere, and Nike—most of the fund's major holdings are involved in health, computers, or communications.

Over the past ten years, the fund has grown at an average annual rate of 14 percent. A $10,000 investment in the fund 10 years ago would now be worth about $37,000.

The fund, which was opened in 1972, has about $2 billion in assets. But Malevich keeps the fund's portfolio at a manageable level with about 70 stock holdings. She takes a conservative buy-and-hold approach, with an annual portfolio turnover ratio of 30 percent.

Malevich looks for companies that have above-average potential for long-term growth as a result of new management, marketing opportunities, or technological superiority.

The fund's leading industrial sectors include communications, 17 percent of assets; health care, 14 percent; computer and office equipment, 11 percent; and electronics, 8 percent.

PERFORMANCE

The fund has enjoyed excellent growth over the past five years. Including dividends and capital gains distributions, the IDS Growth Fund has provided a total return for the past five years of 141 percent. A $10,000 investment in 1991 would have grown to about $24,000 five years later. Average annual return: 19.3 percent.

CONSISTENCY

The fund has been very consistent, outperforming the Dow Jones Industrial Average four of the five years from 1991 through 1995 (and it was about even with the Dow through the first half of 1996). The fund's biggest gains came in 1991 and 1995 when it rose 46.9 percent and 41.2 percent, respectively.

FEES/SERVICES/MANAGEMENT

The fund has a front-end load of 5 percent, and a low annual expense ratio of 0.98 percent (with no 12b-1 fee).

The fund offers all the standard services such as retirement account availability, automatic withdrawal, and automatic checking account deduction. Its minimum initial investment of $2,000 and minimum subsequent investment of $100 are in line with other funds

Mitzi Malevich has managed the fund since 1992. The IDS fund family includes 30 funds and allows shareholders to switch from fund to fund by telephone.

Top Ten Holdings

1. HEALTHSOUTH	6. Boston Scientific
2. Tellabs	7. First Data
3. Andrew	8. Deere
4. MFS Communications	9. Oracle Systems
5. Nucor	10. Nike

Asset Mix: Common stocks: 94%; Cash/equivalents: 6%
Total Net Assets: $2 billion

Fees

Front-end load	5.00%
Redemption fee (max)	*None*
12b-1 fee	*None*
Management fee	0.60
Other expenses	0.38
Total annual expense	0.98%
Minimum initial investment	$2,000
Minimum subsequent investment	$100

Services

Telephone exchanges	*Yes*
Automatic withdrawal	*Yes*
Automatic checking deduction	*Yes*
Retirement plan/IRA	*Yes*
Instant redemption	*Yes*
Financial statements	*Annual*
Income distributions	*Annual*
Capital gains distributions	*Annual*
Portfolio manager—years	5
Number of funds in family	30

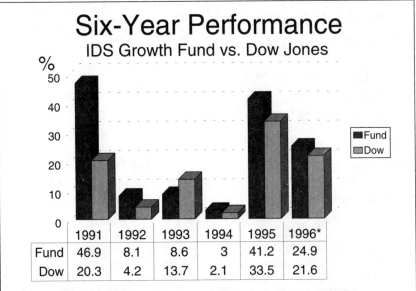

Six-Year Performance
IDS Growth Fund vs. Dow Jones

	1991	1992	1993	1994	1995	1996*
Fund	46.9	8.1	8.6	3	41.2	24.9
Dow	20.3	4.2	13.7	2.1	33.5	21.6

% Annual Total Return
Fund vs. Dow Jones Industrial Avg.

*1996 returns through 11/10/96
(5-year return through 7/96: 141%)

74

Twentieth Century Vista Investors Fund

AGGRESSIVE

Twentieth Century Family of Funds
4500 Main Street
Kansas City, MO 64141-6200

Fund managers: Glen Fogle
and James Stowers III
Fund objective: Aggressive growth

Toll-free: 800-345-2021
In-state: 816-531-5575
Fax: 816-340-4753

Performance	★ ★
Consistency	★ ★ ★
Fees/Services	★ ★ ★ ★ ★
TWCVX	**10 Points**

The Vista Investors Fund focuses on fast-growing small and midsized companies. Fund managers Glen Fogle and James Stowers III look particularly for companies with accelerating earnings and revenue growth.

The fund is very aggressive, maintaining a portfolio that usually consists of at least 90 percent stocks. About 5 to 10 percent of its assets are in foreign stocks, although Fogle downplays the foreign aspect of the fund. "Our international holdings are mostly multinational businesses with sizable operations in the United States and a large number of U.S. shareholders."

Over the past ten years, the fund has had an average annual return of 14 percent. A $10,000 investment in the fund ten years ago would now be worth about $36,000.

High tech stocks have been the driving force behind the fund's growth. "We see the most innovation and the greatest potential for earnings acceleration in the technology sector," says Fogle. "We were also attracted by the continuous development of new markets and opportunities within the sector."

The fund's leading sectors include business services and supplies, 20 percent of assets; computer software and services, 17 percent; communications equipment, 9 percent; health care, 8 percent; and pharmaceuticals, 7 percent.

The fund managers are fairly active traders, with an 89 percent annual portfolio turnover ratio.

PERFORMANCE

The Vista Investors Fund has experienced solid growth over the past five years. Including dividends and capital gains distributions, the fund has provided a total return for the past five years (through mid-1996) of 138 percent. A $10,000 investment in 1991 would have grown to about $24,000 five years later. Average annual return: 18.9 percent.

CONSISTENCY

The fund has been fairly consistent, outperforming the Dow Jones Industrial Average three of the five years through 1995 (but it trailed the Dow through the first half of 1996). The fund's biggest gain came in 1991, when it rose 73.7 percent (compared with a 20.3 percent rise in the Dow).

FEES/SERVICES/MANAGEMENT

Like all Twentieth Century funds, the Vista Investors Fund is a true no-load fund—no fee to buy, no fee to sell. The fund has a very low total annual expense ratio of 1.0 percent (with no 12b-1 fee).

The fund offers all the standard services such as retirement account availability, automatic withdrawal, and automatic checking account deduction. The fund requires a minimum initial investment of $2,500 and a minimum subsequent investment of $50.

The fund has been team-managed since 1983. The Twentieth Century fund family includes 23 funds and allows shareholders to switch from fund to fund by telephone.

Top Ten Holdings

1. Pairgain Technologies	6. Shiva
2. HFS	7. Medaphis
3. HBO	8. Healthsource
4. Centocor	9. Cognos (ADR)
5. Corporate Express	10. OfficeMax

Asset Mix: Common stocks: 93%; Cash/equivalents: 7%
Total Net Assets: $2.2 billion

Fees

Front-end load	*None*
Redemption fee	*None*
12b-1 fee	*None*
Management fee	1.00%
Other expenses	*None*
Total annual expense	1.00%
Minimum initial investment	$2,500
Minimum subsequent investment	$50

Services

Telephone exchanges	*Yes*
Automatic withdrawal	*Yes*
Automatic checking deduction	*Yes*
Retirement plan/IRA	*Yes*
Instant redemption	*Yes*
Financial statements	*Semiannual*
Income distributions	*Annual*
Capital gains distributions	*Annual*
Portfolio managers—years	14
Number of funds in family	23

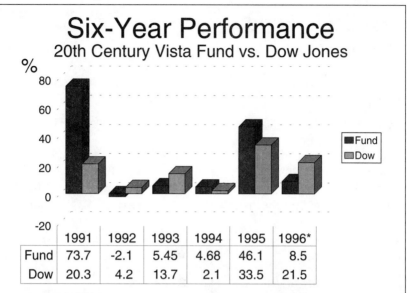

Six-Year Performance
20th Century Vista Fund vs. Dow Jones

	1991	1992	1993	1994	1995	1996*
Fund	73.7	-2.1	5.45	4.68	46.1	8.5
Dow	20.3	4.2	13.7	2.1	33.5	21.5

% Annual Total Return
Fund vs. Dow Jones Industrial Avg.

*1996 returns through 11/10/96
(5-year return through 7/96: 138%)

75

First Eagle Fund of America

First Eagle Funds
45 Broadway
New York, NY 10006

Fund managers: Harold Levy
and David Cohen
Fund objective: Long-term growth

Toll-free: 800-451-3623
In-state: 212-943-9200
Fax: 212-248-8861

Performance	★ ★
Consistency	★ ★ ★ ★
Fees/Services	★ ★ ★ ★
FEAFX	**10 Points**

The First Eagle Fund of America invests in stocks of large and midsized companies that are selling at prices well below their intrinsic value. "We value businesses on the basis of what a private investor would be willing to pay to own the enterprise," explains fund manager Harold Levy.

The portfolio includes some of America's biggest blue chips, such as Lockheed Martin, Chase Manhattan, and General Signal Corp.

Because the fund is considered a "nondiversified investment company," Levy and comanager David Cohen may invest as much as 25 percent of the fund's assets in a single stock that they really like. The policy can lead to short-term volatility, but over the long term, the fund has provided strong, steady performance. Since it opened in 1987, the fund has grown at an average annual rate of 14.6 percent. A $10,000 investment in the fund in 1987 would have grown to $34,000 by mid-1996.

In all, the fund has about 50 stock holdings. The fund managers take a fairly conservative trading approach, with an annual portfolio turnover ratio of 81 percent.

The fund is not particularly well diversified. The holdings are concentrated primarily in just six main industrial groups, including medical, 20 percent of assets; financial, 22 percent; aerospace and defense, 11 percent; consumer products, 11 percent; industrial products, 8 percent; and technology, 7 percent.

PERFORMANCE

The First Eagle Fund of America has experienced strong growth over the past five years. Including dividends and capital gains distributions, the fund has provided a total return for the past five years (through mid-1996) of 138 percent. A $10,000 investment in 1991 would have grown to about $24,000 five years later. Average annual return: 18.9 percent.

CONSISTENCY

The fund has been relatively consistent, outperforming the Dow Jones Industrial Average four of the five years through 1995 (but it was trailing the Dow through the first half of 1996). The fund's biggest gain came in 1995, when it rose 36.4 percent.

FEES/SERVICES/MANAGEMENT

This is a no-load fund that's not exactly going out of its way to win your business. It is a true no-load—no fee to buy, no fee to sell—and its total annual expense ratio of 1.75 percent (with no 12b-1 fee) is in line with other funds. But it offers none of the standard services provided by most fund companies, such as automatic withdrawal, automatic checking account deduction, and instant redemption. Its minimum initial investment of $5,000 and minimum subsequent investment of $1,000 are both very high compared with other funds.

The First Eagle Fund of America is the only fund in the First Eagle family.

Harold Levy has managed the fund since its inception in 1987. David Cohen joined the fund as comanager in 1989.

Top Ten Holdings

1. Tejas Gas
2. Finova Group
3. Wells Fargo
4. McDonnell Douglas
5. Varian Associates

6. First Empire State
7. Premark International
8. Lockheed Martin
9. Aetna Life & Casualty
10. Cooper Industries

Asset Mix: Common stocks: 98%; Cash/equivalents: 2%
Total Net Assets: $154 million

Fees

Front-end load	*None*
Redemption fee	*None*
12b-1 fee	*None*
Management fee	1.25%
Other expenses	0.50
Total annual expense	1.75%
Minimum initial investment	$5,000
Minimum subsequent investment	$1,000

Services

Telephone exchanges	*No*
Automatic withdrawal	*No*
Automatic checking deduction	*No*
Retirement plan/IRA	*Yes*
Instant redemption	*No*
Financial statements	*Semiannual*
Income distributions	*Annual*
Capital gains distributions	*Annual*
Portfolio manager—years	10
Number of funds in family	1

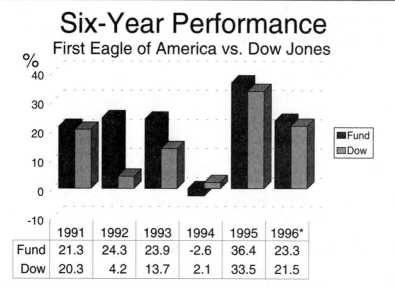

Six-Year Performance
First Eagle of America vs. Dow Jones

	1991	1992	1993	1994	1995	1996*
Fund	21.3	24.3	23.9	-2.6	36.4	23.3
Dow	20.3	4.2	13.7	2.1	33.5	21.5

% Annual Total Return   *1996 returns through 11/10/96
Fund vs. Dow Jones Industrial Avg.   (5-year return through 7/96: 138%)

76

UAM Sirach Special Equity Portfolio

AGGRESSIVE

UAM Funds
One International Place, 44th Floor
100 Oliver Street
Boston, MA 02110

Fund managers: Harvey G. Bateman
  and Stefan W. Cobb
Fund objective: Aggressive growth

Toll-free: 800-638-7983
In-state: 206-624-3800
Fax: 617-557-8610

Performance	★ ★
Consistency	★ ★ ★ ★
Fees/Services	★ ★ ★ ★
SSEPX	**10 Points**

The UAM Sirach Special Equity fund managers screen thousands of small to midsized stocks to narrow the field to the approximately 100 issues that make it into the portfolio. Fund managers Harvey Bateman and Stefan Cobb use five key "buying tests" to cut through the pretenders and settle on the winners.

The criteria include solid earnings growth rates, earnings acceleration, prospective earnings "surprise" possibilities, relative price strength, and solid cash reinvestment rates. The managers put the most emphasis on stocks that have accelerating earnings momentum or have had recent earnings growth that exceeded analysts' expectations.

The fund has grown at a rate of about 16 percent per year since its inception in 1989. A $10,000 investment in the fund at its inception would now be worth about $26,000.

Most of the stocks in the fund have market capitalizations of $100 million to $2 billion. The median market cap is about $1 billion. The fund stays almost fully invested in stocks most of the time. The fund managers are fairly aggressive in their trading approach, with an annual portfolio turnover ratio of 137 percent.

The fund is fairly diverse, although high tech stocks have had the most prominent presence in the portfolio. Leading sectors include computers and related technology, 19 percent of assets; health and medical-related, 13 percent; electronics, 6 percent; lodging and restaurants, 7 percent; retail, 9 percent; and telecommunications, 6 percent.

PERFORMANCE ★ ★

The Special Equity Fund has experienced strong growth over the past five years. Including dividends and capital gains distributions, the fund has provided a total return for the past five years (through mid-1996) of 137 percent. A $10,000 investment in 1991 would have grown to about $24,000 five years later. Average annual return: 18.8 percent.

CONSISTENCY ★ ★ ★ ★

The fund has been very consistent, outperforming the Dow Jones Industrial Average four of the five years through 1995 (and it was ahead of the Dow again through the first half of 1996). The fund's biggest gain came in 1991, when it rose 53.6 percent (compared with a 20.3 percent rise in the Dow).

FEES/SERVICES/MANAGEMENT ★ ★ ★ ★

The UAM Sirach Special Equity Fund is a no-load fund—no fee to buy, no fee to sell, but you must buy it through a brokerage company (either a full service broker or a discounter), which normally would add to your expense. The fund has a very low total annual expense ratio of 0.85 percent (with no 12b-1 fee).

The fund offers most of the standard services such as retirement account availability, automatic withdrawal, and automatic checking account deduction. Its minimum initial investment of $2,500 and minimum subsequent investment of $100 are a little higher than average.

Harvey Bateman has managed the fund since 1989. Stefan Cobb joined the fund as a comanager in 1994. The UAM fund family includes 18 funds.

Top Ten Holdings

1. United Waste Systems
2. Robert Half International
3. Corporate Express
4. Watson Pharmaceuticals
5. McAfee Associates
6. HBO
7. PhyCor
8. Nautica Enterprises
9. Cognos
10. Sanifill

Asset Mix: Common stocks: 94%; Cash/equivalents: 6%
Total Net Assets: $566 million

Fees

Front-end load	*None*
Redemption fee	*None*
12b-1 fee	*None*
Management fee	0.70%
Other expenses	0.15
Total annual expense	0.85%
Minimum initial investment	$2,500
Minimum subsequent investment	$100

Services

Telephone exchanges	*Yes*
Automatic withdrawal	*No*
Automatic checking deduction	*Yes*
Retirement plan/IRA	*Yes*
Instant redemption	*Yes*
Financial statements	*Semiannual*
Income distributions	*Quarterly*
Capital gains distributions	*Annual*
Portfolio manager—years	7
Number of funds in family	18

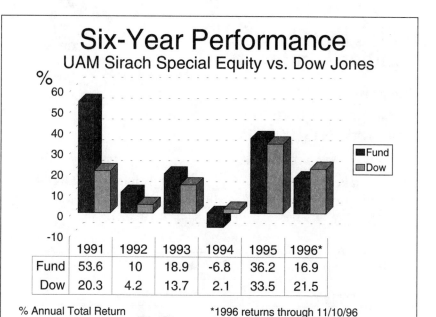

Six-Year Performance
UAM Sirach Special Equity vs. Dow Jones

	1991	1992	1993	1994	1995	1996*
Fund	53.6	10	18.9	-6.8	36.2	16.9
Dow	20.3	4.2	13.7	2.1	33.5	21.5

% Annual Total Return
Fund vs. Dow Jones Industrial Avg.

*1996 returns through 11/10/96
(5-year return through 7/96: 137%)

77

Bull & Bear Special Equities Fund

AGGRESSIVE

Bull & Bear Funds
11 Hanover Square
New York, NY 10005

Fund manager: Brett B. Sneed
Fund objective: Aggressive growth

Toll-free: 800-847-4200
In-state: 212-363-1100
Fax: 212-363-1103

Performance	★ ★
Consistency	★ ★ ★ ★
Fees/Services	★ ★ ★ ★
BBSEX	**10 Points**

"Special equities" may sound like stocks of very special growing companies, but in the unique jargon of the mutual fund industry, "special" normally refers to companies that are embattled, beleaguered or even bankrupt. Bull & Bear Special Equities Fund manager Brett Sneed rummages through these wounded warriors, looking for stocks that appear poised for a comeback.

The fund invests primarily in small companies that are in the midst of liquidations, reorganizations, recapitalizations, mergers, litigation, or management changeovers.

The fund has had wide swings in its performance the past few years. For instance, after climbing 42 percent in 1989, it dropped 36 percent in 1990; it was up 40.5 percent in both 1991 and 1995, but down 16.5 percent in 1994. Its five-year growth of 136 percent (18.7 percent per year) is almost as great as its ten-year growth of 142 percent (just 9.3 percent per year).

The fund stays almost entirely invested in stocks most of the time. It recently had 98 percent of its assets in stocks. Sneed maintains an extremely aggressive trading policy, with an annual portfolio turnover ratio of 319 percent.

The fund, with assets of just $61 million, has about 40 stock holdings. The portfolio is heavily weighted in the high tech area. Leading segments include medical, 26 percent of assets; computer products and services, 29 percent; and finance, 13 percent.

PERFORMANCE

The fund has enjoyed solid growth over the past five years. Including dividends and capital gains distributions, the Special Equities Fund has provided a total return for the past five years (through mid-1996) of 136 percent. A $10,000 investment in 1991 would have grown to about $24,000 five years later. Average annual return: 18.7 percent.

CONSISTENCY

The fund has been fairly consistent in recent years, outperforming the Dow Jones Industrial Average four of the five years through 1995 (but it trailed the Dow through the first half of 1996). The fund's biggest years were 1991 and 1995 when it moved up 40.5 percent (both years).

FEES/SERVICES/MANAGEMENT

The Special Equities Fund is a no-load fund, but what it lacks in front-end or redemption fees, it makes up for in annual fees. Its total annual expense ratio of 2.92 percent (including a 1 percent 12b-1 fee and a 0.85 percent management fee) is the highest among all "Best 100" funds.

The fund offers all the usual mutual fund services such as retirement account availability, automatic withdrawal, and automatic checking account deduction. Its minimum initial investment of $1,000 and minimum subsequent investment of $100 are in line with other funds.

Brett Sneed has managed the fund since 1988. The Bull & Bear fund family includes seven funds and allows shareholders to switch from fund to fund by telephone.

Top Ten Holdings

1. AmeriCredit
2. Neoprobe
3. Employee Solutions
4. Utah Medical Products
5. Ameridata Technologies

6. Newbridge Networks
7. System Software Associates
8. Elan
9. Apria HealthCare Group
10. PLATINUM Technology

Asset Mix: Common stocks: 98%; Cash/equivalents: 2%
Total Net Assets: $61 million

Fees

Front-end load	*None*
Redemption fee (max)	*None*
12b-1 fee	1.00%
Management fee	0.85
Other expenses	1.07
Total annual expense	2.92%
Minimum initial investment	$1,000
Minimum subsequent investment	$100

Services

Telephone exchanges	*Yes*
Automatic withdrawal	*Yes*
Automatic checking deduction	*Yes*
Retirement plan/IRA	*Yes*
Instant redemption	*Yes*
Financial statements	*Annual*
Income distributions	*Annual*
Capital gains distributions	*Annual*
Portfolio manager—years	9
Number of funds in family	7

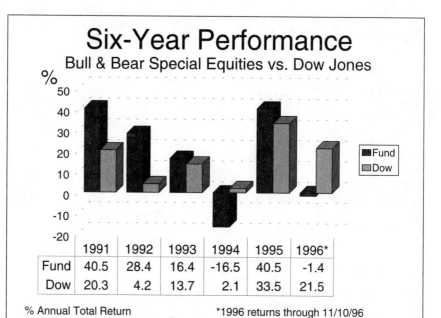

Six-Year Performance
Bull & Bear Special Equities vs. Dow Jones

	1991	1992	1993	1994	1995	1996*
Fund	40.5	28.4	16.4	-16.5	40.5	-1.4
Dow	20.3	4.2	13.7	2.1	33.5	21.5

% Annual Total Return   *1996 returns through 11/10/96
Fund vs. Dow Jones Industrial Avg.   (5-year return through 7/96: 136%)

78

Berwyn Fund

Berwyn Group of Funds
1189 Lancaster Avenue
Berwyn, PA 19312

LONG TERM

Fund manager: Robert E. Killen
Fund objective: Long-term growth

Toll-free: 800-992-6757
In-state: 610-296-7222
Fax: 610-296-5057

Performance	★ ★
Consistency	★ ★ ★ ★
Fees/Services	★ ★ ★ ★
BERWX	**10 Points**

The Berwyn Fund invests in very small stocks that fund manager Robert Killen believes are trading at prices well below their true value. On average, the stocks in the portfolio have market capitalizations of about $200 million (although many are much smaller).

Although it specializes in small stocks, the fund's policy is to invest only in companies that have been in business at least five years, and that have assets of at least $10 million.

The fund stays almost fully invested in stocks most all the time. It always keeps at least 80 percent of assets in stocks. Recently 99 percent of its assets were in stocks. Killen is conservative in his trading policy, with an annual portfolio turnover ratio of 32 percent.

Killen selects stocks that fall into one of three categories: those selling substantially below their book value; those selling at a low valuation to their present earnings level; and stocks selling at a small premium to book value or at a modest valuation based on their present earnings level.

The fund has about 75 stock holdings, spread across a broad range of industries. Leading sectors include computer-related companies, 10 percent of total assets; automotive, 8 percent; banking, 7 percent; oil and gas,

7 percent; steel, 7 percent; metals and mining, 6 percent; and insurance, 5 percent.

PERFORMANCE

The fund has enjoyed strong growth over the past five years. Including dividends and capital gains distributions, the Berwyn Fund has provided a total return for the past five years (through mid-1996) of 129 percent. A $10,000 investment in 1991 would have grown to about $23,000 five years later. Average annual return: 18 percent.

CONSISTENCY

The fund has been very consistent, outperforming the Dow Jones Industrial Average four of the five years from 1991 through 1995 (but it narrowly trailed the Dow through the first half of 1996). The fund's biggest year was 1991 when it jumped 43.5 percent.

FEES/SERVICES/MANAGEMENT

The Berwyn Fund has no front-end load and a maximum 1 percent redemption fee that is waived after the first year. It has a low annual expense ratio of 1.23 percent (with no 12b-1 fee).

The fund offers all the usual mutual fund services such as retirement account availability, automatic withdrawal, and automatic checking account deduction.

The biggest drawback is its minimum initial investment of $10,000, which puts it out of reach for many small investors. Its minimum subsequent investment of $250 is in line with other funds.

Robert Killen has managed the fund since 1984. Berwyn has only two funds.

Top Ten Holdings

1. C-Tec
2. InaCom
3. AK Steel Holding
4. AO Smith "B"
5. Whittaker

6. Riser Foods
7. First American Financial
8. Western Digital
9. Hughes Supply
10. BSB Bancorp

Asset Mix: Common stocks: 99%; Cash/equivalents: 1%
Total Net Assets: $102 million

Fees

Front-end load	*None*
Redemption fee (max)	1.00%
12b-1 fee	*None*
Management fee	1.00
Other expenses	0.23
Total annual expense	1.23%
Minimum initial investment	$10,000
Minimum subsequent investment	$250

Services

Telephone exchanges	*Yes*
Automatic withdrawal	*Yes*
Automatic checking deduction	*Yes*
Retirement plan/IRA	*Yes*
Instant redemption	*Yes*
Financial statements	*Annual*
Income distributions	*Annual*
Capital gains distributions	*Annual*
Portfolio manager—years	13
Number of funds in family	2

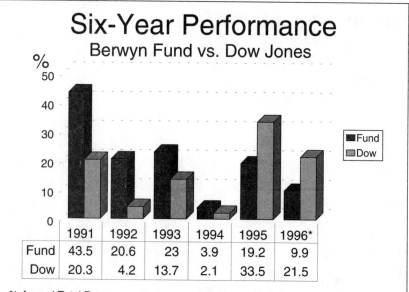

Six-Year Performance
Berwyn Fund vs. Dow Jones

	1991	1992	1993	1994	1995	1996*
Fund	43.5	20.6	23	3.9	19.2	9.9
Dow	20.3	4.2	13.7	2.1	33.5	21.5

% Annual Total Return
Fund vs. Dow Jones Industrial Avg.

*1996 returns through 11/10/96
(5-year return through 7/96: 129%)

79

Vanguard Explorer Fund

AGGRESSIVE

Vanguard Group
P.O. Box 2600
Valley Forge, PA 19482

Fund managers: John Granahan
and Kenneth Abrams
Fund objective: Aggressive growth

Toll-free: 800-635-1511
In-state: 610-669-1000
Fax: 610-640-1371

Performance	★ ★
Consistency	★ ★ ★
Fees/Services	★ ★ ★ ★ ★
VEXPX	**10 Points**

The Vanguard Explorer Fund invests in a broad range of fast-growing small emerging companies, most of which of have market capitalizations of $100 to $500 million. The fund has about $2 billion in total assets, and holds some 200 different stocks.

Fund managers John Granahan and Kenneth Abrams focus on stocks with strong growth potential and a growing market niche, but that are not yet widely held or widely followed by the big institutions on Wall Street. The fund stays about 85 to 90 percent invested in stocks most of the time.

The fund managers have been fairly modest in their trading approach, with a 66 percent annual portfolio turnover ratio.

Since its inception in 1972, the fund has produced an average annual return of about 12 percent. A $10,000 investment in the fund in 1972 would now be worth about $175,000.

The fund has stock holdings in a wide range of industries. Leading sectors include computers and technology, 26 percent of total assets; health care, 17 percent; retail and consumer cyclicals, 17 percent; financial, 8 percent; and capital goods, 6 percent.

PERFORMANCE

The Vanguard Explorer Fund has experienced solid growth over the past five years. Including dividends and capital gains distributions, the fund has provided a total return for the past five years (through mid-1996) of 128 percent. A $10,000 investment in 1991 would have grown to about $23,000 five years later. Average annual return: 18 percent.

CONSISTENCY

The fund has been somewhat consistent, outperforming the Dow Jones Industrial Average three of the five years from 1991 through 1995 (and it was ahead of the Dow again through the first half of 1996). The fund's biggest gain came in 1991, when it rose 55.9 percent (compared with a 20.3 percent rise in the Dow).

FEES/SERVICES/MANAGEMENT

The Explorer Fund is a true no-load fund—no fee to buy, no fee to sell. It has a very low total annual expense ratio of 0.68 percent (with no 12b-1 fee).

The fund offers all the standard services such as retirement account availability, automatic withdrawal, and automatic checking account deduction. Its minimum initial investment of $3,000 is higher than most funds; its minimum subsequent investment of $100 is in line with other funds.

John Granahan has managed the fund since 1985. (He also managed it from 1972 to 1979.) Kenneth Abrams joined the fund as a manager in 1994. The Vanguard fund family includes 90 funds and allows shareholders to switch from fund to fund by telephone.

Top Ten Holdings

1. Dionex	6. BMC Industries
2. Dallas Semiconductor	7. Magellan Health Services
3. Itron	8. Genetics Institute
4. Air Express International	9. Vencor
5. Catalina Marketing	10. Input/Output

Asset Mix: Common stocks: 88%; Cash/equivalents: 12%
Total Net Assets: $2 billion

Fees

Front-end load	*None*
Redemption fee	*None*
12b-1 fee	*None*
Management fee	0.36%
Other expenses	0.32
Total annual expense	0.68%
Minimum initial investment	$3,000
Minimum subsequent investment	$100

Services

Telephone exchanges	*Yes*
Automatic withdrawal	*Yes*
Automatic checking deduction	*Yes*
Retirement plan/IRA	*Yes*
Instant redemption	*Yes*
Financial statements	*Semiannual*
Income distributions	*Annual*
Capital gains distributions	*Annual*
Portfolio manager—years	12
Number of funds in family	90

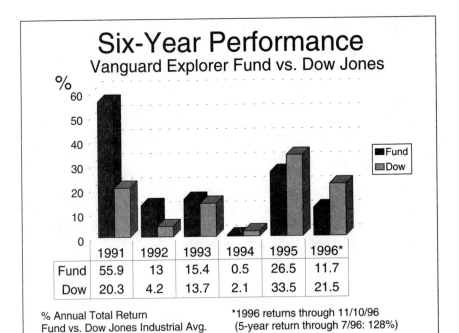

Six-Year Performance
Vanguard Explorer Fund vs. Dow Jones

	1991	1992	1993	1994	1995	1996*
Fund	55.9	13	15.4	0.5	26.5	11.7
Dow	20.3	4.2	13.7	2.1	33.5	21.5

% Annual Total Return
Fund vs. Dow Jones Industrial Avg.

*1996 returns through 11/10/96
(5-year return through 7/96: 128%)

AGGRESSIVE

Westcore Midco Growth Fund

Westcore Funds
370 Seventeenth Street, Suite 2700
Denver, CO 80202

Fund manager: Todger Anderson
Fund objective: Aggressive growth

Toll-free: 800-392-2673
In-state: 303-623-2577
Fax: 303-623-7850

Performance	★ ★
Consistency	★ ★ ★
Fees/Services	★ ★ ★ ★ ★
WTMGX	**10 Points**

Todger Anderson is always looking for the next home run. He goes to bat 200 times, with 200 small emerging growth stocks in his Westcore Midco Growth Fund portfolio, and he says he swings for the fence on every pick. "I'm looking for the next Gap, the next Microsoft, the next Home Depot."

In his search for superior performers, Anderson wants companies with 20 to 30 percent annual earnings growth and a solid product or service that is going to continue to push earnings higher. He also wants stocks of companies that have proven to be successful business models. "For instance, Home Depot and Payless Cashways are in the same business, but Home Depot is clearly the better stock. Payless simply hasn't been able to develop a business model with the same level of earnings growth as Home Depot," Anderson says.

Another comparison Anderson points to is Apple Computer—a respected company, but a ho-hum stock—with Microsoft, which has been the nation's top-performing stock over the past decade. "Apple has a great operating system, but it chose to sell it as a proprietary hardware product rather than as software. Its business has not been a very profitable model. Microsoft, on the other hand, went into the software business and dominates that market. It has been the more successful business model, and it has been a much better stock than Apple."

One complicating factor, Anderson admits, is that the company with the best product does not always win the marketing war. "Look at video recorders. Beta was the better product, but VHS won the war. That was the product consumers bought."

Another factor Anderson considers in selecting stocks is the size of the market. He wants companies that have big markets for their products or services.

In deciding when to sell a stock, Anderson considers several checkpoints:

- *Too much.* If a stock grows quickly and ultimately accounts for more than 5 percent of the fund's total assets, he will sell out a portion of the holdings.
- *Too high.* If a stock is overvalued—with a PE ratio that is too high relative to the company's growth rate—he will sell the stock.
- *Nonquantifiable information.* Every quarter, Anderson and his staff call the managers of each of the 140 companies in the fund's portfolio. "When we ask how the company is doing, if he starts to stutter, or hesitates in answering our questions, we suspect that something has changed, so we sell out some or all of our holdings in that stock."
- *Bad judgment.* "If it turns out that our judgment was incorrect and the company comes out with an unexpectedly low earnings report, we'll get out of the stock."

The stocks he likes best are those he can hold for three to five years. But those are very rare. "That's our goal, but it doesn't happen very often. We let our winners run, and we weed our losers out of the portfolio." The fund has a 50 percent annual portfolio turnover ratio.

Anderson stays fully invested in the stock market at all times. "We don't do any market timing. There has never been any evidence that any money manager who uses market timing has been able to outperform the market over a number of cycles."

The fund has a strong high tech orientation. Health and medical stocks make up 17 percent of total assets, computers and electronics account for 20 percent, and telecommunications makes up 10 percent. Other leading segments include retail, 7 percent; consumer services, 6 percent; hotels and leisure, 6 percent; financial-related, 8 percent.

PERFORMANCE

The Westcore Midco Growth Fund has posted solid growth over the past five years. Including dividends and capital gains distributions, the fund has provided a total return for the past five years (through mid-1996) of 128 percent. A $10,000 investment in 1991 would have grown to about $23,000 five years later. Average annual return: 17.9 percent.

CONSISTENCY

The fund has been relatively consistent, outperforming the Dow Jones Industrial Average three of the five years through 1995 (and it was ahead of the Dow again through the first half of 1996). The fund's biggest gain came in 1991, when it rose 67 percent (compared with a 20.3 percent rise in the Dow).

FEES/SERVICES MANAGEMENT

The fund is inexpensive to buy and inexpensive to hold. It is a true no-load fund—no fee to buy or to sell—and has a total annual expense ratio of just 0.94 percent (with no 12b-1 fee).

The fund offers all the standard services such as retirement account availability, automatic withdrawal, and automatic checking account deduction. Its minimum initial investment of $1,000 and minimum subsequent investment of $50 are in line with other funds.

Todger Anderson has managed the fund since its inception in 1986. The Westcore fund family includes seven funds and allows shareholders to switch from fund to fund by telephone.

Top Ten Holdings

1. Oxford Health Plans
2. HFS
3. CUC International
4. WorldCom
5. Oracle Systems
6. First Data
7. 3Com
8. Infinity Broadcasting "A"
9. Broderbund Software
10. Loewen Group

Asset Mix: Common stocks: 95%; Cash/equivalents: 3%;
U.S. government securities: 2%
Total Net Assets: $638 million

Fees

Front-end load	*None*
Redemption fee	*None*
12b-1 fee	*None*
Management fee	0.65%
Other expenses	0.29
Total annual expense	0.94%
Minimum initial investment	$1,000
Minimum subsequent investment	$50

Services

Telephone exchanges	*Yes*
Automatic withdrawal	*Yes*
Automatic checking deduction	*Yes*
Retirement plan/IRA	*Yes*
Instant redemption	*Yes*
Financial statements	*Semiannual*
Income distributions	*Quarterly*
Capital gains distributions	*Annual*
Portfolio manager—years	11
Number of funds in family	7

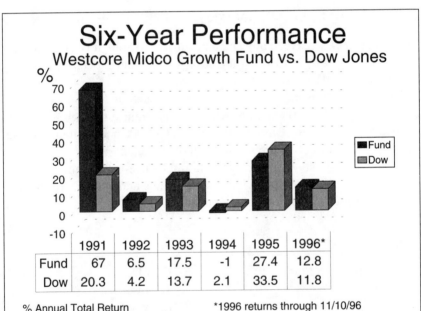

Six-Year Performance
Westcore Midco Growth Fund vs. Dow Jones

	1991	1992	1993	1994	1995	1996*
Fund	67	6.5	17.5	-1	27.4	12.8
Dow	20.3	4.2	13.7	2.1	33.5	11.8

% Annual Total Return
Fund vs. Dow Jones Industrial Avg.

*1996 returns through 11/10/96
(5-year return through 7/96: 128%)

LONG TERM

81
Berger 100 Fund

The Berger Funds
210 University Avenue, Suite 900
Denver, CO 80206

Fund manager: Rod Linafelter
Fund objective: Long-term growth

Toll-free: 800-333-1001
In-state: 303-329-0200
Fax: 303-329-8719

Performance	★ ★
Consistency	★ ★ ★
Fees/Services	★ ★ ★ ★ ★
BEONX	**10 Points**

Most of the day-to-day responsibilities of the Berger Funds have shifted from William Berger to fund manager Rod Linafelter and his staff, but Berger's philosophy still guides the buying and selling strategies of the funds. "Our philosophy has always been to stick with the best companies in terms of success and profitability," Berger says.

Berger is a pioneer in the mutual fund business. He took his first job managing money in 1950 when his boss at Colorado National Bank asked him to manage the institution's $100 million stock portfolio.

Through the 1960s he managed mutual funds and even invented a new breed of fund, the tax-free exchange fund, which is used to convert nonmonetary assets into mutual fund shares. For the past two decades, the Berger 100 Fund has managed to outperform the market on a consistent basis. Berger attributes that success to his obsession with buying the all-star stocks of the market, companies such as Boeing, Merck, and Motorola that increase their sales and earnings year after year. Although the bigger blue chip stocks kept the fund ahead of the pack in the past, its shift in emphasis to the smaller high tech issues such as Solectron and Amgen is driving the growth of the fund today.

"We're seeing some of these small companies growing at clips of 50 percent or more a year. Technology is the area that seems to have the best growth possibilities in this country. That's the area we can prevail in the global market. We will continue to lead the world through new advancements in technology."

The fund focuses not only on stocks with high growth potential, but also on stocks that are appropriately valued in relation to the market. The fund managers consider a wide variety of factors such as price-to-earnings ratio in selecting stocks. "We have so many screens," Berger quips, "a fly couldn't get near us."

As for selling strategies, the fund sells out when the company's earnings momentum begins to ebb or "when the company has earnings surprises that disappoint us. It's the cockroach theory. We think one surprise may beget another surprise, so we get rid of the stock."

Over the past ten years, the Berger 100 Fund has compiled an average annual return of 16 percent. A $10,000 investment in the fund ten years ago would now be worth about $43,000.

More than 50 percent of the fund's total assets are in emerging growth companies, about 25 percent are midcap stocks and 12 percent are in the larger blue chips. The Berger 100 Fund holds about 80 stocks.

In terms of industrial sectors, the fund is heavily weighted in high tech stocks, with about 16 percent in computer and software stocks, 5 percent in electronics, and 7 percent in telecommunications. Health care-related stocks make up about 20 percent of the portfolio, and financial and investment stocks make up 7 percent.

PERFORMANCE

The Berger 100 Fund has experienced solid growth over the past five years. Including dividends and capital gains distributions, the fund has provided a total return for the past five years (through mid-1996) of 126 percent. A $10,000 investment in 1991 would have grown to $23,000 five years later. Average annual return: 17.7 percent.

CONSISTENCY

The fund has lost some momentum in recent years after strong gains in 1991, 1992 and 1993. It outperformed the Dow Jones Industrial Average three of the five years from 1991 to 1995, trailing the market in 1994, 1995, and through the first half of 1996. Its biggest gain came in 1991, when it jumped 88.8 percent (compared with a 20.3 percent rise in the Dow).

FEES/SERVICES MANAGEMENT   ★ ★ ★ ★ ★

The fund offers investors a lot for a little. It is a pure no-load fund—no fees to buy, no fees to sell. Its annual expense ratio of 1.47 percent (including a 0.25 percent 12b-1 fee) is in line with other no-load funds.

The fund offers all the standard services such as retirement account availability, automatic withdrawal, and automatic checking account deduction. Its minimum initial investment of $500 and minimum subsequent investment of $50 compare very favorably with other funds.

Rod Linafelter has been a manager with the fund since 1990. The Berger fund family includes only three other funds: the Berger 101 Fund, the Berger Small Company Growth Fund (which the company introduced in 1994) and the Berger New Generation Fund (an emerging growth stock fund introduced in 1996). The company allows free exchanges between its funds.

Top Ten Holdings

1. Sonat Offshore Drilling
2. Amgen
3. Solectron
4. Merck
5. Boeing
6. WorldCom
7. Luxottica Group (ADR)
8. Halliburton
9. Federal National Mortgage Association
10. Columbia/HCA Healthcare

Asset Mix: Common stocks: 93%; Cash/equivalents: 7%
Total Net Assets: $2.2 billion

Fees

Front-end load	*None*
Redemption fee	*None*
12b-1 fee	0.25%
Management fee	0.75
Other expenses	0.47
Total annual expense	1.47%
Minimum initial investment	$500
Minimum subsequent investment	$50

Services

Telephone exchanges	*Yes*
Automatic withdrawal	*Yes*
Automatic checking deduction	*Yes*
Retirement plan/IRA	*Yes*
Instant redemption	*Yes*
Financial statements	*Semiannual*
Income distributions	*Annual*
Capital gains distributions	*Annual*
Portfolio manager—years	7
Number of funds in family	4

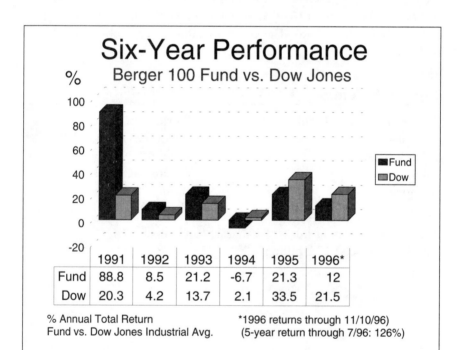

Six-Year Performance
Berger 100 Fund vs. Dow Jones

	1991	1992	1993	1994	1995	1996*
Fund	88.8	8.5	21.2	-6.7	21.3	12
Dow	20.3	4.2	13.7	2.1	33.5	21.5

% Annual Total Return
Fund vs. Dow Jones Industrial Avg.

*1996 returns through 11/10/96)
(5-year return through 7/96: 126%)

LONG TERM

Fidelity Blue Chip Growth Fund

Fidelity Investments
82 Devonshire Street
Boston, MA 02109

Fund manager: John McDowell
Fund objective: Long-term growth

Toll-free: 800-544-8888
In-state: 801-534-1910
Fax: 617-476-9753

Performance	★ ★ ★
Consistency	★ ★ ★ ★
Fees/Services	★ ★ ★
FBGRX	**10 Points**

True to its name, the Fidelity Blue Chip Growth Fund invests in some of the largest, most well-known names in corporate America. Its largest holdings include such familiar household names as General Motors, Chrysler, Allstate, Philip Morris, and Digital Equipment.

Blue chip stocks have not exactly been the hottest sector of the market in recent years, but former fund manager Michael Gordon and current manager John McDowell, who took over the fund in 1996, have managed to keep the portfolio growing at a respectable clip. Since the inception of the fund in 1988, it has grown at an average annual rate of about 19 percent. A $10,000 investment in the fund when it opened would have grown to about $43,000 over the next nine years.

The fund's strategy is to invest in a diversified portfolio of established companies, maintaining at least 65 percent of assets in blue chip stocks. Most of its stock holdings are included in the Standard & Poor's 500. The fund may also invest in some smaller emerging companies.

The fund maintains an active trading policy, with an annual portfolio turnover ratio of about 180 percent.

In all, the fund has about 250 stock holdings. At one time, the fund was heavily weighted in technology stocks, which comprised about one-third of the portfolio. But the fund shifted focus in late 1995, moving more money into financial stocks (17 percent of assets), durables (11 percent), energy (8 percent), and industrial equipment (7 percent).

PERFORMANCE

The fund has enjoyed excellent growth over the past five years. Including dividends and capital gains distributions, the Fidelity Blue Chip Growth Fund has provided a total return for the past five years (through mid-1996) of 151 percent. A $10,000 investment in 1991 would have grown to $25,000 five years later. Average annual return: 20.2 percent.

CONSISTENCY

The fund has been fairly consistent recently, outperforming the Dow Jones Industrial Average four of the five years through 1995 (but it trailed the Dow through the first half of 1996). Its best year was in 1991 when it jumped 54.8 percent.

FEES/SERVICES MANAGEMENT

The fund has a low front-end load of 3 percent, and a comparatively low annual expense ratio of 1.02 percent (with no 12b-1 fee).

The fund offers all the standard services such as retirement account availability, automatic withdrawal, and automatic checking account deduction. Its minimum initial investment of $2,500 and minimum subsequent investment of $250 are a little high compared with other funds.

Fund manager John McDowell has only been with the fund since 1996. The Fidelity fund family includes about 210 funds.

Top Ten Holdings

1. General Motors	6. Philip Morris Companies
2. Home Depot	7. Caterpillar
3. Chrysler	8. Deere & Co.
4. Allstate	9. Computer Sciences
5. MGIC Investment	10. Digital Equipment

Asset Mix: Common stocks: 83%; Corporate bonds: 10%; Cash/equivalents: 7%
Total Net Assets: $8.4 billion

Fees

Front-end load	3.00%
Redemption fee	*None*
12b-1 fee	*None*
Management fee	0.69
Other expenses	0.33
Total annual expense	1.02%
Minimum initial investment	$2,500
Minimum subsequent investment	$250

Services

Telephone exchanges	*Yes*
Automatic withdrawal	*Yes*
Automatic checking deduction	*Yes*
Retirement plan/IRA	*Yes*
Instant redemption	*Yes*
Financial statements	*Semiannual*
Income distributions	*Semiannual*
Capital gains distributions	*Semiannual*
Portfolio manager—years	1
Number of funds in family	210

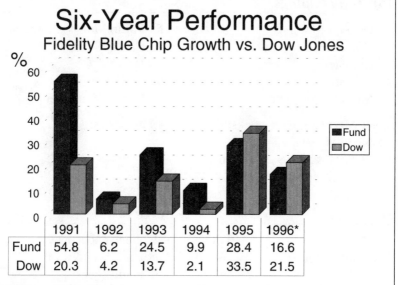

Six-Year Performance
Fidelity Blue Chip Growth vs. Dow Jones

	1991	1992	1993	1994	1995	1996*
Fund	54.8	6.2	24.5	9.9	28.4	16.6
Dow	20.3	4.2	13.7	2.1	33.5	21.5

% Avg. Annual Total Return
Fund vs. Dow Jones Industrial Avg.

*1996 returns through 11/10/96
(5-year return through 7/96: 151%)

83

United Science and Technology Fund

United Funds, Inc.
6300 Lamar Avenue
Shawnee Mission, KS 66201-9217

Fund manager: Abel Garcia
Fund objective: Sector Fund

Toll-free: 800-366-5465
In-state: 913-236-2000
Fax: 913-236-1595

Performance	★ ★ ★ ★
Consistency	★ ★ ★
Fees/Services	★ ★ ★
UNSCX	**10 Points**

Formerly known as the "Science and Energy Fund," the United Science and Technology Fund has changed its name and its focus in recent years to take advantage of the tremendous growth in the technology sector.

The fund invests in a wide range of technology-related industies including aerospace, communications, electronic equipment, computer systems and software, electronics, business machines, medical supplies, and biotechnology.

Over the past ten years, the fund has grown at an average annual rate of about 17 percent. A $10,000 investment in the fund ten years ago would now be worth about $48,000.

Fund manager Abel Garcia takes a conservative buy-and-hold approach, with an annual portfolio turnover ratio of just 33 percent.

In all, the fund has about 100 stock holdings. Its leading segment is computers and office equipment, which accounts for about 43 percent of total assets. Other leading segments include electronics, 17 percent; telecommunications, 15 percent; drugs and hospital supplies, 4 percent; and consumer and business services, 4 percent.

The fund stays almost fully invested in the stock market most of the time. Typically, at least 80 percent of assets are invested in technology companies.

PERFORMANCE

The fund has enjoyed exceptional growth over the past five years. Including dividends and capital gains distributions, the United Science and Technology fund has provided a total return for the past five years (through mid-1996) of 176 percent. A $10,000 investment in 1991 would have grown to about $27,600 five years later. Average annual return: 22.6 percent.

CONSISTENCY

The fund has been fairly consistent, outperforming the Dow Jones Industrial Average three of the five years through 1995 (and the fund was just ahead of the Dow through the first half of 1996). The fund's biggest years were 1991 and 1995 when it moved up 59.3 percent and 55.6 percent, respectively.

FEES/SERVICES MANAGEMENT

The fund has a 5.75 percent front-end sales load, and a very low annual expense ratio of 0.92 percent (including a 0.13 percent 12b-1 fee and a 0.61 percent management fee).

The fund offers most of the standard services such as retirement account availability, automatic withdrawal, and automatic checking account deduction, but it does not offer instant telephone redemption or switching between funds by phone. Its minimum initial investment of $500 and subsequent minimum investment of $1 compares very favorably with other funds.

Abel Garcia has managed the fund since 1984. The United fund family includes 17 funds. United is part of Waddell & Reed, a financial planning subsidiary of Torchmark.

Top Ten Holdings

1. Ascend Communications
2. Cascade Communications
3. HBO
4. Cisco Systems
5. Parametric Technology

6. America Online
7. Informix
8. Macromedia
9. Shiva
10. General Motors "E"

Asset Mix: Common stocks: 92%; Cash/equivalents: 8%
Total Net Assets: $1 billion

Fees

Front-end load	5.75%
Redemption fee	*None*
12b-1 fee	0.13
Management fee	0.61
Other expenses	0.18
Total annual expense	0.92%
Minimum initial investment	$500
Minimum subsequent investment	$1

Services

Telephone exchanges	*No*
Automatic withdrawal	*Yes*
Automatic checking deduction	*Yes*
Retirement plan/IRA	*Yes*
Instant redemption	*No*
Financial statements	*Semiannual*
Income distributions	*Semiannual*
Capital gains distributions	*Annual*
Portfolio manager—years	13
Number of funds in family	17

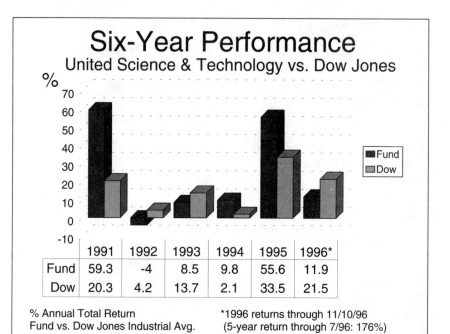

Six-Year Performance
United Science & Technology vs. Dow Jones

	1991	1992	1993	1994	1995	1996*
Fund	59.3	-4	8.5	9.8	55.6	11.9
Dow	20.3	4.2	13.7	2.1	33.5	21.5

% Annual Total Return   *1996 returns through 11/10/96
Fund vs. Dow Jones Industrial Avg.   (5-year return through 7/96: 176%)

SECTOR

Fidelity Select Industrial Equipment Portfolio

Fidelity Investments
82 Devonshire Street
Boston, MA 02109

Fund manager: Paul Antico
Fund objective: Sector fund

Toll-free: 800-544-8888
In-state: 801-534-1910
Fax: 617-476-9753

Performance	★ ★ ★
Consistency	★ ★ ★ ★
Fees/Services	★ ★ ★
FSCGX	**10 Points**

Generally industrial equipment stocks are considered to be about as slow and plodding as the forklifts and cranes that characterize their industry. But the Fidelity Select Industrial Equipment Portfolio—which has shunned the glitz and glamor of high tech stocks in favor of such segments as pumping equipment, machine tools, and farm machinery—has enjoyed exceptional growth the past few years.

Over the past five years, the fund has provided an average annual return of about 20 percent. Since it opened in 1986, the fund has grown at a rate of about 12 percent per year. A $10,000 investment in the fund in 1986 would have grown to $37,000 ten years later.

The fund invests primarily in industrial equipment manufacturers, parts suppliers, and subcontractors. The fund maintains a fairly active trading policy, with a 131 percent annual portfolio turnover ratio. In all, the fund has about 40 stock holdings.

The fund's leading segments include general industrial machinery, 22 percent of assets; farm machinery, 11 percent; construction equipment, 8 percent; electrical machinery, 8 percent; and computer and office equipment, 7 percent.

PERFORMANCE

The fund has enjoyed exceptional growth over the past five years. Including dividends and capital gains distributions, the Fidelity Select Industrial Equipment Portfolio has provided a total return for the past five years (through mid-1996) of 151 percent. A $10,000 investment in 1991 would have grown to $25,000 five years later. Average annual return: 20.3 percent.

CONSISTENCY

The fund has been fairly consistent, outperforming the Dow Jones Industrial Average four of the five years through 1995 (and it was about even with the Dow through the first half of 1996). Its best year was 1993, when it moved up 43.8 percent (compared with a 13.7 percent rise in the Dow).

FEES/SERVICES MANAGEMENT

The fund has a low front-end load of 3 percent and a maximum redemption fee of 0.75 percent, if shares are sold off within 30 days of purchase. Otherwise a $7.50 fee is charged upon redemption. The fund's total annual expense ratio of 1.65 percent (with no 12b-1 fee) is about average among load funds.

The fund offers all the standard services such as retirement account availability, automatic withdrawal, and automatic checking account deduction. Its minimum initial investment of $2,500 and minimum subsequent investment of $250 are a little high compared with other funds.

Fund manager Paul Antico has only been with the fund since 1996. The Fidelity fund family includes about 210 funds.

Top Ten Holdings

1. Caterpillar
2. Ingersoll Rand
3. IBM
4. Harnischfeger Industries
5. Dresser Industries
6. Deere & Co.
7. Compaq Computer
8. Dover
9. General Electric
10. Case

Asset Mix: Common stocks: 87%; Cash/equivalents: 13%
Total Net Assets: $337.6 million

Fees

Front-end load	3.00%
Redemption fee	$7.50
12b-1 fee	*None*
Management fee	0.61
Other expenses	1.04
Total annual expense	1.65%
Minimum initial investment	$2,500
Minimum subsequent investment	$250

Services

Telephone exchanges	*Yes*
Automatic withdrawal	*Yes*
Automatic checking deduction	*Yes*
Retirement plan/IRA	*Yes*
Instant redemption	*Yes*
Financial statements	*Semiannual*
Income distributions	*Semiannual*
Capital gains distributions	*Semiannual*
Portfolio manager—years	1
Number of funds in family	210

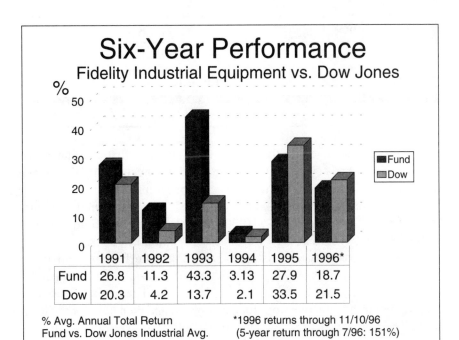

Six-Year Performance
Fidelity Industrial Equipment vs. Dow Jones

	1991	1992	1993	1994	1995	1996*
Fund	26.8	11.3	43.3	3.13	27.9	18.7
Dow	20.3	4.2	13.7	2.1	33.5	21.5

% Avg. Annual Total Return
Fund vs. Dow Jones Industrial Avg.

*1996 returns through 11/10/96
(5-year return through 7/96: 151%)

85

Davis New York Venture Fund "A"

LONG TERM

Davis Funds
124 East Marcy Street
Sante Fe, NM 87504-1688

Fund managers: Shelby Davis
and Christopher Davis
Fund objective: Long-term growth

Toll-free: 800-279-0279
In-state: 505-820-3101
Fax: 505-820-3002

Performance	★ ★
Consistency	★ ★ ★ ★
Fees/Services	★ ★ ★
NYVTX	**9 Points**

There are few managers in the mutual fund business that can match the experience of Davis New York Venture Fund manager Shelby Davis. He has run the long-term growth fund since it opened in 1969.

During that period, the fund has compiled an average annual growth rage of about 14 percent. A $10,000 investment in the fund when it opened in 1969 would now be worth about $385,000.

Davis and comanager Christopher Davis take a fairly conservative approach, investing primarily in undervalued large, established companies that the fund manager believes to be undervalued. The managers use extensive research to uncover top stock prospects, and then hold for the long term. The fund has a very low annual portfolio turnover ratio of just 15 percent.

"Like most portfolio managers, we believe in understanding the financial condition of companies inside and out," says Christopher Davis. "Where we gain an edge is by focusing on the quality of top management teams that are innovatively responsive to change, have proven records, and build business through their long-term vision. We separate the doers from the bluffers."

The fund is not particularly well diversified. It has substantial holdings in stocks of financial and insurance companies, which account for 42 percent of total assets. No other industrial segment accounts for more than 5 percent of assets. In all, the fund has about 120 stock holdings.

According to the prospectus, the fund's policy is to invest in stocks "that have capital growth potential due to factors such as undervalued assets or earnings potential, product development and demand, favorable operating ratios, resources for expansion, management abilities, reasonableness of market price, and favorable overall business prospects."

PERFORMANCE

The fund has posted solid growth over the past five years. Including dividends and capital gains distributions, the Venture Fund has provided a total return for the past five years (through mid-1996) of 139 percent. A $10,000 investment five years ago would have grown to about $24,000. Average annual return: 19 percent.

CONSISTENCY

The fund has been very consistent, outperforming the Dow Jones Industrial Average four of the five years from 1991 through 1995 (although it trailed the Dow through the first half of 1996). The fund's biggest gains came in 1991 and 1995, when it climbed 40.6 percent (both years).

FEES/SERVICES MANAGEMENT

The fund has a front-end load of 4.75 percent, and a very low total annual expense ratio of just 0.9 percent (including a 0.12 percent 12b-1 fee and a 0.75 management fee).

The fund offers all the standard services such as retirement account availability, automatic withdrawal, and automatic checking account deduction. Its minimum initial investment of $1,000 and minimum subsequent investment of $25 compare favorably with other funds.

Shelby Davis has managed the fund since its inception in 1969. Co-manager Christopher Davis recently joined the fund after managing other Davis funds. He has been with the company since 1989. The Davis fund family includes nine funds and allows shareholders to switch from fund to fund by telephone.

Top Ten Holdings

1. Intel
2. American Express
3. Wells Fargo
4. Citicorp
5. Morgan Stanley Group

6. Hewlett-Packard
7. Travelers Group
8. Coca-Cola
9. Equitable
10. First Bank System

Asset Mix: Common stocks: 86%; Preferred stock: 2%;
Cash/equivalents: 12%
Total Net Assets: $2.2 billion

Fees

Front-end load	4.75%
Redemption fee	*None*
12b-1 fee	0.12
Management fee	0.75
Other expenses	0.03
Total annual expense	0.90%
Minimum initial investment	$1,000
Minimum subsequent investment	$25

Services

Telephone exchanges	*Yes*
Automatic withdrawal	*Yes*
Automatic checking deduction	*Yes*
Retirement plan/IRA	*Yes*
Instant redemption	*Yes*
Financial statements	*Annual*
Income distributions	*Annual*
Capital gains distributions	*Annual*
Portfolio manager—years	28
Number of funds in family	9

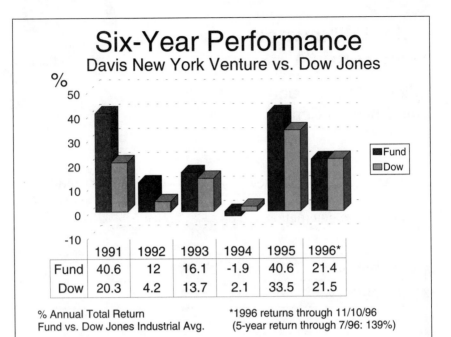

Six-Year Performance
Davis New York Venture vs. Dow Jones

	1991	1992	1993	1994	1995	1996*
Fund	40.6	12	16.1	-1.9	40.6	21.4
Dow	20.3	4.2	13.7	2.1	33.5	21.5

% Annual Total Return
Fund vs. Dow Jones Industrial Avg.

*1996 returns through 11/10/96
(5-year return through 7/96: 139%)

86

Colonial Newport Tiger Fund "A"

Colonial Mutual Funds
One Financial Center
Boston, MA 02111-2621

Fund managers: John Mussey
and Tim Tuttle
Fund objective: International equity

Toll-free: 800-248-2828
In-state: 617-426-3750
Fax: 617-426-1219

Performance	★ ★
Consistency	★ ★ ★ ★
Fees/Services	★ ★ ★
CNTAX	**9 Points**

Asia's explosive growth has been the driving force behind the strong, steady performance of the Colonial Newport Tiger Fund. Over the past eight years, the Tiger Fund, which invests strictly in the Asian stock market, has been the nation's best-performing international mutual fund.

Since its inception in 1989, the fund has grown at an average annual rate of about 15 percent. A $10,000 investment in the fund in 1989 would have grown to about $27,000 seven years later.

"A basic investment philosophy we've had since the beginning has been to take advantage of Asia's unusually rapid growth," explains Tim Tuttle, who manages the fund along with Jack Mussey. "The rate of economic growth in that area has been far faster than in Europe and North America. That faster economic growth translates into faster stock growth."

In managing the fund, Tuttle believes less is more. He and Mussey take a very conservative buy-and-hold approach, with an annual portfolio turnover ratio of just 8 percent.

"Our strategy has been very simple and very straightforward: Establish a sound investment philosophy and stick with it. Don't try to get too

cute. Some of the younger portfolio managers try to use very sophisti-
cated trading strategies. That may work well in a good market, but they
can get killed in a down market."

The fund buys stocks of very large companies (averaging $8 billion
in market capitalization) and holds for the long term. It invests strictly in
stocks of Southeast Asia, including China, Hong Kong, Singapore, Ma-
laysia, Korea, Taiwan, Thailand, and Indonesia. The fund does not invest
in Japan.

The fund generally stays at least 90 percent invested in stocks, and recently had a full 100 percent of assets in stocks. The fund has about 50
stock holdings. The leading sectors include finance, 23 percent of assets;
real estate-related stocks, 21 percent; manufacturing, 13 percent; communications 9 percent; and gas and electric services, 9 percent.

Tuttle attributes the strong performance of the Asian stock market to
the rapid economic growth rates of the Asian countries. He offers several
reasons for the growing strength of the Asian economy:

- *Education.* "It's almost an obsession with them. Their children spend
  3,000 hours a year in school compared with 1,500 hours a year for
  U.S. children."
- *Work ethic.* "Asians have always been hard workers. Their average
  work week is 55 hours compared with an average work week here of
  36 hours. In parts of China, they work 70 hours a week."
- *Savings ethic.* Asians save one-third of their income versus about 3
  percent personal savings for Americans. "That provides huge liquidity for the Asian economies."
- *Wage rates.* Most of Asia pays factory workers about one-fifth the sal-
  ary that American workers receive. (In Japan, by contrast, workers
  make 50 percent more than American workers.)
- *Probusiness government.* Governments work with businesses, sometimes offering tax concessions and other advantages to make them
  more competitive internationally.

Tuttle expects a few problems with the Asian economy as China
struggles to switch from a centrally planned economy to a free market
economy. Over the long term, however, he's convinced that the best bet
for stock market investors is the Asian market.

PERFORMANCE

The fund has enjoyed exceptional growth over the past five years. Including dividends and capital gains distributions, the Tiger Fund has provided a total return for the past five years (through mid-1996) of 139 percent. A $10,000 investment in 1991 would have grown to about $24,000 five years later. Average annual return: 19.1 percent.

CONSISTENCY

The fund has been fairly consistent, outperforming the Dow Jones Industrial Average three of the five years through 1995 (but it trailed the Dow through the first half of 1996). The fund has fared even better compared with the MSCI/EAFE International Index, outperforming the index four of the five years through 1995, and again through the first half of 1996.

FEES/SERVICES MANAGEMENT

The Colonial Newport Tiger "A" shares have a front-end load of 5.75 percent. Its total annual expense ratio of 1.80 percent (with a 0.25 12b-1 fee and a 0.8 percent management fee) is slightly above average.

The fund offers all the standard services such as retirement account availability and automatic checking account deduction. Its minimum initial investment of $1,000 and minimum subsequent investment of $50 compare favorably with other funds.

John Mussey and Tim Tuttle have managed the fund since 1989. The Colonial family includes 30 funds and allows shareholders to switch from fund to fund by telephone.

Top Ten Holdings

1. Citic Pacific
2. Hang Seng Bank
3. Cheung Kong Holdings
4. City Developments
5. Sun Hung Kai Properties
6. Hong Kong & China Gas
7. Singapore Press Holdings
8. HSBC Holdings
9. Development Bk Singapore
10. Swire Pacific "A"

Asset Mix: Common stocks: 100%
Total Net Assets: $441 million

Fees

Front-end load	5.75%
Redemption fee	*None*
12b-1 fee	0.25
Management fee	0.80
Other expenses	0.75
Total annual expense	1.80%
Minimum initial investment	$1,000
Minimum subsequent investment	$50

Services

Telephone exchanges	*Yes*
Automatic withdrawal	*Yes*
Automatic checking deduction	*Yes*
Retirement plan/IRA	*Yes*
Instant redemption	*Yes*
Financial statements	*Semiannual*
Income distributions	*Annual*
Capital gains distributions	*Annual*
Portfolio managers—years	7
Number of funds in family	30

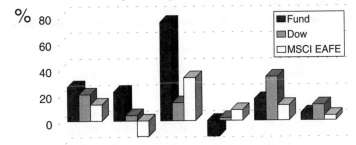

Six-Year Performance
Colonial Newport Tiger vs. Dow & World index

	1991	1992	1993	1994	1995	1996*
Fund	26	22.1	75.2	-12	16.3	5.7
Dow	20.3	4.2	13.7	2.1	33.5	11.8
MSCI EAFE	12.5	-11.9	32.9	8.1	11.6	3.7

% Annual Total Return   *1996 returns through 7/1/96
Fund vs. Dow Jones Industrial Avg.   (5-year return through 7/96: 139%)
MSCI EAFE refers to Morgan Stanley world index

87

Scudder Development Fund

AGGRESSIVE

Scudder Group of Funds
Two International Place
Boston, MA 02110

Fund manager: Roy C. McKay
Fund objective: Aggressive growth

Toll-free: 800-225-2470
In-state: 617-295-1000
Fax: 617-295-4072

Performance	★ ★
Consistency	★ ★
Fees/Services	★ ★ ★ ★ ★
SCDVX	**9 Points**

In selecting stocks for his Scudder Development Fund, manager Roy McKay tries to beat Wall Street's heavy hitters to the punch. He looks for small to midsized emerging growth companies that haven't yet attracted the interest of the big institutions, then cashes in when Wall Street discovers them and bids up the price.

Investors need to take a long-term perspective with this fund—it can be very volatile. In the past six years, the Development Fund has had two losing years and two years when it had gains of 50 percent or more.

Over the past 20 years the fund has had an average annual return of 16 percent. A $10,000 investment in the fund 20 years ago would now be worth about $200,000.

The fund has about 120 stock holdings, primarily in growing industries. Computer-related stocks make up 27 percent of assets; health-related, 14 percent; retail and consumer, 10 percent; business services, 13 percent; manufacturing, 11 percent; and telecommunications, 6 percent. The median market capitalization of the stocks in the portfolio is about $1 billion.

McKay is fairly conservative in his trading strategy, with an annual portfolio turnover ratio of 42 percent. The fund stays fully invested in stocks most of the time.

PERFORMANCE

The Scudder Development Fund has experienced solid growth over the past five years. Including dividends and capital gains distributions, the fund has provided a total return for the past five years (through mid-1996) of 136 percent. A $10,000 investment in 1991 would have grown to about $24,000 five years later. Average annual return: 18.8 percent.

CONSISTENCY

The fund has been very inconsistent, trailing the Dow Jones Industrial Average three of the five years from 1991 through 1995 (but it was ahead of the Dow through the first half of 1996). However, when things go well for the fund, they go very well. It soared 71.8 percent in 1991 and 50.6 percent in 1995—but suffered losses of 2 percent in 1992 and 5.3 percent in 1994.

FEES/SERVICES/MANAGEMENT

Like all Scudder funds, the Development Fund is a true no-load fund—no fee to buy, no fee to sell. The fund's total annual expense ratio of 1.32 percent (with no 12b-1 fee) is in line with other funds.

The fund offers all the standard services such as retirement account availability, automatic withdrawal, and automatic checking account deduction. Its minimum initial investment of $1,000 and minimum subsequent investment of $100 is in line with other funds.

Roy McKay has managed the fund since 1988. The Scudder fund family includes 37 funds and allows shareholders to switch from fund to fund by telephone.

Top Ten Holdings

1. Parametric Technology		6. G&K Services	
2. Cintas		7. Atmel	
3. Grand Casinos		8. Informix	
4. Ascend Communications		9. STERIS	
5. U.S. Robotics		10. Viking Office Products	

Asset Mix: Common stocks: 97%; Cash/equivalents: 3%
Total Net Assets: $941 million

Fees

Front-end load	*None*
Redemption fee	*None*
12b-1 fee	*None*
Management fee	0.99%
Other expenses	0.33
Total annual expense	1.32%
Minimum initial investment	$1,000
Minimum subsequent investment	$100

Services

Telephone exchanges	*Yes*
Automatic withdrawal	*Yes*
Automatic checking deduction	*Yes*
Retirement plan/IRA	*Yes*
Instant redemption	*Yes*
Financial statements	*Quarterly*
Income distributions	*Semiannual*
Capital gains distributions	*Semiannual*
Portfolio manager—years	9
Number of funds in family	37

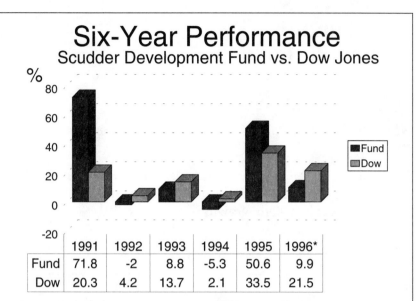

Six-Year Performance
Scudder Development Fund vs. Dow Jones

	1991	1992	1993	1994	1995	1996*
Fund	71.8	-2	8.8	-5.3	50.6	9.9
Dow	20.3	4.2	13.7	2.1	33.5	21.5

% Annual Total Return
Fund vs. Dow Jones Industrial Avg.

*1996 returns through 11/10/96
(5-year return through 7/96: 136%)

88

Alger Fund
Growth Portfolio

LONG TERM

The Alger Fund
75 Maiden Lane
New York, NY 10038

Fund managers: David Alger,
  Seilai Khoo, Ronald Tartaro
Fund objective: Long-term growth

Toll-free: 800-992-3863
In-state: 201-547-3600
Fax: 201-434-1459

Performance	★ ★
Consistency	★ ★ ★ ★
Fees/Services	★ ★ ★
AFGPX	**9 Points**

The Alger Fund Growth Portfolio invests most of its assets in fast-paced companies with more than $1 billion in market capitalization. By investing in a broad portfolio of these stable but growing companies, the fund has carved out a long-term record of strong consistent growth.

The fund has grown at a rate of about 16 percent per year since its inception in 1986. A $10,000 investment in the Alger Growth Portfolio when it opened in 1986 would have grown to about $40,000 ten years later.

Lead fund manager David Alger is fairly aggressive in his trading strategy, with an annual portfolio turnover ratio of 118 percent.

Although the fund does invest in some smaller growth stocks, by charter it must keep at least 65 percent of its assets in stocks of companies with over $1 billion in market capitalization. The fund stays almost fully invested in stocks most of the time.

Alger looks for stocks of companies that are either still in the developmental stage or are entering a new stage of growth as a result of a change in management or the development of new technology, new products, or broader services.

In all, the fund has about 75 stock holdings, heavily weighted in technology-related issues. Computers and business equipment account for 16 percent of total assets; health care stocks account for 21 percent; semiconductors make up 11 percent; communications makes up 6 percent and financial services also accounts for 6 percent.

PERFORMANCE

The fund has enjoyed solid growth over the past five years. Including dividends and capital gains distributions, the Alger Growth Portfolio has provided a total return for the past five years (through mid-1996) of 136 percent. A $10,000 investment in 1991 would have grown to about $24,000 five years later. Average annual return: 18.8 percent.

CONSISTENCY

The fund has been very consistent, outperforming the Dow Jones Industrial Average four of the five years through 1995 (but it trailed the Dow through the first half of 1996). Its biggest gain came in 1991, when it jumped 43.8 percent (compared with a 20.3 percent rise in the Dow).

FEES/SERVICES/MANAGEMENT

The fund has no front-end load, but it carries a 5 percent redemption fee that declines one percent each year. Its total annual expense ratio of 2.09 percent (including a 0.75 percent 12b-1 fee and a 0.75 percent management fee) is higher than most of the funds featured here.

The fund offers all the standard services such as retirement account availability, automatic withdrawal, and automatic checking account deduction. It has no minimum investment requirements, which compares very favorably with other funds.

David Alger has managed the fund since its inception in 1986. The Alger fund family includes six funds and allows shareholders to switch from fund to fund by telephone.

Top Ten Holdings

1. Digital Equipment
2. Cisco Systems
3. Lone Star Steakhouse/Saloon
4. Altera
5. First Data

6. Maxim Integrated Products
7. Healthsource
8. Oxford Health Plans
9. OfficeMax
10. Cardinal Health

Asset Mix: Common stocks: 90%; Cash/equivalents: 10%
Total Net Assets: $249 million

Fees

Front-end load	*None*
Redemption fee (Max)	5.00%
12b-1 fee	0.75
Management fee	0.75
Other expenses	0.59
Total annual expense	2.09%
Minimum initial investment	$1
Minimum subsequent investment	$1

Services

Telephone exchanges	*Yes*
Automatic withdrawal	*Yes*
Automatic checking deduction	*Yes*
Retirement plan/IRA	*Yes*
Instant redemption	*Yes*
Financial statements	*Annual*
Income distributions	*Annual*
Capital gains distributions	*Annual*
Portfolio manager—years	11
Number of funds in family	6

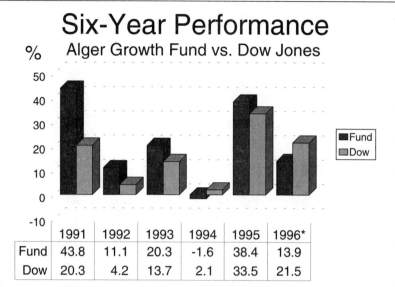

Six-Year Performance
% Alger Growth Fund vs. Dow Jones

	1991	1992	1993	1994	1995	1996*
Fund	43.8	11.1	20.3	-1.6	38.4	13.9
Dow	20.3	4.2	13.7	2.1	33.5	21.5

% Annual Total Return
Fund vs. Dow Jones Industrial Avg.

*1996 returns through 11/10/96)
(5-year return through 7/96: 136%)

89

Cowen Opportunity Fund "A"

AGGRESSIVE

Cowen Family of Funds
1 Financial Square
New York, NY 10005-3597

Fund managers: William Church
and Jarrod Cowen
Fund objective: Aggressive growth

Toll-free: 800-262-7116
In-state: 212-495-6000
Fax: 212-495-5638

Performance	★ ★
Consistency	★ ★ ★ ★
Fees/Services	★ ★ ★
CWNOX	**9 Points**

Cowen Opportunity Fund manager William Church likes to rummage through Wall Street's back alleys, searching for the tarnished, forgotten stocks that the market has beaten down and abandoned.

"Most growth companies hit a point in their development when they begin to stumble," says Church. "Everybody's looking for the next Microsoft, but it's very rare for a company to go straight to the moon as Microsoft did. When a stock stumbles, people stop following it. The stock just lays there by the wayside. We like to trawl through those types of stocks and look for companies that may be on the verge of a comeback."

The Opportunity Fund is an aggressive growth fund that invests primarily in small to midsized growth stocks. "We like to focus on small stocks because the smaller the company, the less research is done on it and the greater edge we have on the market."

Young growth companies stumble for two reasons, says Church. First, they stumble because they have to expand beyond the tight base of the entrepreneurial group that founded the company, with new people, new strategies, and new products that don't always pan out as well as the originals. "Growth is often its own worst enemy," says Church.

Young companies also stumble because their success tends to attract competition, often from larger corporations with deeper pockets. When a company's profits begin to wane, the glare of Wall Street dims as well. The stock price drops, investors lose interest, and analysts stop tracking the stock. As the song says, nobody loves you when you're down and out—except William Church. Church looks for companies that have fallen out of favor and are no longer tracked closely by Wall Street. When those companies seem ready to rebound, he wants to be the first on board.

Church also has a few sell rules. If insiders are selling aggressively, he'll get out of the stock. If the company's stock price gets too high relative to its earnings or book value, he'll sell. If the company is not meeting its objectives, he'll sell. "We listen carefully when the management of a company is describing what it plans to do. Then we monitor their progress. On the newer companies, we may allow for a little slippage in reaching their goals, but not too much. If it slides too much, we get out."

In selecting stocks, Church runs a variety of screens to uncover companies that fit his model. He looks for the following:

- Companies that are trading near their all-time lows or at least 50 percent below their highs of the past two years.
- Companies that are trading at less than two times book value.
- Companies that have suddenly shown some growth after two or three years of flat revenue.
- Companies in which the management team is actively buying the stock. "To us that's a positive. That's real money."

Once he finds a stock that meets his initial approval, Church looks at its financial reports and pays a visit to the company. "Normally, I wouldn't buy a stock until I visit the company and meet the management face to face," he says.

The Opportunity Fund has about 60 stock holdings. Its leading industrial sectors include oil and gas-related companies, 24 percent of assets; health and medical, 15 percent; computer-related, 12 percent. Church is an aggressive trader, with an annual portfolio turnover ratio of 148 percent.

PERFORMANCE

The fund has experienced solid growth over the past five years. Including dividends and capital gains distributions, the Cowen Opportunity Fund has provided a total return for the past five years (through mid-1996) of

134 percent. A $10,000 investment in 1991 would have grown to $23,000 five years later. Average annual return: 18.5 percent.

CONSISTENCY

The fund has been very consistent, outperforming the Dow Jones Industrial Average four of the five years from 1991 through 1995 (and it was even with the Dow through the first half of 1996).

FEES/SERVICES/MANAGEMENT

The fund has a front-end load of 4.75 percent and a total annual expense ratio of 1.45 percent (including a 0.25 percent 12b-1 fee and a 0.9 percent management fee), which is in line with other load funds.

The fund offers all the standard services such as retirement account availability, automatic withdrawal, and automatic checking account deduction. Its minimum initial investment requirement of $1,000 and minimum subsequent investment of $100 are about average among all mutual funds.

William Church has managed the fund since its inception in 1988. Jarrod Cowen was added as manager in 1994. The Cowen Fund family includes four funds and allows investors to switch from fund to fund by telephone.

Top Ten Holdings

1. Oryx Energy
2. Parker & Parsley Petroleum
3. Weatherford Enterra
4. Dravo
5. Control Data Systems
6. Petroleum Geo-Services
7. Kinder Care Learning Centers
8. Downey Financial
9. Evans & Sutherland Computer
10. Chiquita Brands Int'l

Asset Mix: Common stocks: 95%; Cash/equivalents: 5%
Total Net Assets: $42 million

Fees

Front-end load	4.75%
Redemption fee	*None*
12b-1 fee	0.25
Management fee	0.90
Other expenses	0.30
Total annual expense	1.45%
Minimum initial investment	$1,000
Minimum subsequent investment	$100

Services

Telephone exchanges	*Yes*
Automatic withdrawal	*Yes*
Automatic checking deduction	*Yes*
Retirement plan/IRA	*Yes*
Instant redemption	*Yes*
Financial statements	*Semiannual*
Income distributions	*Annual*
Capital gains distributions	*Annual*
Portfolio manager—years	9
Number of funds in family	4

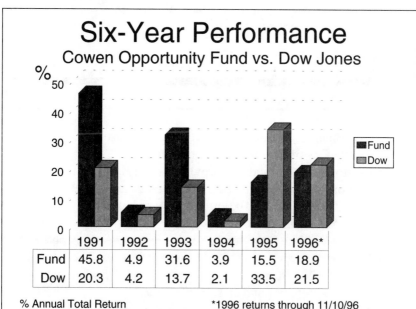

Six-Year Performance
Cowen Opportunity Fund vs. Dow Jones

	1991	1992	1993	1994	1995	1996*
Fund	45.8	4.9	31.6	3.9	15.5	18.9
Dow	20.3	4.2	13.7	2.1	33.5	21.5

% Annual Total Return
Fund vs. Dow Jones Industrial Avg.

*1996 returns through 11/10/96
(5-year return through 7/96: 134%)

90

Princor Emerging Growth Fund "A"

AGGRESSIVE

Princor Financial Group
P.O. Box 10423
Des Moines, IA 50306

Fund manager: Mike Hamilton
Fund objective: Aggressive growth

Toll-free: 800-247-4123
In-state: 515-246-7503
Fax: 515-248-2453

Performance	★ ★
Consistency	★ ★ ★ ★
Fees/Services	★ ★ ★
PEMGX	**9 Points**

The Princor Emerging Growth Fund focuses primarily on young, fast-growing companies from a wide range of industries.

Started in 1987, the fund has provided steady growth for its share-holders over the past ten years, posting an average annual return since its inception of 17 percent. A $10,000 investment held since 1987 would now be worth $38,000.

Fund manager Mike Hamilton has built very a diversified portfolio of 100 small stocks covering about 50 different industries. The fund generally stays about 80 to 90 percent invested in stocks. It also maintains a small position in preferred and convertible issues.

The label "aggressive growth" is a bit misleading for this fund, which takes a very conservative buy-and-hold approach. Its annual portfolio turnover ratio is a very modest 13 percent. The fund's stated investment policy is to "invest for any period of time, in any industry, and in any kind of growth-oriented company."

The fund's leading industrial sectors include commercial banks, 7 percent of total assets; drugs and medical products, 8 percent; computer services, 7 percent; and electronic components, 6 percent.

PERFORMANCE

The fund has enjoyed exceptional growth over the past five years. Including dividends and capital gains distributions, the Princor Emerging Growth Fund has provided a total return for the past five years (through mid-1996) of 134 percent. A $10,000 investment in 1991 would have grown to about $23,000 five years later. Average annual return: 18.5 percent.

CONSISTENCY

The fund has been very consistent, outperforming the Dow Jones Industrial Average four of the five years from 1991 through 1995 (but it trailed the Dow through the first half of 1996). The fund's biggest year was 1991 when it jumped 52.8 percent.

FEES/SERVICES/MANAGEMENT

The fund has a front-end load of 4.75 percent. Its total annual expense ratio of 1.47 percent (including a 0.25 percent 12b-1 fee and a management fee of 0.64 percent) is about average among load funds.

The fund offers all the standard services such as retirement account availability, automatic withdrawal, and automatic checking account deduction. Its minimum initial investment of $300 and minimum subsequent investment of $50 compare very favorably with other funds.

Mike Hamilton has managed the fund since 1987. The Princor fund family includes 13 funds and allows shareholders to switch freely from fund to fund by telephone.

Top Ten Holdings

1. Oracle Systems
2. Cisco Systems
3. Microsoft
4. AirTouch Communications
5. DSC Communications
6. 3Com
7. Compaq Computer
8. Nokia (ADR)
9. Silicon Graphics
10. Vanguard Cellular Systems

Asset Mix: Common stocks: 83%; Preferred stock: 1%;
Corporate bonds: 3%; Cash/equivalents: 13%
Total Net Assets: $213 million

Fees

Front-end load	4.75%
Redemption fee	*None*
12b-1 fee	0.25
Management fee	0.64
Other expenses	0.58
Total annual expense	1.47%
Minimum initial investment	$300
Minimum subsequent investment	$50

Services

Telephone exchanges	*Yes*
Automatic withdrawal	*Yes*
Automatic checking deduction	*Yes*
Retirement plan/IRA	*Yes*
Instant redemption	*Yes*
Financial statements	*Semiannual*
Income distributions	*Annual*
Capital gains distributions	*Annual*
Portfolio manager—years	10
Number of funds in family	13

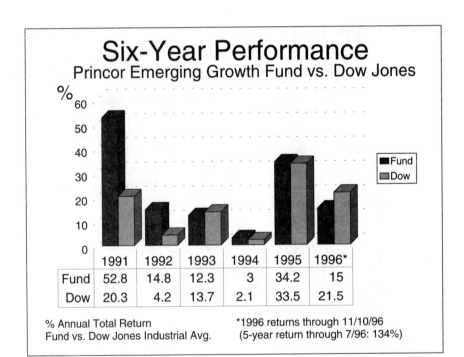

Six-Year Performance
Princor Emerging Growth Fund vs. Dow Jones

	1991	1992	1993	1994	1995	1996*
Fund	52.8	14.8	12.3	3	34.2	15
Dow	20.3	4.2	13.7	2.1	33.5	21.5

% Annual Total Return
Fund vs. Dow Jones Industrial Avg.

*1996 returns through 11/10/96
(5-year return through 7/96: 134%)

GROWTH

Mutual Series
Qualified Fund

Mutual Series Funds
51 John F. Kennedy Parkway
Short Hills, NJ 07078

Fund manager: Michael Price
Fund objective: Growth and Income

Toll-free: 800-448-3863
In-state: 201-912-2000
Fax: 201-376-6922

Performance	★ ★
Consistency	★ ★ ★ ★
Fees/Services	★ ★ ★
MQIFX	**9 Points**

Mutual Series Qualified Fund manager Michael Price rifles through the market's bargain bins, searching for, in his words, "cheap stocks"—companies trading at substantial discounts to their net asset value, securities of companies involved in mergers, acquisitions, and spinoffs, and companies in financial distress or bankrupcy.

Price's cheap stocks approach has helped the fund produce solid long-term returns and consistent year-to-year performance. The fund had annual returns in excess of 20 percent four of the five years from 1991 to 1995. But its growth chart bears little resemblance to that of the overall market. For instance, in 1992, when the Dow Jones Industrial Average was up 4.2 percent, the fund was up 22.7 percent; in 1993, when the market was up 13.7 percent, the fund was up 22.7 percent again; and in 1995, when the market was up 33.5 percent, the fund was up 26.6 percent. "The portfolio is designed for bad markets as well as good," explains Price, "and we will clearly sacrifice some upside potential in exchange for downside protection."

Over the past ten years, the fund has had an average annual return of about 15 percent. A $10,000 investment in the fund ten years ago would now be worth about $39,000.

The fund is made up primarily of large blue chip stocks such as cigarette-maker RJR Nabisco, Chase Manhattan bank, and U.S. West phone service. The fund also invests in some foreign stocks such as Volvo, tire-maker Pacific Dunlop, and tobacco giant Rothmans. In all, the portfolio has about 200 stock holdings.

While stocks usually make up most of the fund's assets, cash and liquid assets may at times account for about 25 percent of total assets. The Qualified Fund has more than $3 billion in total assets.

The fund is well diversified across industry sectors. Leading sectors include banking, 7 percent; consumer products and services, 11 percent; insurance, 5 percent; and health care, 6 percent.

PERFORMANCE

The Mutual Qualified Fund has experienced strong growth over the past five years. Including dividends and capital gains distributions, the fund has provided a total return for the past five years (through mid-1996) of 133 percent. A $10,000 investment in 1991 would have grown to about $23,000 five years later. Average annual return: 18.5 percent.

CONSISTENCY

The fund has been fairly consistent, outperforming the Dow Jones Industrial Average four of the five years through 1995 (but it trailed the Dow through the first half of 1996). The fund had gains of more than 20 percent four of the five years from 1991 to 1995.

FEES/SERVICES/MANAGEMENT

In 1996, the Mutual Series Funds were sold to Franklin Resources. Michael Price will continue as fund manager. However, the bad news for investors is that, beginning in 1997, the funds have been changed from no-load to load funds. (Load fees had not been announced as of this writing.)

The fund offers many of the standard services such as retirement account availability, automatic withdrawal, and automatic checking account deduction, but it does not offer the instant redemption option most other funds provide. Its minimum initial investment of $1,000 and minimum subsequent investment of $50 compare favorably with other funds. Michael Price has managed the fund since its inception in 1980.

Top Ten Holdings

1. Chase Manhattan	6. Pacific Dunlop Ltd.
2. RJR Nabisco Holdings	7. Sprint
3. U.S. West Media Group	8. Tenet HealthCare
4. Investor AB, B	9. MSCW Investors II, LLC
5. Sunbeam	10. Volvo AB, B

Asset Mix: Common stocks: 76%; Cash/equivalents: 24%
Total Net Assets: $3.8 billion

Fees

Front-end load	*None*
Redemption fee (max)	*None*
12b-1 fee	*None*
Management fee	0.60%
Other expenses	0.12
Total annual expense	0.72%
Minimum initial investment	$1,000
Minimum subsequent investment	$50

Services

Telephone exchanges	*No*
Automatic withdrawal	*Yes*
Automatic checking deduction	*Yes*
Retirement plan/IRA	*Yes*
Instant redemption	*No*
Financial statements	*Annual*
Income distributions	*Annual*
Capital gains distributions	*Annual*
Portfolio manager—years	17
Number of funds in family	5

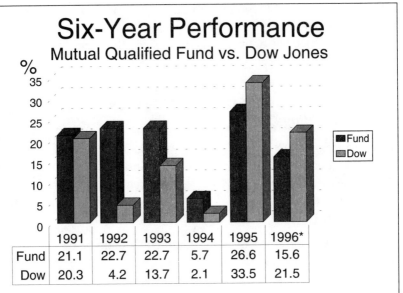

Six-Year Performance
Mutual Qualified Fund vs. Dow Jones

	1991	1992	1993	1994	1995	1996*
Fund	21.1	22.7	22.7	5.7	26.6	15.6
Dow	20.3	4.2	13.7	2.1	33.5	21.5

% Annual Total Return   *1996 returns through 11/10/96
Fund vs. Dow Jones Industrial Avg.   (5-year return through 7/96: 133%)

AGGRESSIVE

Meridian Fund

Meridian Fund, Inc.
60 E. Sir Francis Drake Blvd.
Wood Island, #306
Larkspur, CA 94939

Fund manager: Richard F. Aster Jr.
Fund objective: Aggressive growth

Toll-free: 800-446-6662
In-state: 415-461-6237
Fax: 415-461-0856

Performance	★ ★
Consistency	★ ★
Fees/Services	★ ★ ★ ★ ★
MERDX	**9 Points**

Meridian Fund manager Richard F. Aster Jr. looks for small to midsized companies with above-average growth in earnings and revenue. But, though the fund specializes in small, speculative stocks, Aster takes a fairly conservative approach in his investment policy.

Aster, who has been with the fund since its inception in 1984, does not always keep the fund fully invested in stocks. Recently, its asset mix was 78 percent stocks and 22 percent cash and cash equivalents. That strategy can stave off losses in a market downturn, but it can hurt a fund's performance in a raging bull market. For instance, in 1995 when the Dow Jones Industrial Average climbed 33.5 percent, the Meridian Fund gained only 22.4 percent.

Aster also maintains a conservative buy-and-hold approach, with a 29 percent annual turnover ratio.

Over the past ten years, the fund has had an average annual return of 12.3 percent. A $10,000 investment in the fund ten years ago would now be worth about $32,000.

The fund is heavily weighted in technology stocks. Cellular communications stocks account for 10 percent of total assets; health services make up 18 percent; technology accounts for 8 percent; retail makes up 12 percent; and consumer services comprise 8 percent. The fund holds only about 40 stocks.

PERFORMANCE

The fund has enjoyed strong growth over the past five years. Including dividends and capital gains distributions, the Meridian Fund has provided a total return for the five-year period (through mid-1996) of 129 percent. A $10,000 investment in 1991 would have grown to about $23,000 five years later. Average annual return: 18.1 percent.

CONSISTENCY

The Meridian Fund has been somewhat inconsistent trailing the Dow Jones Industrial Average three of the five years from 1991 through 1995 (and it trailed the Dow again through the first half of 1996). The fund's biggest year was 1991, when it moved up 58 percent (compared with a 20.3 percent rise in the Dow).

FEES/SERVICES/MANAGEMENT

Meridian Fund is a true no-load fund—no fee to buy, no fee to sell. It also has a low annual expense ratio of 1.06 percent (with no 12b-1 fee).

The fund offers all the standard services such as retirement account availability, automatic withdrawal, and automatic checking account deduction. Its minimum initial investment of $1,000 and minimum subsequent investment of $50 compare favorably with other funds.

Richard F. Aster Jr. has managed the fund since its inception in 1984. The Meridian Fund is one of two funds offered by Meridian Fund, Inc.

Top Ten Holdings

1. Vivra
2. Service Corp. Int'l
3. Cellular Communications Services
4. Quorum Health Group
5. Community Health Systems

6. AirTouch Communications
7. Vanguard Cellular Systems
8. Kohl's
9. Bed, Bath & Beyond
10. National Data

Asset Mix: Common stocks: 80%; U.S. Treasury bills: 20%
Total Net Assets: $393 million

Fees

Front-end load	*None*
Redemption fee (max)	*None*
12b-1 fee	*None*
Management fee	0.80%
Other expenses	0.26
Total annual expense	1.06%
Minimum initial investment	$1,000
Minimum subsequent investment	$50

Services

Telephone exchanges	*Yes*
Automatic withdrawal	*Yes*
Automatic checking deduction	*Yes*
Retirement plan/IRA	*Yes*
Instant redemption	*Yes*
Financial statements	*Annual*
Income distributions	*Annual*
Capital gains distributions	*Annual*
Portfolio manager—years	13
Number of funds in family	2

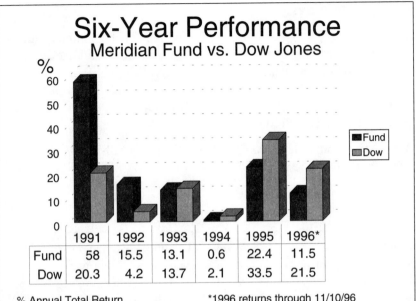

Six-Year Performance
Meridian Fund vs. Dow Jones

	1991	1992	1993	1994	1995	1996*
Fund	58	15.5	13.1	0.6	22.4	11.5
Dow	20.3	4.2	13.7	2.1	33.5	21.5

% Annual Total Return   *1996 returns through 11/10/96
Fund vs. Dow Jones Industrial Avg.   (5-year return through 7/96: 129%)

AGGRESSIVE

93

Dean Witter Developing Growth Securities Fund

Dean Witter Reynolds Inc.
2 World Trade Center
New York, NY 10048

Fund manager: Jayne Stevligson
Fund objective: Aggressive growth

Toll-free: 800-869-3863
In-state: 212-392-2550
Fax: 212-392-7204

Performance	★ ★ ★ ★
Consistency	★ ★ ★
Fees/Services	★ ★
DWDGX	**9 Points**

The Dean Witter Developing Growth Securities Fund is an aggressive growth fund that focuses on small stocks with annual sales in the range of $50 million to $400 million.

In selecting stocks for the portfolio, fund manager Jayne Stevligson looks for companies with certain key traits: a commitment to quality in their product or service; a competitive edge in their respective markets; hands-on managers who own a large stake in the company; the ability to maintain pricing and business flexibility; the ability to respond quickly to market shifts; and above-average price appreciation potential.

Over the past ten years, the fund has posted average annual returns of about 12 percent. A $10,000 investment in the fund ten years ago would now be worth about $32,000.

Stevligson is fairly aggressive in her trading policies, with an annual portfolio turnover ratio of 114 percent. In all, the fund has about 120 stock holdings. The fund almost fully invested in stocks most of the time.

The fund is well diversified across several growing industrial segments. The leading segments include computer software, 8 percent; communications, 10 percent; semiconductors, 5 percent; and health care and medical, 15 percent.

PERFORMANCE

The fund has enjoyed outstanding growth over the past five years. Including dividends and capital gains distributions, the Developing Growth Fund has provided a total return for the past five years (through mid-1996) of 165 percent. A $10,000 investment in 1991 would have grown to about $26,500 five years later. Average annual return: 21.5 percent.

CONSISTENCY

The fund has been fairly consistent, outperforming the Dow Jones Industrial Average three of the five years through 1995 (and again through the first half of 1996). The fund's biggest years were 1991 and 1995 when it jumped 48.2 percent and 47.7 percent respectively.

FEES/SERVICES/MANAGEMENT

The fund has a 5 percent redemption fee, and an annual expense ratio of 1.77 percent (including a 1 percent 12b-1 fee and a 0.5 percent management fee), which is a little bit above average.

The fund offers all the standard services such as checking account deduction and automatic withdrawal. Its minimum initial investment of $1,000 and minimum subsequent investment of $100 are in line with other funds.

Fund manager Jayne Stevligson has only been with the fund since 1994. Dean Witter offers a total of 41 funds and allows shareholders to switch from fund to fund by telephone.

Top Ten Holdings

1. U.S. Robotics	6. Bay Networks
2. Boston Scientific	7. Medaphis
3. HFS	8. Omnicare
4. PeopleSoft	9. Macromedia
5. PhyCor	10. HEALTHSOUTH

Asset Mix: Common stocks: 92%; Cash/equivalents: 3%;
U.S. government agency obligations: 5%
Total Net Assets: $783.4 million

Fees

Front-end load	*None*
Redemption fee	5.00%
12b-1 fee	1.00
Management fee	0.50
Other expenses	0.27
Total annual expense	1.77%
Minimum initial investment	$1,000
Minimum subsequent investment	$100

Services

Telephone exchanges	*Yes*
Automatic withdrawal	*Yes*
Automatic checking deduction	*Yes*
Retirement plan/IRA	*Yes*
Instant redemption	*Yes*
Financial statements	*Semiannual*
Income distributions	*Annual*
Capital gains distributions	*Annual*
Portfolio manager—years	3
Number of funds in family	41

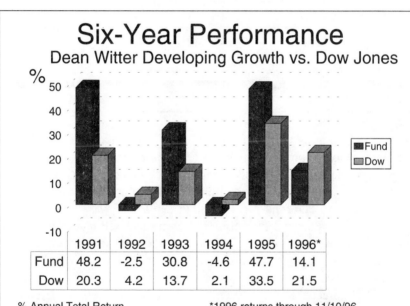

Six-Year Performance
Dean Witter Developing Growth vs. Dow Jones

	1991	1992	1993	1994	1995	1996*
Fund	48.2	-2.5	30.8	-4.6	47.7	14.1
Dow	20.3	4.2	13.7	2.1	33.5	21.5

% Annual Total Return
Fund vs. Dow Jones Industrial Avg.

*1996 returns through 11/10/96
(5-year return through 7/96: 165%)

94

Sierra Trust Emerging Growth Fund "A"

AGGRESSIVE

Sierra Trust Funds
9301 Corbin Avenue, Suite 333
Northridge, CA 91328-1160

Fund manager: James P. Goff
Fund objective: Aggressive growth

Toll-free: 800-222-5852
In-state: 818-725-0400
Fax: 617-248-6006

Performance	★ ★ ★
Consistency	★ ★ ★
Fees/Services	★ ★ ★
SREMX	**9 Points**

The Sierra Emerging Growth Fund invests in small stocks that fund manager James Goff expects will achieve accelerated growth in earnings and revenue, or that are undervalued relative to the market.

Over the past five years, the fund has grown at the rate of about 20 percent per year. The fund was opened in 1990.

Goff follows a strict discipline in buying and selling stocks for the portfolio. "When stocks hit their valuation targets or experience a difficult earnings period, the positions are either quickly sold or cut back." Goff is very aggressive in his trading strategy, with an annual portfolio turnover ratio of 181 percent. The fund stays fully invested in stocks almost all the time.

In all, the fund has about 70 stock holdings. Leading segments include health care, 18 percent; financial services, 14 percent; consumer, 15 percent; telecommunications, 10 percent; automotive, 10 percent; and materials and processing, 7 percent.

On average, the stocks in the portfolio have a market capitalization of about $500 million.

PERFORMANCE

The fund has enjoyed exceptional growth over the past five years. Including dividends and capital gains distributions, the Sierra Emerging Growth Fund has provided a total return for the past five years (through mid-1996) of 152 percent. A $10,000 investment in 1991 would have grown to about $25,000 five years later. Average annual return: 20.3 percent.

CONSISTENCY

The fund has been fairly consistent, outperforming the Dow Jones Industrial Average three of the five years through 1995 (and again through the first half of 1996). The fund's biggest year was 1991 when it moved up 39.3 percent.

FEES/SERVICES/MANAGEMENT

The Sierra Emerging Growth Fund has a front-end load of 5.75 percent. Its total annual expense ratio of 1.7 percent (including a 0.25 percent 12b-1 fee and a 0.88 percent management fee) is about average among load funds.

The fund offers all the usual mutual fund services such as retirement account availability, automatic withdrawal, and automatic checking account deduction. Its minimum initial investment of $250 and minimum subsequent investment of $100 compare very favorably with other funds.

James Goff has managed the fund since 1993. The Sierra fund family includes 15 funds and allows shareholders to switch from fund to fund by telephone.

Top Ten Holdings

1. Insignia Financial Group "A"
2. RP Scherer
3. Paging Network
4. JD Wetherspoon
5. Petco Animal Supplies
6. Exide
7. HFS
8. Trigen Energy
9. APS Holding "A"
10. CommNet Cellular

Asset Mix: Common stocks: 97%; Cash/equivalents: 3%
Total Net Assets: $286 million

Fees

Front-end load	5.75%
Redemption fee	*None*
12b-1 fee	0.25
Management fee	0.88
Other expenses	0.57
Total annual expense	1.70%
Minimum initial investment	$250
Minimum subsequent investment	$100

Services

Telephone exchanges	*Yes*
Automatic withdrawal	*Yes*
Automatic checking deduction	*Yes*
Retirement plan/IRA	*Yes*
Instant redemption	*Yes*
Financial statements	*Annual*
Income distributions	*Annual*
Capital gains distributions	*Annual*
Portfolio manager—years	4
Number of funds in family	15

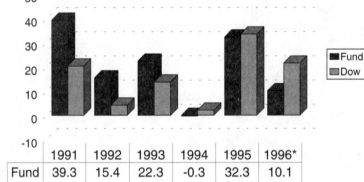

Six-Year Performance
Sierra Emerging Growth Fund vs. Dow Jones

	1991	1992	1993	1994	1995	1996*
Fund	39.3	15.4	22.3	-0.3	32.3	10.1
Dow	20.3	4.2	13.7	2.1	33.5	21.5

% Annual Total Return
Fund vs. Dow Jones Industrial Avg.

*1996 returns through 11/10/96
(5-year return through 7/96: 152%)

95
Fidelity Growth Company Fund

Fidelity Investments
82 Devonshire Street
Boston, MA 02109

Fund manager: Lawrence Greenburg
Fund objective: Long-term growth

Toll-free: 800-544-8888
In-state: 801-534-1910
Fax: 617-476-9753

Performance	★ ★
Consistency	★ ★ ★ ★
Fees/Services	★ ★ ★
FDGRX	**9 Points**

The portfolio list of the Fidelity Growth Company Fund reads like a Who's Who of American growth stocks. It is loaded with perennial favorites such as Microsoft, Bristol-Myers Squibb, PepsiCo, the Gap, Home Depot, General Electric, and Wal-Mart.

In all, the portfolio includes some 250 mid- to large-sized growth stocks that have helped make this one of the nation's most consistent funds. The fund has outperformed the Dow Jones Industrial Average seven of the last ten years.

Along with the big names, the fund invests in some up-and-coming growth companies such as Cisco Systems, Starbucks, and Medtronic. It also invests in a few turnaround opportunities such as IBM, Texas Instruments, and Sears. Fund manager Lawrence Greenburg is not shy about investing in tobacco stocks either. The fund owns stock in both Philip Morris and RJR Nabisco, the nation's two largest cigarette makers.

Greenburg maintains a fairly aggressive trading approach, with a 97 percent annual portfolio turnover ratio.

Although the fund is well diversified, with holdings across a broad range of industrial sectors, technology is the dominant group. The technology sector accounts for 32 percent of assets. Other leading sectors include finance, 10 percent; health, 9 percent; retail and wholesale, 8 percent; and utilities 7 percent. About 10 percent of the portfolio is in foreign stocks. The fund stays about 80 to 90 percent invested in stocks most of the time.

PERFORMANCE

The Growth Company Fund has experienced solid growth over the past five years. Including dividends and capital gains distributions, the fund has provided a total return for the past five years (through mid-1996) of 130 percent. A $10,000 investment in 1991 would have grown to about $23,000 five years later. Average annual return: 18.2 percent.

CONSISTENCY

The fund has been very consistent, outperforming the Dow Jones Industrial Average four of the five years through 1995 (but it narrowly trailed the Dow through the first half of 1996). The fund's biggest gain came in 1991, when it rose 48.3 percent (compared with a 20.3 percent rise in the Dow).

FEES/SERVICES/MANAGEMENT

The fund is a low load fund with a front-end fee of 3 percent. It has a very low total annual expense ratio of 0.96 percent (with no 12b-1 fee).

The fund offers all the standard services such as retirement account availability, automatic withdrawal, and automatic checking account deduction. Its minimum initial investment of $2,500 and minimum subsequent investment of $250 are a little high compared with other funds.

Larry Greenburg has only managed the fund since 1996. The Fidelity fund family includes 210 funds.

Top Ten Holdings

1. General Electric
2. Cisco Systems
3. Philip Morris
4. Compaq Computer
5. Oracle Systems
6. IBM
7. Federal National Mortgage Association
8. Citicorp
9. American Express
10. Microsoft

Asset Mix: Common stocks: 83%; Cash/equivalents: 17%
Total Net Assets: $8.5 billion

Fees

Front-end load	3.00%
Redemption fee	*None*
12b-1 fee	*None*
Management fee	0.69
Other expenses	0.27
Total annual expense	0.96%
Minimum initial investment	$2,500
Minimum subsequent investment	$250

Services

Telephone exchanges	*Yes*
Automatic withdrawal	*Yes*
Automatic checking deduction	*Yes*
Retirement plan/IRA	*Yes*
Instant redemption	*Yes*
Financial statements	*Semiannual*
Income distributions	*Semiannual*
Capital gains distributions	*Semiannual*
Portfolio manager—years	1
Number of funds in family	210

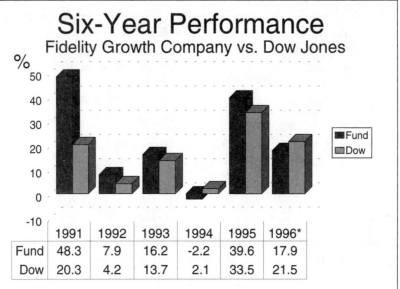

Six-Year Performance
Fidelity Growth Company vs. Dow Jones

	1991	1992	1993	1994	1995	1996*
Fund	48.3	7.9	16.2	-2.2	39.6	17.9
Dow	20.3	4.2	13.7	2.1	33.5	21.5

% Annual Total Return   *1996 returns through 11/10/96
Fund vs. Dow Jones Industrial Avg.   (5-year return through 7/96: 130%)

96
Alliance Growth Fund "A"

Alliance Capital Group
P.O. Box 1520
Secaucus, NJ 07096-1520

Fund manager: Tyler Smith
Fund objective: Long-term growth

Toll-free: 800-227-4618
or 800-221-5672
In-state: 201-319-4000
Fax: 201-319-4139

Performance	★ ★ ★
Consistency	★ ★ ★
Fees/Services	★ ★
AGRFX	**8 Points**

Stock market behemoths such as Sears, Texas Instruments, and Loews have been largely ignored on Wall Street recently in the wake of the high tech feeding frenzy. But Alliance Growth Fund manager Tyler Smith has built a solid track record the past few years by uncovering undervalued large cap stocks on the verge of a turnaround.

The Growth Fund combines undervalued megastocks with fast-paced emerging growth stocks. Smith keeps about 20 percent of his portfolio invested in high tech growth stocks. The fund has posted an average annual return over the past five years of about 20 percent.

Smith takes a fairly conservative long-term approach, with an annual portfolio turnover ratio of 61 percent. The fund is chartered to invest some of its assets in bonds and money markets, but stocks dominate the port-folio, often accounting for 95 to 98 percent of the fund's assets.

The fund's objective is to invest "primarily in equity securities of companies with favorable earnings outlooks and whose long-term growth rates are expected to exceed that of the U.S. economy."

The fund invests in a broad range of stocks led by financial stocks, which account for about 33 percent of total assets; consumer durables, 15 percent; and services, 9 percent.

PERFORMANCE

The fund has enjoyed exceptional growth over the past five years. Including dividends and capital gains distributions, the Alliance Growth Fund has provided a total return for the past five years (through mid-1996) of 149 percent. A $10,000 investment in 1991 would have grown to about $25,000 five years later. Average annual return: 20 percent.

CONSISTENCY

The fund has been fairly consistent, outperforming the Dow Jones Industrial Average three of the five years from 1991 through 1995 (but the fund trailed the Dow through the first half of 1996). The fund's biggest year was 1991 when it jumped 62 percent.

FEES/SERVICES/MANAGEMENT

The fund has a 4.25 percent front-end sales load, and an annual expense ratio of 1.35 percent (including a 0.3 percent 12b-1 fee and a 0.75 percent management fee), which is about average among all funds.

On the negative side, while the fund offers all the standard services such as retirement account availability, automatic withdrawal, and automatic checking account deduction, its service leaves something to be desired. The company was unable to send us an annual report, claiming the reports were out of print—with more than six months to go before the new reports were due.

The fund's minimum initial investment of $250 and minimum subsequent investment of $50 compare very favorably with other funds.

Tyler Smith has managed the fund since its inception in 1987. The Alliance fund family includes 44 funds and allows shareholders to switch from fund to fund by telephone.

Top Ten Holdings

1. Cisco Systems
2. Travelers Group
3. Philip Morris
4. Mannesmann
5. American International Group

6. Texas Instruments
7. Sears Roebuck
8. Loews
9. Oracle Systems
10. ITT

Asset Mix: Common stocks: 96%; Cash/equivalents: 4%;
Convertible Issues: 1%
Total Net Assets: $415 million

Fees

Front-end load	4.25%
Redemption fee	*None*
12b-1 fee	0.30
Management fee	0.75
Other expenses	0.30
Total annual expense	1.35%
Minimum initial investment	$250
Minimum subsequent investment	$50

Services

Telephone exchanges	*Yes*
Automatic withdrawal	*Yes*
Automatic checking deduction	*Yes*
Retirement plan/IRA	*Yes*
Instant redemption	*Yes*
Financial statements	*Semiannual*
Income distributions	*Quarterly*
Capital gains distributions	*Annual*
Portfolio manager—years	10
Number of funds in family	44

Six-Year Performance
% Alliance Growth Fund vs. Dow Jones

	1991	1992	1993	1994	1995	1996*
Fund	62	10.4	28.2	-1.8	29.5	20.1
Dow	20.3	4.2	13.7	2.1	33.5	21.5

% Annual Total Return   *1996 returns through 11/10/96)
Fund vs. Dow Jones Industrial Avg.   (5-year return through 7/96: 149%)

GROWTH

97
Kemper-Dreman High Return Fund "A"

Kemper Funds
120 S. LaSalle Street
Chicago, IL 60603

Fund manager: David N. Dreman
Fund objective: Growth and income

Toll-free: 800-621-1048
In-state: 312-781-1121
Fax: 312-499-1644

Performance	★ ★
Consistency	★ ★ ★
Fees/Services	★ ★ ★
KDHAX	**8 Points**

The Kemper-Dreman High Return Fund is a growth and income fund that tends to put a lot more emphasis on the growth than it does the income. The 1.1 percent annual dividend shareholders collect is chump change compared with the stellar 19 percent average annual total return the fund has produced over the past five years.

Fund manager David Dreman, who has run the fund since its inception in 1988, invests primarily in stocks of sound companies that appear to be undervalued. Dreman looks for stocks with low PE ratios, a record of solid earnings and dividend growth, reasonable returns on equity, and sound finances. As part of this strategy, the fund sells call options on stocks it holds and put options on stocks it may wish to acquire. It also buys and sells securities index futures and options, although most of its assets are in common stocks.

Dreman takes a conservative buy-and-hold approach, with an annual portfolio turnover ratio of just 18 percent.

The fund's 50 stock holdings have a decidedly nontech flavor, primarily because high tech stocks don't pay dividends. The High Return Fund is one of the few top performing funds without a single computer or telecommunications stock in the portfolio. It is heavily concentrated in banks and financial stocks, which make up 35 percent of total assets. Other leading segments include medical, 13 percent; energy, 7 percent; retailing, 6 percent; and tobacco, 4 percent.

PERFORMANCE

The fund has experienced strong growth over the past five years. Including dividends and capital gains distributions, the Kemper-Dreman High Return Fund has provided a total return for the past five years (through mid-1996) of 139 percent. A $10,000 investment in 1991 would have grown to about $24,000 five years later. Average annual return: 19 percent.

CONSISTENCY

The fund has been fairly consistent, outperforming the Dow Jones Industrial Average three of the five years through 1995 (and the fund narrowly trailed the Dow through the first half of 1996). The fund's biggest years were 1991 and 1995 when it climbed 47.6 percent and 46.9 percent, respectively.

FEES/SERVICES/MANAGEMENT

The High Return Fund has a front-end load of 5.75 percent. Its annual expense ratio of 1.57 percent (with no 12b-1 fee) is about average among funds.

   The fund offers all the usual mutual fund services such as retirement account availability, automatic withdrawal, and automatic checking account deduction. Its minimum initial investment of $1,000 and minimum subsequent investment of $100 is in line with other funds.

   David Dreman has managed the fund since its inception in 1988. The Kemper fund family includes 30 funds and allows shareholders to switch freely from fund to fund by telephone.

Top Ten Holdings

1. Federal National Mortgage Association
2. Federal Home Loan Mortgage Corp.
3. Columbia Gas Systems
4. Intel
5. Philip Morris
6. General Electric
7. Compaq Computer
8. PNC Bank
9. First Union
10. Texas Instruments

Asset Mix: Common stocks: 81%; Cash/equivalents: 19%
Total Net Assets: $154 million

Fees

Front-end load	5.75%
Redemption fee	*None*
12b-1 fee	*None*
Management fee	0.75
Other expenses	0.82
Total annual expense	1.57%
Minimum initial investment	$1,000
Minimum subsequent investment	$100

Services

Telephone exchanges	*Yes*
Automatic withdrawal	*Yes*
Automatic checking deduction	*Yes*
Retirement plan/IRA	*Yes*
Instant redemption	*Yes*
Financial statements	*Semiannual*
Income distributions	*Annual*
Capital gains distributions	*Annual*
Portfolio manager—years	9
Number of funds in family	30

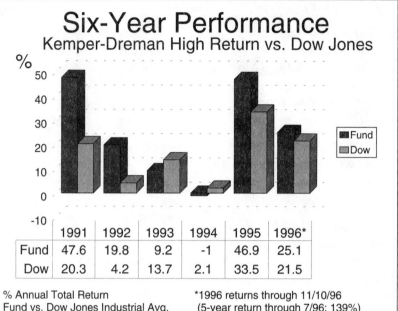

Six-Year Performance
Kemper-Dreman High Return vs. Dow Jones

	1991	1992	1993	1994	1995	1996*
Fund	47.6	19.8	9.2	-1	46.9	25.1
Dow	20.3	4.2	13.7	2.1	33.5	21.5

% Annual Total Return
Fund vs. Dow Jones Industrial Avg.

*1996 returns through 11/10/96
(5-year return through 7/96: 139%)

98

GAM International Fund

GAM Funds
135 East 57th Street, 25th Floor
New York, NY 10022

Fund manager: John R. Horseman
Fund objective: International equity

Toll-free: 800-426-4685
In-state: 212-407-4700
Fax: 212-407-4684

Performance	★ ★
Consistency	★ ★ ★
Fees/Services	★ ★ ★
GAMNX	**8 Points**

This is a fund that passes itself off as an international "equity" fund, but in truth, the fund has been taking a pretty lame approach to the stock market. Only 37 percent of the fund's assets are in stocks. The rest are in bonds, cash equivalents, and convertible issues.

To its credit, the GAM International Fund has been one of the better-performing international funds the past five years, thanks largely to an 80 percent gain in 1993. But if you're looking for a true play in the international stock market, you won't find it here.

However, for a conservative international play, this would certainly be a suitable find. Most of its stock holdings are in large blue chip companies in major markets such as Toshiba in Japan, Banco Popular in Spain, and Barclays in Britain. Its bond holdings are primarily in government bonds of major countries such as Britain, France, and Germany.

The fund only has about 35 stock holdings. Fund manager John Horseman maintains a conservative trading approach, with a 35 percent annual portfolio turnover ratio.

The fund is invested across a broad range of industry groups. By country, about 30 percent of its assets are invested in Germany, 15 percent in the United Kingdom, 11 percent in Switzerland, 11 percent in Japan, 10 percent in the Netherlands, and 8 percent in France.

PERFORMANCE

The fund has posted strong growth over the past five years. Including dividends and capital gains distributions, the GAM International Fund has provided a total return for the past five years (through mid-1996) of 132 percent. A $10,000 investment in 1991 would have grown to $23,000 five years later. Average annual return: 18.3 percent.

CONSISTENCY

The fund has been fairly consistent. Although it trailed the Dow Jones Industrial Average four of the five years from 1991 through 1995 (and again through the first half of 1996), it outpaced the MSCI/EAFE international index four of the five years through 1995. (But it was trailing the index through the first half of 1996.) The fund's biggest year was 1993, when it soared 80 percent.

FEES/SERVICES/MANAGEMENT

The fund has a front-end load of 5.0 percent and total annual expense ratio of 1.6 percent (with no 12b-1 fee), which is fairly low for an international fund. Its minimum initial investment of $10,000 and minimum subsequent investment of $1,000 are very high compared with most other funds.

The fund offers all of the standard services customarily provided by mutual funds including telephone redemption, checking account deduction, automatic withdrawal, retirement accounts, and telephone fund switching.

John Horseman has managed the fund since 1987. The GAM fund family includes seven funds.

Top Ten Holdings

1. Republic of Germany government bonds (6.25%)
2. Sandoz
3. Government of France bonds (6.00%)
4. Government of France (6.00%)
5. Fortis AMEV
6. Roche Holding
7. Barclays
8. Republic of Austria (6.50%)
9. Government of Netherlands (7.50%)
10. Government of Netherlands (7.50%)

Asset Mix: Government bonds: 50%; Convertible issues: 4%; Foreign equities: 37%; Cash/equivalents: 9%
Total Net Assets: $828 million

Fees

Front-end load	5.00%
Redemption fee (max)	*None*
12b-1 fee	*None*
Management fee	1.00
Other expenses	0.60
Total annual expense	1.60%
Minimum initial investment	$10,000
Minimum subsequent investment	$1,000

Services

Telephone exchanges	*Yes*
Automatic withdrawal	*Yes*
Automatic checking deduction	*Yes*
Retirement plan/IRA	*Yes*
Instant redemption	*Yes*
Financial statements	*Quarterly*
Income distributions	*Annual*
Capital gains distributions	*Annual*
Portfolio manager—years	10
Number of funds in family	9

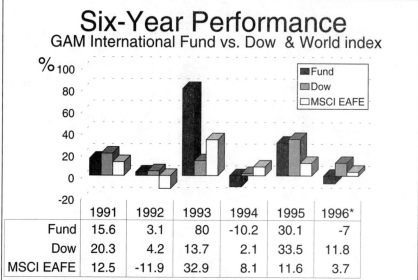

Six-Year Performance
GAM International Fund vs. Dow & World index

	1991	1992	1993	1994	1995	1996*
Fund	15.6	3.1	80	-10.2	30.1	-7
Dow	20.3	4.2	13.7	2.1	33.5	11.8
MSCI EAFE	12.5	-11.9	32.9	8.1	11.6	3.7

% Annual Total Return   *1996 returns through 7/1/96
Fund vs. Dow Jones Industrial Avg.   (5-year return through 7/96: 132%)
MSCI EAFE refers to Morgan Stanley world index

LONG TERM

99
Alger Small
Capitalization Portfolio

The Alger Fund
75 Maiden Lane
New York, NY 10038

Fund managers: David Alger,
Seilai Khoo, Ronald Tartaro
Fund objective: Long-term growth

Toll-free: 800-992-3863
In-state: 201-547-3600
Fax: 201-434-1459

Performance	★ ★
Consistency	★ ★ ★
Fees/Services	★ ★ ★
ALSCX	**8 Points**

The Alger Small Cap Portfolio invests in small fast-growing companies with innovative products, services, or technologies. While those stocks are often very volatile, they tend to offer strong long-term performance.

Since its inception in 1986, the Small Capitalization Portfolio has provided an average annual return of about 19 percent. A $10,000 investment in the fund when it opened in 1986 would have grown to about $52,000 ten years later.

Fund managers David Alger (who has managed the fund since its inception), Seilai Khoo and Ronald Tartaro are fairly aggressive in their trading strategy, with an annual portfolio turnover ratio of 133 percent. The fund stays almost fully invested in stocks most of the time.

Most of the approximately 100 stocks in the portfolio range in size from $20 million in market capitalization to $2.2 billion.

The portfolio is heavily weighted in technology stocks. Leading sectors include communications (15 percent of total assets), computer-related stocks (22 percent), health care (13 percent), and semiconductors, 19 percent.

PERFORMANCE

The fund has enjoyed strong growth over the past five years. Including dividends and capital gains distributions, the Alger Small Cap Portfolio has provided a total return for the past five years (through mid-1996) of 132 percent. A $10,000 investment in 1991 would have grown to $23,200 five years later. Average annual return: 18.4 percent.

CONSISTENCY

The fund has been somewhat inconsistent, trailing the Dow Jones Industrial Average three of the five years from 1991 through 1995—although it was within 1 percent of the Dow two of those three years. (It also trailed the Dow through the first half of 1996.) Its biggest gains came in 1991 and 1995 when it jumped 54.6 percent and 48.9 percent, respectively.

FEES/SERVICES/MANAGEMENT

The fund has no front-end load, but it carries a 5 percent redemption fee that declines one percentage point for each year you hold the fund. Its total annual expense ratio of 2.11 percent (including a 0.75 percent 12b-1 fee and a 0.85 percent management fee) is higher than most of the funds featured here.

The fund offers all the standard services such as retirement account availability, automatic withdrawal and automatic checking account deduction. It has no minimum investment requirements, which compares very favorably with other funds.

David Alger has managed the fund since its inception in 1986. The Alger fund family includes six funds and allows shareholders to switch from fund to fund by telephone.

Top Ten Holdings

1. Maxim Integrated Products
2. Glenayre Technologies
3. Bay Networks
4. Digital Equipment
5. Ascend Communications
6. BioChem Pharma
7. Healthsource
8. Linear Technology
9. Electronics For Imaging
10. U.S. Robotics

Asset Mix: Common stocks: 96%; Cash/equivalents: 4%
Total Net Assets: $584 million

Fees

Front-end load	*None*
Redemption fee (max)	5.00%
12b-1 fee	0.75
Management fee	0.85
Other expenses	0.51
Total annual expense	2.11%
Minimum initial investment	$1
Minimum subsequent investment	$1

Services

Telephone exchanges	*Yes*
Automatic withdrawal	*Yes*
Automatic checking deduction	*Yes*
Retirement plan/IRA	*Yes*
Instant redemption	*Yes*
Financial statements	*Annual*
Income distributions	*Annual*
Capital gains distributions	*Annual*
Portfolio manager—years	11
Number of funds in family	6

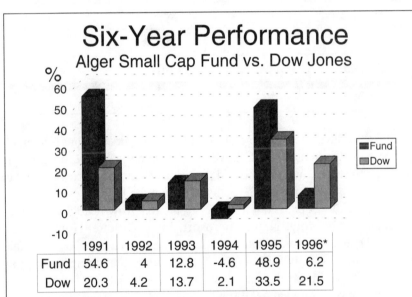

Six-Year Performance
Alger Small Cap Fund vs. Dow Jones

	1991	1992	1993	1994	1995	1996*
Fund	54.6	4	12.8	-4.6	48.9	6.2
Dow	20.3	4.2	13.7	2.1	33.5	21.5

% Avg. Annual Total Return
Fund vs. Dow Jones Industrial Avg.

*1996 returns through 11/10/96
(5-year return through 7/96: 132%)

100

Enterprise Growth Portfolio

LONG TERM

Enterprise Funds
3343 Peachtree Road NE
Suite 450
Atlanta, GA 30326

Fund manager: Ronald E. Canakaris
Fund objective: Long-term growth

Toll-free: 800-432-4320
In-state: 404-261-1116
Fax: 404-261-1118

Performance	★ ★
Consistency	★ ★ ★
Fees/Services	★ ★ ★
ENGRX	**8 Points**

Small stocks have been the rage on Wall Street this decade, but fund manager Ronald Canakaris still believes in the potential of the bigger blue chip growth stocks that have helped propel his Enterprise Growth Fund to strong, stready gains in the 17 years he has run the fund.

The portfolio is packed with many of the top growth stocks in America, such as Motorola, Nike, Microsoft, Intel, Gillette, Home Depot, Coca-Cola, and Johnson & Johnson. Canakaris takes a pure buy-and-hold approach, staying fully invested in stocks while maintaining a very low 15 percent annual portfolio turnover ratio.

Over the past ten years, the fund has posted an average annual return of about 14 percent. A $10,000 investment in the fund ten years ago would now be worth about $36,000.

Canakaris looks for companies with rapid strong earnings growth that are positioned to benefit from the expansion of global markets.

The fund has only about 35 stock holdings, primarily in fast-growth industries. Leading sectors include computer-related, 30 percent of assets; food and beverages, 11 percent; communications, 6 percent; consumer nondurables, 15 percent; retail, 6 percent; and pharmaceuticals, 10 percent.

PERFORMANCE

The fund has enjoyed exceptional growth over the past five years. Including dividends and capital gains distributions, the Enterprise Growth Fund has provided a total return for the past five years (through mid-1996) of 132 percent. A $10,000 investment in 1991 would have grown to about $23,000 five years later. Average annual return: 18.4 percent.

CONSISTENCY

The fund has been fairly consistent, outperforming the Dow Jones Industrial Average three of the five years through 1995 (and again through the first half of 1996). The fund's biggest years were 1991 and 1995 when it moved up 41.8 percent and 40 percent, respectively.

FEES/SERVICES/MANAGEMENT

The Enterprise Growth Fund has a front-end load of 4.75 percent. Its total annual expense ratio of 1.6 percent (including a 0.45 percent 12b-1 fee and a 0.75 percent management fee) is about average among load funds.

The fund offers all the usual mutual fund services such as retirement account availability, automatic withdrawal, and automatic checking account deduction. Its minimum initial investment of $1,000 and minimum subsequent investment of $50 compare favorably with other funds.

Ronald Canakaris has managed the fund since 1980. The Enterprise fund family includes 10 funds and allows shareholders to switch from fund to fund by telephone.

Top Ten Holdings

1. Intel	6. Seagate Technology
2. Coca-Cola	7. General Motors "E"
3. Procter & Gamble	8. Oracle Systems
4. Microsoft	9. U.S. Robotics
5. Cisco Systems	10. Johnson & Johnson

Asset Mix: Common stocks: 97%; Cash/equivalents: 3%
Total Net Assets: $150 million

Fees

Front-end load	4.75%
Redemption fee	*None*
12b-1 fee	0.45
Management fee	0.75
Other expenses	0.40
Total annual expense	1.60%
Minimum initial investment	$1,000
Minimum subsequent investment	$50

Services

Telephone exchanges	*Yes*
Automatic withdrawal	*Yes*
Automatic checking deduction	*Yes*
Retirement plan/IRA	*Yes*
Instant redemption	*Yes*
Financial statements	*Annual*
Income distributions	*Annual*
Capital gains distributions	*Annual*
Portfolio manager—years	17
Number of funds in family	10

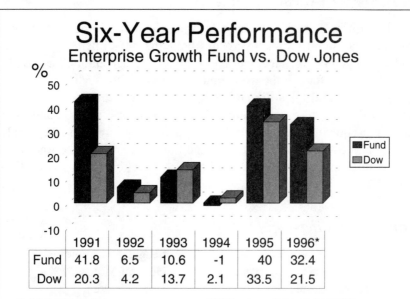

Six-Year Performance
Enterprise Growth Fund vs. Dow Jones

	1991	1992	1993	1994	1995	1996*
Fund	41.8	6.5	10.6	-1	40	32.4
Dow	20.3	4.2	13.7	2.1	33.5	21.5

% Annual Total Return
Fund vs. Dow Jones Industrial Avg.

*1996 returns through 11/10/96
(5-year return through 7/96: 132%)

Honorable Mentions

Bond Funds

Fund	Load	Average Annual Return 3-yr.	5-yr.	Annual Expense Ratio	Minimum Investment	Telephone
Loomis Sayles Bond Fund	None	10.2%	14.0%	0.79%	$2,500	800-633-3330
Alliance Corporate Bond Fund	4.25%	6.4	13.1	1.24	250	800-221-5672
Federated Bond Fund	1.00	6.1	10.9	1.03	1,500	800-245-0242
Janus Flexible Income Fund	None	7.1	10.9	0.96	2,500	800-525-3713
Strong Corporate Bond Fund	None	8.7	10.7	1.00	2,500	800-368-3863
IDS Bond Fund	5.00	6.4	10.3	0.78	2,000	800-328-8300
Smith Barney Investment Grade Bond	4.50R	5.1	10.2	1.61	1,000	800-221-8806
Vanguard Fixed: Long Term Corp.	None	5.5	10.1	0.31	3,000	800-635-1511
Ivy Bond Fund	4.75	6.2	9.8	1.50	1,000	800-777-6472

Equity Income

Fund	Load	Average Annual Return 3-yr.	5-yr.	Annual Expense Ratio	Minimum Investment	Telephone
T. Rowe Price Equity Income	None	15.9%	15.0%	0.85%	$1,000	800-225-5132
Federated Equity Income	5.50%	12.5	14.5	1.03	500	800-245-0242
Benham Equity Income & Growth	None	14.4	14.4	0.67	2,500	800-331-8331
IDS Diversified Equity Income	5.00	11.0	14.1	0.94	2,000	800-328-8300
State Street Research Equity Income	4.50	12.3	14.1	1.42	2,500	800-531-0131
Heritage Income Growth Trust	4.75	13.1	13.7	1.64	1,000	800-421-4184
Vanguard Equity Income	None	12.7	13.4	0.45	3,000	800-635-1511
Delaware Decatur Total Return	4.75	13.8	13.3	1.26	1,000	800-362-7500
Managers Funds: Income Equity	None	13.8	11.9	1.45	2,000	800-835-3879
Van Kampen-Amer. Cap Equity Income	5.75	13.2	11.7	0.95	500	800-421-5666

Note: "R" stands for "Redemption Fee."

High-Yield Bond Funds

Fund	Load	Average Annual Return 3-yr.	5-yr.	Annual Expense Ratio	Minimum Investment	Telephone
Dean Witter High Yield Securities	5.50%	8.4%	16.1%	0.79%	$1,000	800-869-3863
Fidelity Spartan High Income Fund	1.00R	11.4	15.7	0.80	10,000	800-544-8888
Mainstay High Yield Corporate Bond	5.00R	11.7	15.7	1.60	500	800-522-4202
Northeast Investors Trust	None	11.6	15.3	0.67	1,000	800-225-6704
Seligman High Yield Bond	4.75	11.0	14.7	1.09	1,000	800-221-2783
Fidelity Capital & Income	1.50R	7.1	14.7	0.98	2,500	800-544-6666
First Investors High Yield Fund	6.25	9.7	14.2	1.56	1,000	800-423-4026
Colonial High Yield Securities	4.75	8.9	14.0	1.21	1,000	800-248-2828
First Investors Fund for Income	6.25	9.7	14.0	1.22	1,000	800-423-4026
IDS Extra Income	5.00	8.7	13.8	0.87	2,000	800-328-8300

International and Global Equity

Fund	Load	Average Annual Return 3-yr.	5-yr.	Annual Expense Ratio	Minimum Investment	Telephone
Hotchkis & Wiley International	None	13.5%	14.5%	1.00%	$5,000	800-346-7301
Dean Witter European Growth	5.00%R	20.2	14.4	2.23	1,000	800-869-3863
Fortis Worldwide Global Growth	4.75	16.1	14.3	1.73	500	800-800-2638
GAM Global Fund	5.00	18.7	14.3	2.16	10,000	800-426-4685
Putnam Europe Growth Fund	5.75	17.9	13.9	1.38	500	800-225-1581
Templeton World Fund	5.75	14.4	13.9	1.05	100	800-237-0738
Alliance New Europe Fund	4.25	16.4	13.9	2.09	250	800-221-5672
SmallCap World Fund	5.75	14.0	13.8	1.13	1,000	800-421-9900
Managers International Equity Fund	None	13.1	13.6	1.58	2,000	800-835-3879
T. Rowe Price European Stock Fund	None	18.2	12.2	1.20	2,500	800-638-5660

Sector Funds

Fund	Load	Average Annual Return 3-yr.	5-yr.	Annual Expense Ratio	Minimum Investment	Telephone
Davis Financial Fund	4.75%	16.4%	21.6%	1.18%	$1,000	800-279-0279
PaineWebber Financial Services Growth	5.00R	14.5	21.1	2.22	1,000	800-647-1568
Fidelity Select Leisure Portfolio	3.00	14.5	18.3	1.62	2,500	800-544-8888
Fidelity Select Brokerage & Investment	3.00	9.2	17.8	2.54	2,500	800-544-8888
Fidelity Select Transportation	3.00	10.8	17.6	2.36	2,500	800-544-8888
Vanguard Specialized Health Care	None	26.4	16.9	0.46	3,000	800-635-1511
Kemper Technology Fund	5.75	19.3	15.4	0.88	1,000	800-621-1048
Cohen & Steers Realty Shares	None	9.5	15.4	1.12	10,000	800-437-9912
Fidelity Select Insurance	3.00	15.1	11.1	2.34	2,500	800-544-8888
Fidelity Select Food and Agriculture	3.00	18.9	10.5	1.68	2,500	800-544-8888

Tax-Exempt Bond Funds

Fund	Load	Average Annual Return 3-yr.	5-yr.	Annual Expense Ratio	Minimum Investment	Telephone
Executive Insured Tax-Exempt	4.75%	6.8%	9.8%	0.5%	$1,000	800-423-4026
Smith Barney Managed Municipals	4.00	6.5	9.4	0.71	1,000	800-221-8806
Excelsior Long Term Tax Exempt	4.50	6.8	9.3	0.77	500	800-446-1012
United Municipal Bond Fund	4.25	5.6	8.4	0.65	500	800-366-5465
Vista Tax Free Income Fund	4.50	4.1	8.4	0.85	2,500	800-648-4782
Flagship All American Tax Exempt	4.20	5.2	8.4	0.76	3,000	800-227-4648
Vanguard Municipal Bond: High Yield	None	5.8	8.4	0.21	3,000	800-635-1511
Vanguard Municipal Bond: Long Term	None	5.9	8.3	0.21	3,000	800-635-1511
Warburg Pincus Tax Free Bond	None	5.3	8.2	0.48	1,000	800-257-5614
Benham National Tax Free: Long Term	None	4.7	7.9	0.66	1,000	800-331-8331

Glossary

American Depositary Receipt (ADR) A foreign stock sponsored by a U.S. bank and re-issued on a U.S. stock exchange. Although ADRs do not trade at the same price in the United States as they trade for at home (because the sponsoring bank issues them at a different price), their prices move exactly with the price movements of the original stock.

annual expense ratio Yearly mutual fund fee assessed to cover the fund's expenses, including management fees, transaction fees, and marketing expenses. Annual expense ratios usually vary from 0.6 percent to about 3.0 percent of the fund's net asset value. The expense ratio is deducted directly from each shareholder's holdings.

assets The amount of money invested in a mutual fund by shareholders. The largest mutual fund is Fidelity Magellan, which boasts about $30 billion in total assets. Most funds have in the range of $25 million to $3 billion.

back-end load A fee charged by some mutual funds to investors when they sell their shares in the fund. The fees, which range from about 1 to 6 percent, typically diminish about 1 percent each year the investor holds the fund. For instance, a fund with a maximum 5 percent back-end load will charge the full 5 percent the first year. But the fee normally drops to 4 percent the second year, 3 percent the third, 2 percent the fourth, 1 percent the fifth, and zero after the fifth year. There are two types of back-end loads, *deferred sales charges* and *redemption fees*. Deferred are definitely the preferred. Funds with deferred sales fees base the charges on the net asset value of the shares when you bought them, while redemption fees are based the price of your shares at the time you sell. So if your fund has a strong gain, you'll pay much more in redemption fees than you would in deferred sales charges. (See also *load, no-load, front-end load, redemption fee,* and *deferred sales charge.*)

bottom up Investment method in which an investor selects stocks based on the merits of each individual stock without regard to the overall economy. Opposite of a "top-down" approach in which an investor looks at broad economic patterns to determine which investment sectors would make the most timely investments. Most stock mutual fund managers use a *bottom-up* approach, although some use a blend of both. (See also *top down.*)

cash equivalent An investment that has a monetary value equal to a specified sum.

cash equivalent investments Interest-bearing securities of high liquidity and safety—such as commercial paper, certificates of deposit, and Treasury bills—that are considered virtually as good as cash. Money market funds invest almost exclusively in cash equivalents. When stock mutual fund managers sense a looming downturn in the market, they often lighten their stock portfolios and move more assets to cash equivalents. That provides safety and a little income for the short term while they await a turnaround in the market.

classes of mutual fund shares Mutual fund companies often issue fund shares of several classifications. The shares, which normally are referred to as "A" class, "B" class, "C" class, "D" class, and so on, usually have the same asset mix but different investor requirements. For instance, "A" shares may have a front-end sales load and a low annual expense ratio, whereas "B" shares may have a back-end load and a slightly higher annual expense ratio. "C" shares may have no sales load but a very high annual expense ratio, and "D" shares may be geared to institutional and affluent investors and may require a minimum investment of $100,000 or more.

deferred sales charge A sales fee or "back-end load" charged by some mutual funds to shareholders when they sell their fund shares. See *back-end load.*

dividend A portion of a company's earnings that is paid to its shareholders. Funds holding dividend-paying stocks pass those dividends onto shareholders in lump payments either quarterly, semiannually, or annually, depending on the fund. Investors in most funds may have dividends automatically reinvested in additional shares.

dividend yield The annual dividend payment divided by its market price per share. If a stock is trading at $100 a share, and it pays a $10 dividend, the dividend yield is 10 percent.

equity investment A security (usually common stock or preferred stock) that represents a share of ownership in a business entity (usually a corporation).

front-end load The sales fee a mutual fund charges investors to buy shares of the fund. The fee (usually in the range of 3 to 8.5 percent) is deducted directly from the investor's contribution. For instance, a $1,000 investment in a fund with a 5 percent front-end load would result in $50 in load fees and $950 in actual fund shares. (See also *load, no-load,* and *back-end load.*)

load A sales fee charged to mutual fund investors. Loads normally vary from about 3 percent to 8.5 percent of the total purchase amount. (See *no-load, front-end load, back-end load,* and *redemption fee.*)

money market fund A mutual fund that invests in high-quality short-term debt instruments such as treasury bills or certificates of deposit. Money market fund investors earn a steady stream of interest income that varies with short-term interest rates. Generally, investors may cash out at any time.

Morgan Stanley Capital Investment and Europe, Australasia, Far East Index (MSCI/EAFE) gauges the performance of the foreign stock market.

net asset value (NAV) The total worth of all the investments of a mutual fund. The NAV changes daily to reflect fluctuations in the price of its stock and bond holdings.

no-load fund A mutual fund that charges no sales fee to buy and no sales fee to sell. (Also see *load, front-end load,* and *back-end load.*)

open-end mutual fund A mutual fund that allows investors to buy shares directly from the mutual fund company and stands ready to redeem shares whenever shareholders are ready to sell. Open-end funds may issue new shares any time there is a demand for more shares from investors. Shareholders buy and sell shares at the fund's net asset value (plus sales fees), in contrast to a "closed-end mutual fund," which trades like stock on a stock exchange. Rather than selling at net asset value, closed-end fund shares trade at whatever price the market is willing to pay.

price-earnings ratio (PE) Specifically: a company's stock price divided by its earnings per share over the past 12 months. It is Wall Street's most commonly used ratio to determine a stock's value to investors. P/Es are a lot like golf scores—the lower the better. For instance, a company with a stock price of $20 and earnings-per-share of $1 has a 20 P/E ($20 divided by $1), while a company with a stock price of $10 and the same $1 in earnings-per-share has a 10 P/E. The higher a stock's P/E, the more expensive the stock is relative to its earnings.

redemption fee Sales fee or "back-end load" charged by some mutual funds to shareholders when they sell their shares. (Also see *back-end load.*)

top down An investment strategy in which the investor looks at broad economic trends to decide which types of investments appear to be best positioned for growth, and then selects individual investments based on that economic assessment. It is the opposite of a *bottom-up* strategy, in which an investor assesses an individual investment strictly on its own merits irrespective of the overall economy. (Also see *bottom up.*)

12b-1 fee A small fee assessed annually by some mutual funds to cover advertising and marketing expenses. The fee is deducted directly from each shareholder's holdings and usually represents less than 1 percent of net asset value.

For investors with patience and persistence, mutual funds can be a simple and effective way to enjoy a lifetime of success in the investment market.

Index

New
CD-ROM Money Maker Kits
from Dearborn Multimedia

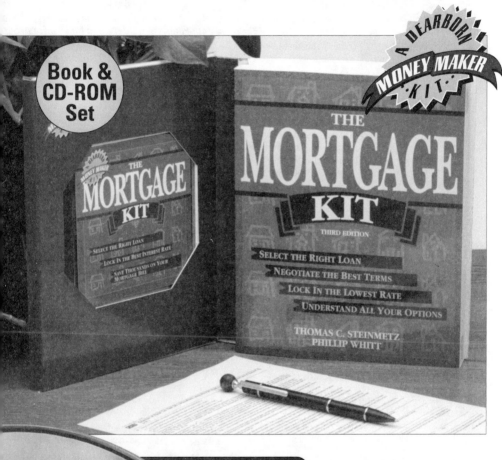

Book & CD-ROM Set

A DEARBORN MONEY MAKER KIT

THE MORTGAGE KIT

THIRD EDITION

SELECT THE RIGHT LOAN
NEGOTIATE THE BEST TERMS
LOCK IN THE LOWEST RATE
UNDERSTAND ALL YOUR OPTIONS

THOMAS C. STEINMETZ
PHILLIP WHITT

Features:

- *25 minute video help with the author*
- *12-28 interactive printable forms per CD-ROM*
- *On-Line glossary of terms*
- *Quick-start video tutorial*
- *Interactive printable book on CD-ROM*
  (Print out sections you like for closer reading or writing notes.)

Start Enjoying Greater Financial Freedom
Triple Your Investment Portfolio

SAVE Thousands on Real Estate as a Buyer or Seller

Successfully Start & Manage a NEW Busine